SLIPPERY BEAST

ALSO BY ELLEN RUPPEL SHELL

A Child's Place: A Year in the Life of a Day Care Center

The Hungry Gene: The Science of Fat and the Future of Thin

Cheap: The High Cost of Discount Culture

The Job: Work and Its Future in a Time of Radical Change

SLIPPERY BEAST

A True Crime Natural History, with Eels

ELLEN RUPPEL SHELL

Abrams Press, New York

Library of Congress Control Number: 2024933732

ISBN: 978-1-4197-6585-8
eISBN: 978-1-64700-893-2

Printed and bound in the United States
10 9 8 7 6 5 4 3 2 1

ABRAMS The Art of Books
195 Broadway, New York, NY 10007
abramsbooks.com

For Avery and Aiden, Alison and Jo

I discovered in nature the nonutilitarian delights that I sought in art. Both were a form of magic; both were a game of intricate enchantment and deception.

—Vladimir Nabokov,
"Butterflies"

CONTENTS

PROLOGUE

MONSTERS IN THE POND

Alone
In her millions, the moon's pilgrim,
The nun of water.

—Ted Hughes, "An Eel"

I LIVE PART OF THE year in Maine, just down the Pemaquid Peninsula in the fishing hamlet of Bremen. Often my husband joins me. Our neighbors are lobstermen, boatbuilders, crafters. Most seem to have a side hustle—snowplowing, landscaping, crab picking. A mile up the hill an emergency room doc breeds cashmere goats, and a mile or so farther a felt maker and her husband moonlight as blacksmiths. It's the sort of place outsiders come to escape their past and to reinvent themselves as heartier, more independent, more *American*. Some arrive determined to stake their claim, only to flee within a year or so when the blackflies and sullen winters bring them low. Others score a hunting license, join the volunteer fire department, and settle in for the long run. My husband and I have found a way to split the difference.

Our place squats low beneath copses of spindly oaks and firs at the dead end of a dirt road that washes out every spring. The backyard slopes down to a 240-acre stream-fed pond choked with water lilies and flanked by beaver dams the size of igloos. The pond favors kayaks and canoes over powerboats, but that's not to say the place is quiet. Most mornings seagulls squawk up a racket, and cormorant chicks squeal, their mothers standing guard with unfurled wings. Geese cackle conspiratorially as they anoint our back lawn with poop, and on early summer evenings the loons wail like wolves in heat. Deer and the occasional moose crash by. That's about it for action, though some days do bring surprises. Like the day Jill appeared, unbidden, at our door.

Jill (who prefers we skip her last name) lived less than a mile from us, which by rural Maine standards made her a close neighbor. Well coiffed and casually chic, she was hard to miss in the land of L.L.Bean and Carhartt. I'd seen her out trotting her golden retriever, but we'd never spoken. Ushering her in, I wondered what she had in mind.

Perched lightly on the edge of her seat, Jill declined coffee and assured me that this was no social call, more like a mission of mercy. She felt duty bound to warn rookies like me of the town's lurking dangers. This sounded serious, but could she be more specific? Well, for starters, the peninsula was crawling with bad actors, especially drug dealers. Did I know about them? Why yes I did, if she meant the "secret" marijuana farm up the hill, the one with the barn shrouded in the jumbo Confederate flag. Pretty shady, I know, but to be honest the weed worried me a bit less than the flag.

Jill pressed on. Did I know that vandals on snowmobiles swoop down every winter like vultures to rob the homes of summer people?

That was bad, I agreed, but we weren't exactly summer people (it was early April, which in Maine cannot be mistaken for the Fourth of July). Plus, look around: there wasn't much here worth stealing. She shrugged. Did I know about the ticks and the Lyme disease? Oh, yeah. The poison ivy? Ditto. The great horned owls that preyed on cats? Ugh, that sounded gruesome. But I'd read somewhere that something like four billion birds are murdered by cats every year, so perhaps that's nature's just retribution? Also, we had no cats.

Gathering the threads of her frayed patience, Jill leaned back to lob the big one: Did I know that the pond was roiling with eels?

BINGO!

My relationship with nature is best described as an uneasy truce built on a shaky foundation of fear: of kamikaze wasps, venomous spiders, rabid rodents, and most decidedly snakes. So, eels . . . pretty much snakes in the water, right? I feigned indifference and saw Jill to the door. But after she left, I silently vowed to keep the eel infestation under wraps.

As summer approached, I felt a little guilty about not sharing Jill's intel with our guests. Were eels viperous? Did they have razor-sharp teeth like the shrieking variety in *The Princess Bride*? Could an eel entangle a human ankle in its coils and yank the victim to a watery grave? Who knew?

As it turned out, none of that mattered: many visitors cannonballed into the pond that summer and not a single eel took the bait. Nor did we spot one. As time passed I pretty much forgot about the eels.

AND THEN, SOME YEARS LATER, Sam sauntered into our lives.

Sam (let's keep his real name out of this) was a jack-of-all-trades who worked wonders with power tools. Or so he claimed. But if that was ever true, Sam's wonders ceased with us. We'd hired him to fix our leaking roof and moldy basement, tasks for which his initial enthusiasm waned steadily with the passage of time. Some days he'd go missing on the pretext that his ex-wife had hauled him into family court in pursuit of still more child support. (He saw this as simple harassment, as his kids were mostly grown.) Some days he'd arrive late, offering no explanation. And some days he'd quit early, pull off his work boots, and pad into the kitchen toting a four-pack of Mainiac Gold cider. We'd each pop a can and he'd gripe, mostly about his ex-wife, who—in his telling—was harder on a man's constitution than a wicked bout of the crud. Sam didn't have much good to say about most other people in his life either—his former coworkers, his competitors, his adult daughter. But he was proud as heck of his eight-year-old grandson. He coached the boy in T-ball and horseshoes and had plans to teach him to fish. He'd do that, he said, once he put together the money to buy a decent boat. That sounded about right to me.

At forty-nine, Sam clearly knew his own mind. It wasn't too late to live the dream! I asked him why not mix business with pleasure and invest in a commercial fishing license to go with that boat? "I could do that," he said, looking thoughtful. "I have done that. But that was years ago. These days it's too risky. You know, with the eels."

This from a man who thought nothing of hauling buckets of nails up a sixteen-foot ladder. What was he scared of? Was it the razor-sharp teeth, I probed?

Sam cracked open a third can of cider and swigged it nearly dry. Eels didn't bite people, as far as he knew, he said, but it wouldn't matter if they did. He wasn't talking about eels big enough to draw blood. In Maine, grown eels taste of river-bottom mud and are best used as fish bait. What mattered were the glass eels, or—as they are often called—elvers, baby eels about the length and shape of a waterlogged toothpick. (As we will see, elvers and glass eels, though often conflated, technically represent different stages in the eel's long life.) Those little critters were worth a bundle, ounce for ounce close to what a farmer would charge for the weed growing up the road. Only two states—Maine and South Carolina—had a legal glass eel fishery, but South Carolina's was too small to matter. That left Maine as the only serious elver-hunting ground in the United States. Elver fishers could barely keep ahead of the demand, especially from China, where, for some reason Sam couldn't quite fathom, elvers were known as "white gold." The little devils were so prized, he said, that poachers were risking jail time or worse to get their hands on them.

Clearly, I'd touched a nerve. Still, I was skeptical: What kind of money were we talking about here? I mean, lobster retails for twelve or thirteen dollars a pound. But lobsters are delicious, and a luxury. Who would pay serious money for a tangled mess of baby eels? "Let's put it this way," Sam said. On a cool, moonless night of the sort that infant eels favored, a man could catch $40,000 worth, maybe more. With money like that on the table a lot of folks had gotten greedy, and some folks had gotten mean. "Eel is a dirty business, always has been," he told me. "But in the old days it was dirty and safe. Now it's just dirty."

Sam was no angel; he'd seen his share of trouble, and not just with his ex-wife. But he wanted no part of the eel wars. Eels brought mischief and worse. Knives had been flashed and guns drawn, lives threatened. "And don't get me started on the Indians," he said. "There was a standoff with the fish and wildlife Down East. And from what I heard; the Passamaquoddy won that fight."

The sun was low and the four-pack was empty. Sam muttered something about returning early the next morning to make up for lost time. He jammed on his boots, edged his way out the door toward his pickup, hunched in, and drove off. I never saw him again, though I imagine he did buy that boat with the advance money we'd been foolish enough to fork over. It occurred to me that it wasn't fear of elver thieves that was keeping Sam off the water, and that his ex-wife probably had good reason to gripe. I felt duped but also a tiny bit grateful. Sam was one slippery guy, and as a rule I believed less than half of what he said. But when it came to eels, what he'd told me that late September afternoon wasn't the half of it. I didn't know it at the time, but Sam had cracked open a cabinet of wonders. And like so many curious souls before me, I could not avert my gaze.

INTRODUCTION

LOVE'S ARROW

> the selfsame eel, a firebrand now, a scourge,
> the arrow shaft of Love on earth . . .
>
> —Eugenio Montale, "The Eel"

"EEL PEOPLE," AS THEY CALL themselves, tend to get hooked at an early age, typically while fishing with their fathers. That would not be me. In the whole of my childhood, I can recall casting a fishing rod only once, and promptly embedding the hook in my thigh. So, perhaps like you, I did not grow up fishing eels. I stumbled upon them unexpectedly and with some trepidation. Maybe you too feel some unease? If so, you are in good company. Eels are nature's Rorschach test; what we think of them reveals not much about them and a lot about us. Mystery? Nuisance? Jackpot? Dinner? Threat? Depending on who you are or who you ask, eels can be all or none of those things. But no matter your feelings about the eel, there's one thing of which I hope to convince you: no living creature is more remarkable.

Emerging some 200 million years ago from the (figurative) primordial slime, the eel survived a fusillade of calamities culminating 66 million years ago in the Cretaceous-Paleogene extinction that vaporized three out of every four species, including the non-avian dinosaurs. The eel weathered continental shifts and an ice age that paralyzed much of the world. And it colonized six of the seven continents, the sole exception being Antarctica. It is perhaps this traumatic evolutionary history that brought the modern eel its uncanny adaptability. Frozen alive, it finds a way to wait out the thaw. Marooned on land, it finds a way to breathe through its skin. Confronted with an obstacle, it finds a way to surmount it.

So durable is the eel, and so willing to adapt, that over time it came to constitute as much as half of the total freshwater fish biomass found in many of the world's waterways. It seems almost certain that no other animal is better equipped to survive on this planet. And yet, somehow we have found ways to imperil it. We've shredded it in hydroelectric turbines and blocked its migration path with dams. We've poisoned its freshwater habitats, and heated the oceans and disrupted the currents on which its life cycle depends. The coup de grâce? We've broiled, grilled, salted, smoked, and jellied it to near oblivion.

Since the 1970s, eel numbers have plummeted, with thirteen of all freshwater species classified as "near threatened" or worse. This is especially true of the three commercially vital freshwater species in the northern hemisphere: the Atlantic eels, both the European and the American, and the Japanese eel. Counts of the European eel, *Anguilla anguilla*, and the Japanese eel, *Anguilla japonica*, have shrunk by at least 90 percent. Counts of the American eel, *Anguilla rostrata*, have withered by half. To cite one concerning example: the St. Lawrence River and Lake Ontario, once eel havens, are now eel wastelands.

Such devastation comes courtesy of abuses, of course. But it also comes by way of neglect.

In Japan and Europe, eel advocates have rallied, and strict regulations are sternly (if unevenly) enforced. But with far fewer champions or protectors, the American eel is mostly on its own. As one European eel scientist blurted, red-faced, when I raised the issue: "You Americans don't give a damn about the eel." Frankly, it was hard to argue his point.

The American eel is the David to our Goliath, its very existence threatened by our own. But really, is this any surprise? After all, we live in what some scientists call the Anthropocene, a geologic period in which humans exert an unprecedented influence on the planet. It's no secret that we've made a mess of things. Confronted with the prospect of any creature's terminal decline, one tends to feel that something has gone terribly wrong. Still, why should we care about the eel? The black rhino, the Sumatran elephant, the lowland gorilla, all are under threat, and these are majestic creatures. Eels are not majestic, and not many of us would mourn their demise. Fewer still would lift a finger to protect them, and not all that long ago, I counted myself among the idle-fingered majority. But I've since learned that playing fast and loose with the eel is like tugging on the bottom block of a Jenga tower. We do so at our peril.

James McCleave, University of Maine professor emeritus of marine sciences and a world-renowned expert on the American eel, was the first to convince me of the eel's central role in nature's plan. We met for breakfast at a McDonald's about an hour's drive from his home in Orono, Maine. McCleave, recently retired from his academic post and looking relaxed in a festive Hawaiian shirt,

Sunset on opening day of elver season near the Old Mill at Pemaquid Falls in Bristol, Maine. A fisherman braves the cold to wade knee-deep in the river to adjust his fyke net, hopeful that the midnight catch will bring him a small fortune. (Ellen Ruppel Shell)

pushed back from his Egg McMuffin and told it plain. "The freshwater eel is a huge contributor to food webs," he said. "In that sense, it's way more important than other fish."

Eels are both predator and prey. In freshwater rivers, lakes, and streams, they eat most any living thing smaller than themselves, thereby shaping and curating the food chain. In saltwater estuaries and seas, they are eaten by a vast array of carnivores, many of which we rely on to keep our world on track. When eels are plentiful in a river, stream, or lake, it's a signal that nature is in balance. When eel numbers decline, it's a sure sign of trouble. But these signals are hard to read, because given their nocturnal habits and slippery ways, keeping track of eels is like trying to track the stars through a cloudy night.

Freshwater eels are contrarians: whatever it is you expect of them, think otherwise. Most migratory fish—Atlantic salmon, river herring, steelhead trout, alewives, sturgeon—are anadromous, meaning they are born in fresh water, spend most of their adult lives in the ocean, and return to fresh water to spawn. But the freshwater eel is catadromous: born at sea, it travels thousands of miles to estuaries, rivers, and lakes where it grows to maturity, then returns to its birthplace years—even decades—later to spawn and die. In the course of this epic journey, eels undergo a series of transformations so dramatic that for centuries no one was sure if young eels were even eels at all. And if that sounds weird, here's what's even weirder: freshwater eels mate only in the final day or two of their lives, and the great majority perish before they have a chance to do so. What this means is that for the freshwater eel to exist at all as a family of fish, an outlandish number of individual eels must be born into this world. And thanks to us, the prospect of this happening is getting dimmer by the day.

No question, then, that the fate of the eel is tightly entangled with our own, the proverbial canary in the coal mine of human hubris. This precarity makes its plight all the more urgent, and its story all the more compelling. And it's no fluke that I've anchored that story in the compelling—and contrarian—state of Maine.

LIFE IN MAINE, THE MOTTO goes, "is the way life should be." Tourist brochures trumpet the state's 17.5 million acres of raw forestland (the densest of any state), spectacular coastline stretching thousands of miles, and mountains majesty towering over roiling seas. Those brochures don't lie: Maine is a paragon of natural beauty, and a mecca for visitors who flock every summer to capture its special something for their Instagram feeds. But as the days grow short and the foliage crumbles, Maine empties out like an upturned box of photographs.

"In the United States," author Gertrude Stein once quipped, "there is more space where nobody is than where anybody is. This is what makes America what it is." It is certainly what made Maine what it is. Crouched like an afterthought in its remote northeast corner, Maine looms all the larger in the public imagination for being geographically out of reach. And like so many out-of-the-way places, it has yet to find firm footing in the Information Age.

In CNBC's 2023 list of top states for business, Maine received an A– in quality of life and a B+ in education, but otherwise performed poorly, with a grade of F in both infrastructure and access to capital, and Ds in technology innovation and economy overall. One might question what such rankings mean or whether they truly matter. Fair enough. Still, the odds are slim to none that Maine will transform into an economic juggernaut anytime soon. A 2020 analysis published in *Maine Policy Review*, an independent journal published by the University of Maine, concluded that "Maine's most valuable export in recent years has not been lumber, lobsters, or blueberries, but its talented young people who have seen the road to prosperity as I-95 South."

So, you may ask, what does all this have to do with eels? Good question. So here's the punch line: the American eel, a high-value fish that has played a notable role in Maine history and traditions, offers the state a genuine economic opportunity. If you are skeptical that eels can make a difference, you have every reason to be. After all, Americans eat relatively little eel—something north of 11 million pounds a year compared with one billion pounds of tuna. But consider this: Fifty years ago, how many Americans paid top dollar for slivers of raw fish atop thimble-size mounds of rice? Tastes change, and eel is having its moment. Since 2022, after lobster, eel fry—glass eels and elvers—have been Maine's most lucrative fishery, outpacing clams, scallops, crab, and other seafood. That's a big deal in a state known for its nautical heritage and inclinations, and an even bigger deal when you consider that eels were all but worthless just a few decades ago.

To be clear, I'm not predicting that eel will unseat fried chicken and burgers on the nation's dinner plates anytime soon. No matter how popular, commercially processed eel is too expensive to fill that role. But while eel is not yet an everyday food, it is widely available in the nation's restaurants and markets, most of it in the form of kabayaki—eel grilled and glazed in a sweet mix of mirin, soy, and sugar. And since European and Japanese eel is increasingly costly and scarce, demand for the American species already outpaces the supply. American eel has become part of the global culinary conversation and by all evidence a growing part of a five-billion-dollar freshwater eel market, a market in which Maine plays a vital but—to many minds—woefully compromised role.

Roughly 90 percent of seafood Americans eat is imported, but much of that seafood began life in the United States. The American eel is a prime example: its life cycle is baffling and fraught, but no more so than the global supply chain cobbled together to exploit it. The bulk of baby eels caught off Maine's craggy coast are not eaten locally or, for that matter, eaten at all, but rather shipped off to be raised to plump adulthood in enormous open fishponds in East Asia. Typically, American glass eels and elvers caught by fishermen in Maine are flown to Hong Kong for passage to Chinese eel farms, where they are plied with greasy balls of fishmeal, hormones, and sometimes other drugs, grown quickly to market size, beheaded, skinned, butchered, cooked, slathered in sauce, and packaged for export, often back to the United States.

Wait, you may well ask, isn't that a cheat? It's one thing to hunt down grown eels in the wild; that seems fair. It's quite another to cultivate eels on Chinese farms from American brood stock and for Maine to devote an entire fishery to the endeavor. I mean, glass eels and elvers are infants that, left to their own devices, have a shot at a long life. If we prefer farmed eels, why not start them from eggs and sperm, as we do catfish and oysters? An excellent question, and one that naturalists and scientists have pondered for centuries. The answer is straightforward: fish farmers don't breed eels because they can't, at least not efficiently. Eels—especially the American eel—all but refuse to reproduce on demand. Granted, heavily dosed with hormones in the cushy confines of a laboratory, they will grudgingly do the deed. But these efforts are more a tease than a commitment, for the resulting larvae—even when pampered and fed on delicacies such as shark egg paste—tend to die off in a few days. Just as gold cannot be spun from straw, freshwater eels cannot be coaxed to reliably procreate in captivity, but stubbornly insist on starting life in the wild.

Growing big eels from baby eels is not easy: it requires skill, determination, patience, and more than a little luck. But cultivation of grown eels from infant eels is simpler—and far more reliable—than attempting to breed eels from eggs and sperm. Properly fed and cared for, farmed eels have a sterling survival rate and reach market size—a third to half a pound—far more quickly than do wild eels. Meanwhile, the alternative—fully grown wild eels—is not a realistic option, as wild eels are no longer favored by most consumers.

My first taste of wild eel came thanks to the generosity of Caroline Durif, an eel scientist stationed on an island near the port city of Bergen, on the west coast of Norway. Eel fishing is banned in Norway, but my host had secured a handsome specimen from a local fisherman who was permitted to catch and sell eels for research purposes. Since we were both doing research, we felt no

A child buys an eel from a bemused street vendor in this etching of unknown provenance. In Europe, Asia, and the Americas eels were not only a popular food but also an ingredient in various folk medicines. Eel oil was a remedy for deafness, and wrapping dried eel skins around one's fingers or thigh was said to prevent cramps and cure rheumatism. In Asia, eel was eaten to combat fatigue and enhance sexual performance, and in North America spiking one's husband's liquor with a live eel warded off alcohol abuse. (Wellcome Collection)

guilt pangs indulging in Norwegian wild eel, and I was thrilled to partake in what I imagined would taste like a cross of lobster and chicken. One bite disabused me of that fantasy. The soapy flavor and wet dishrag texture are difficult to compare with other foods I've tasted, but let's just say that neither chicken nor lobster came to mind.

Sadly, the problem with wild eel goes beyond taste. Many eels spend their formative years trolling in waters laden with things that none of us would choose to swallow—heavy metals, PCBs, microplastics. These contaminants bioaccumulate (a technical term for "build up") in the eel's abundant body fat, the very tissue that carries most of its flavor. Eels lucky enough to spend their lives in pristine waters would of course avoid this problem, and such wild eels would likely be delicious. But not many waters are pristine, especially the relatively stagnant fresh and coastal waters where wild eels spend the bulk of their lives. In fact, wild eel has become so iffy that several scientists I spoke with suggested I caution you the reader against eating it at all. You've been so warned. But don't fret, for unless you have caught it yourself or joined in with someone who has, it's unlikely you've eaten much if any wild freshwater eel. In markets, restaurants, and sushi bars the world over, 98 percent of the freshwater eel sold commercially is farm grown from infant eels.

Eel farming is an art so ancient that Aristotle declared, "The majority subsist in freshwater that the eel-farmers look after." But it's not known whether eel farming was commonplace before being adopted by the Japanese in the late nineteenth century. In Asia the practice spread gradually to the island nation of Taiwan (which Japan acquired from China in 1895), Korea, Malaysia, and, most importantly, China. In the 1980s, when farmed eels began to outsell wild eels in Japan and elsewhere, the Chinese government responded by investing heavily to promote the eel aquaculture industry.

Today, China hosts nearly 90 percent of the world's eel farms, some nine hundred of which cluster in or near Guangdong Province (on the border with Hong Kong) and in Fujian Province. Customs data indicate that imports of baby eels (or eel fry) from the Americas to East Asia surged from two tons in 2004 to a whooping 157 tons in 2022. Though the numbers are difficult to parse, this makes American glass eels and elvers the presumed progenitor of most freshwater eels cultivated and processed in China, and much of that eel is shipped back to the United States. Kabayaki plated on plastic in the sushi case at your local supermarket for Monday night dinner with the kids? Yup. Unagi in the omakase you splurged on to celebrate your friend's thirtieth birthday? Ditto. Europe, too, has developed a taste for American eel, so much so that DNA tests confirm that the American species (most of it fattened and processed in China) now constitutes as much as two-thirds of eel eaten in both the United States and Europe.

China's export-focused eel supply chain squeezes out every ounce of profit, embracing not only eel aquaculture but also the processing of smoked eel, eel jerky, and (don't mock them until you've tried them) honey-roasted eel snacks and other delights. Under the right conditions, farmed eels grow roughly a gram a day—about an ounce a month. Depending on the season, one kilogram (2.2 pounds) of American glass eels or elvers might bring $4,600 to a Maine fisherman. Not bad! But the real profit comes down the road, for in sixteen months or so that single kilogram might grow to one metric ton—2,204 pounds—of market-ready fish worth roughly $35,000. It's hard to imagine a more profitable agricultural endeavor than eel farming, or one more likely to help bring a struggling rural economy to its feet.

The Chinese government's pivot to eel aquaculture was meant to both revitalize rural industry and to incentivize the return of young people to their ancestorial homes in the countryside. The intention is to support opportunity in rural areas, especially for women and young people, and to ease the pressure on China's overcrowded cities, where unemployment and dissatisfaction are on the rise. That logic might also apply to Maine, the source of so much of the brood stock on which China's booming eel business relies. It's commonplace for any rural region's natural endowment—be it timber, minerals, or fish—to be mined or harvested as a raw commodity and sent elsewhere, where the bulk of its value is captured in the processing, marketing, and selling of the finished product. In Maine this is starkly true in the case of eels, which one analyst calculated undergo a *sixtyfold increase in value* between capture and final retail sale in supermarkets and restaurants.

Such calculations have not escaped the notice of members of Maine's business community, some of whom have traveled to Guangdong Province to witness Maine-caught elvers being fattened in murky ponds like so many slithering foie gras ducks. These observers returned informed but pessimistic. China had for decades invested heavily in the art, science, and business of eel aquaculture, and it seemed certain that no American endeavor could compete with its rock-bottom wage structure and turbo-charged efficiencies. But in recent years, matters have changed. The growing complexity and risk of sourcing finished goods from China have created new opportunities for Americans to reclaim the true value of many goods, not least of these the American eel, Maine's very own "white gold."

This book begins and ends in Maine, as it must, but the eel is the hub around which the tale spins. One of the most surprising things about the eel is that the quest to decode its cryptic life cycle so closely parallels and reflects the advance of Western scientific thought. For your amusement and, I hope, amazement, I unveil that natural and not-so-natural history with special attention to the intellectual heavyweights—from Aristotle to Linnaeus to Freud—who struggled to unlock the eel's treasure trove of secrets. Along with this cavalcade of luminaries, we'll meet a cast of contemporary players, the fishermen, scientists, entrepreneurs, visionaries, scoundrels, and dreamers whose lives have been touched and forever changed by the slippery beast. Here's a sampling: The Eel Godfather whose plot to corner Maine's American elver market brought him fame, fortune, and a stint in federal prison. The volleyball coach turned medieval scholar whose cartographical encounters with Dutch eel ships sealed his fate as the Surprised Eel Historian.

The Passamaquoddy fishers fighting to reclaim their sovereign right to eels as a sacred tribal resource. The alleged assassin and drug trafficker who reportedly laundered millions through his booming eel export business in Haiti. The modern-day Captain Ahab who regularly logs tens of thousands of nautical miles in search of the eel's elusive mating grounds. And the redheaded gamine from Indiana who against all odds coaxed millions from the smitten Maine government and other investors to build the nation's first "family farm" for eels.

Since I began mulling over this project years ago, friends, colleagues, and family have asked what it is about the eel, of all animals, that has gripped so many august minds through the ages. I put that question to Sylvie Dufour, research director at the French National Centre for Scientific Research. Dufour met with me in a conference room not far from her cluttered office at the National Museum of Natural History. It was early summer, and as is typical in Paris, there was no air-conditioning. I wilted in the 101-degree heat, furtively sipping tepid tap water from a tiny paper cup I'd swiped from the stash I'd spotted earlier in the bathroom. Dufour sat waterless, crisp, and focused, presumably too captivated by the subject at hand to even notice any personal discomfort.

"Most people who study the eel become addicted," she began, with a look implying that she was one of those people.

In what sense, I thought aloud, is the eel addictive? (It was a question to which I assumed I knew the answer. I was wrong.)

"It's the shape," she said. "It's very suggestive. People make the link very quickly." Dufour paused a beat to let that sink in as I squirmed uncomfortably in my seat. "But mostly, it's the mystery that fascinates us. The story of that mystery is one of the most compelling in natural history. And I leave it to you to tell it."

What follows is my heartfelt effort to do so.

CHAPTER 1

THE EELS OF MAINE

Life isn't all fricasseed frogs and eel pie.
—C. S. Lewis, *The Silver Chair*

IN MAINE, THE AMERICAN EEL reveals itself reluctantly. Maybe that's because its waking hours don't comport with our own. Or because eel season flashes by so quickly. Or because eels lack the star power of lobster, oysters, or even clams. Whatever the reason, eels don't make much of a splash in the Pine Tree State. So it came as a surprise to learn that Maine is a veritable Fort Knox of American eels.

Oh, please, you may be thinking, *it's not just Maine*. And you would be right. Eels are shy and lie low after sunrise, so they are easy to miss. But east of the Mississippi the American eel lurks in countless marshes, creeks, rivers, lakes, streams, and inlets. Maybe you've spotted one while out skinny-dipping on a starry night. Or glimpsed one in the beak of a soaring raptor. Or reeled one in—unbidden—on a fishing line. Or maybe not. It's easy to be fooled, for there are many imposters.

The lamprey, that bloodsucking parasite, looks very much like the eel that it's not. The three species of "electric eels," genus *Electrophorus*, have stronger genetic ties to catfish than to the eel. Sea snakes, reptiles with lungs and paddle-like tails, are often confused for eels. So, that "eel" you see in your mind's eye may not be an eel at all. And then again, it may well be.

A century ago, in some parts of the world, especially England, it was difficult *not* to encounter freshwater eels of some variety. British naturalist Charles J. Cornish observed them swarming "in such tens of millions they made a black margin to the river on either side of the bank, where they swam because the current was the weakest." Chemist and poet Sir Humphrey Davy, president of the British Royal Society, was unparalleled in his keen observations of the natural world, and absolutely fascinated by eels. In his *Salmonia, or Days of Fly Fishing*, composed a year before his death in 1829, he notes this rather gruesome demonstration of eel self-sacrifice and tenacity: "It was a cold backward summer and when I was at Ballyshannon, about the end of July, the mouth of the river, which had been in flood all this month, under the fall, was blackened by millions of little eels about as long as the finger, which were constantly urging their way up the moist rocks by the side of the fall. Thousands died, but their bodies, remaining moist, served as the ladder for others to make their way; and I saw some ascending even perpendicular stones, making their road through the wet moss or adhering to some eels that had died in the attempt."

Clearly, eels are prepared to exist where less determined creatures might perish, and under the most varied—and daunting—conditions. The European eel, once so plentiful on the Thames, is also pleased to find itself inhabiting waterways from the north of Norway to the Sebou River region of Morocco. The Japanese eel sweeps from the northern island of Hokkaido to the Philippines. The American eel feels at home in waters from Greenland to Venezuela. Over time I developed a habit of asking scientists if any other freshwater fish can claim such a far-flung domain. They hesitated, looked skyward, furled their brows. Then came the hedge: "None . . . that I can think of."

So yes, eels seem to be everywhere and are therefore familiar. But if familiarity breeds contempt, eels are the exception at least in the culinary sense: eaters the world over simply cannot get enough of them. In Morocco, eel is steamed into tagines. In Italy, it is threaded on skewers and roasted with bay leaves. In northeastern India, it finds its way into curries. Smoked eel is a delicacy across eastern Europe and parts of Scandinavia, and in Denmark and Belgium, pickled eel is a treat. The British embrace their jellied eel—chopped and boiled in stock that cools and sets and is sometimes baked into a pie. (This delicacy is traced to Victorian London, where in the nineteenth century eel was one of the very few fish to thrive in the River Thames, then known as the "Great Stink.") *Larousse Gastronomique*, the definitive guide to French cooking first published in 1938, lists forty-five different recipes for eel, simply marinated and broiled, say, or long poached in a stew of onions. (Squeamish readers may prefer not to know that aspiring chefs are advised to slaughter the eel by slamming its head repeatedly on a counter and putting a "noose around its base" before peeling off the skin.) Chinese chefs treat eel as they do other animal proteins—steamed with black beans, simmered in soups, stir-fried with ginger and garlic shoots, or used as a stuffing for chicken or duck.

So, what of eel eaters in the United States? In *The American Plate*, published in 2015, the food historian Libby O'Connell surprised me, pointing out that Americans once vastly preferred eel to lobster. To be fair, this was not a high bar: in nineteenth-century Maine, lobster was derided as a "cockroach of the sea," fit mostly for prisoners and indentured servants and as an ingredient in fertilizer. Still, O'Connell describes eel as "a gourmet's dream," so popular it made a cameo appearance in the 1796 classic *American Cookery*, the comprehensive culinary compendium thought to be the first cookbook penned by an American and published in the United States. In 1884, the U.S. Department of Fisheries reported on the nation's eel fishery—Massachusetts alone claimed an annual harvest of 400,000 pounds. Americans happily ate fried, stewed, pickled, and broiled eel until what historians call the Progressive Era, the 1890s to the 1920s, a time of political and economic reform when distinctive ethnic dietary preferences gave way to a homogeneous national cuisine. At the time, wild-caught fish and game of many varieties—though fashionable with the rich and a necessity for the poor—fell off the menu of "respectable" middle-class American households seeking the ease and status of prepared and store-bought foods. Eel, a common fish whose preparation required skill and patience, was first among the causalities. Ogden Nash, famed twentieth-century writer of light verse, compressed common opinion into this snappy scrap of doggerel: "I don't mind eels / except as meals."

By World War II, the ranks of eel aficionados in the United States had all but dwindled to small enclaves of European and Asian immigrants. Some trace the nation's anti-eel sentiment to the "yuck factor" evoked by the industrial-age contaminants tainting the nation's rivers. There is merit to this argument: the widespread use of insecticides led to concerns about chronic ingestion of heavy metals from residues leaking from farmers' fields into lakes and rivers. But this concern did not trickle down to the general public, which remained largely unaware of the dangers. Into the late 1930s and early 1940s, the only analyses carried out for chemical contaminants in foods were for lead arsenate and other arsenical pesticides in fruits. Freshwater fish, it seems, were not really a concern.

A more likely reason for America's collective turn away from eel is that, as a whole, Americans have never been drawn to seafood of any variety. In Iceland, an island nation, residents eat 200 pounds of fish a year. The Spanish consume 101 pounds of seafood annually, the French 75 pounds, the Italians nearly 63 pounds, and the Germans 31 pounds. Americans consume on average just 19 pounds. Why Americans eat so little fish and shellfish is not well understood. But there are clues. The food industry analyst Helene York was only half joking when she said that Americans avoid fish because "despite how it's marketed, most seafood doesn't taste like chicken." I'm not sure I agree: nearly 70 percent of the fish eaten in the United States is purchased in restaurants, and a good portion of that, dunked in batter, deep fried, and served on a bun with sauce and cheese, could easily pass for chicken or almost anything else. So I don't think the question of why Americans eschew seafood can be reduced to a mere matter of taste. In surveys, many of us admit that the real reason we don't eat fish at home is that we don't know how to cook it and don't want to learn, as we can't stomach the smell or feel of it. We are trained by advertisers and marketers to prioritize convenience, and the eel, with its slimy, mucus-coated skin and snakelike torso, is devilishly challenging to prepare at home. For this reason alone, it makes sense that American eel—once so popular—fell out of favor.

Until, that is, we discovered sushi.

America's first taste of raw fish on vinegared rice is often traced to the 1960s or '70s. But the food historian H. D. Miller wants to correct the historical record. From his reading, sushi landed on the American West Coast with a surge of Japanese immigrants sometime closer to 1900. Apparently, wealthy celebrities were especially taken with the exotic dish, which they served at parties and other gatherings featured in the society pages. Imagine the excitement when in 1904 the *Los Angeles Herald* reported socialite Fern Dell Higgins surprising guests with a spread in which "Japanese sushi . . . was the principal feature."

The food fads of the rich are known to trickle down to plebeian tables, but at this time in history, sushi never stood a chance. American interest in the dish cooled quickly after the Immigration Act of 1924 banned the Japanese from entering the United States, and any residual enthusiasm was sharply diminished after Japan's attack on Pearl Harbor in December 1941. It would be more than twenty years before sushi found its rightful place on the American table.

In *The Story of Sushi: An Unlikely Saga of Raw Fish and Rice*, author Trevor Corson reports that interest in the dish was rekindled in 1966, when the food importer Noritoshi Kanai partnered with Chicago businessman Harry Wolff Jr. to open the nation's first modern sushi bar inside Kawafuku, then the "grandest restaurant" in the Little Tokyo neighborhood of Los Angeles. The lavish, L-shaped sushi bar looked boldly out on an ice-lined raw fish display that was particularly popular with wealthy Japanese businessmen, some of whom sent word of it back to their home country. Apparently, this inspired other chefs who felt constrained by Japan's demanding and restrictive sushi culture to try their hand in the United States.

So, what does sushi have to do with eel? That's a bit of a story, so bear with me. Unlike sushi, "unagi" (Japanese for freshwater eel) is never eaten raw. We'll dig into the whys of this later, but for now, let's just think of unagi, which is always served cooked, as a gateway drug to sushi, which is always served raw; and think of sushi, which is often made of familiar fish like salmon, as a gateway drug to the less familiar eel. The owners of Kawafuku understood this symbiotic relationship between sushi and unagi and reasoned that if Japanese restaurants in the United States were persuaded to serve sushi, a lucrative supply chain could be built to support their national cuisine in which pricey eel featured prominently. Vintage Kawafuku menus—still available online—highlight not one but two broiled eel dishes, the restaurant's most expensive items. Meanwhile, sushi was on the rise. Not every American relished the idea of eating raw fish, but enough did to stir the beginnings of a craze. The *New York Times* food writer Craig Claiborne got in early, declaring Japanese food a "trend" in 1963. Claiborne, a sharp observer of culinary trends, noted that "New Yorkers seem to take to the raw fish dishes, sashimi and sushi, with almost the same enthusiasm they display for tempura and sukiyaki." Still, he cautioned that "sushi may seem a bit 'far out' for many American palates," and at the time perhaps it was. But thanks to a cascade of influences—including the resounding success of the television miniseries *Shogun*, based on James Clavell's historical novel set in seventeenth-century Japan—by the early 1980s, sushi was swimming freely in the American gastronomic mainstream. Coast to coast, consumers were swamped in supermarket sushi, truck-stop sushi, vegan sushi, fusion sushi, and nearly two thousand sushi restaurants catering to the craze. (Today, that number is closer to twenty thousand.)

As Kanai and Wolff predicted, eel, too, took off, and not just in LA. In 1983, Mimi Sheraton, Claiborne's successor at the *Times*, singled out "broiled eel wrapped in paper-thin sheaves of cucumber" in a coveted four-star review of Hatsuhana, a Japanese restaurant in Midtown Manhattan. But what Sheraton and other enthusiasts failed to mention (and perhaps did not know) was that by then, the Japanese eel in which they delighted was under threat.

Japan, by far the world's largest consumer of freshwater eel, has a history of favoring its native species, which meant that traditional Asian eel production and cuisine was grounded in Japanese eel. But as international demand for Japanese eel exploded, the species grew scarce and catches plummeted from more than 200 metric tons (440,000 pounds) in 1957 to less than twenty metric tons (44,000 pounds) in the 1980s. When Mimi Sheraton wrote her four-star review of Hatsuhana, the Japanese eel fishery—at about 10 percent of peak—had all but collapsed, while in Japan the price of glass eels and elvers soared. This made baby eels catnip for organized crime. Illicitly sourced glass eels accounted for much of Japanese eel production, which was sometimes linked to yakuza gangs, the Japanese mafia. These illegal operations relied on the patronage of large, industrial eel farms, many of them in China, outfitted with their own processing and packaging facilities to make it easy to skirt official oversight and sell eel products directly to department stores and supermarkets. This practice did not bode well for the survival of the Japanese eel species, which by the turn of the last century was essentially on life support.

It was not until February 2013 that the International Union for Conservation of Nature (IUCN) listed the Japanese eel as endangered, as did the Japanese Ministry of Environment. Exports were—and are—severely limited: today Japan imports 40 percent of the world's traded freshwater eel supply and exports only 1 percent. And again, pretty much all of the eel Japan imports is cultivated from wild-caught eel fry, most of it American eel.

During the 2020 fishing season, government sources reported a combined eleven tons of glass eels caught legally in twenty-four of Japan's forty-seven prefectures. But that number did not square with the seventeen tons of domestically caught glass eels growing in Japan's aquaculture operations that year. The government confessed that six tons, roughly 40 precent of the total, were from "unknown" sources that probably included yakuza gangs. In 2021, a poacher from Shikoku, the smallest of Japan's four main islands, patiently outlined his logic to a reporter: "Official traders are only prepared to buy glass eels at low prices so I sell my catches through unofficial channels where higher prices can be charged." Since the "unofficial" price can be three times that of the official government price, fishermen had every incentive to sell as much eel as possible off the books, a process that hastened the Japanese eel's catastrophic decline. Since 2023 there's been a crackdown on dodgy actors: poachers and dealers who once got barely a slap on the wrist now risk a quarter-million-dollar fine and three years in prison. Of course, no matter how harsh, regulations mean very little without enforcement. Given that roughly 40 percent of glass eels traded in Japan are still obtained from unknown sources, it's assumed that poaching of Japanese eels is rampant, and it remains to be seen whether the species will ever fully recover.

As the Japanese eel dwindled, Asian dealers and farmers pivoted to its European cousin: by the late 1990s, more than 70 percent of Chinese fish farms were growing European eels. With the rising demand and growing pressure, it didn't take long for that fishery, too, to crash. In 2007 the European eel was listed in Appendix II of the Convention on International Trade in Endangered Species (CITES), a multilateral treaty to regulate the trade in endangered species. Three years later, in 2010, the European Union banned the trading of live eels outside the EU, and limited trade by non-EU eel exporting countries like Tunisia and Morocco. These measures, while effective, came far too late—in 2013, the IUCN declared the European species "critically endangered," which is to say, at risk of extinction in the wild.

Ironically, in its attempts to regulate the eel trade, Europe unwittingly cleared a path for illegal actors. The calculus comes down to this: the tighter the regulations, the scarcer the glass eels

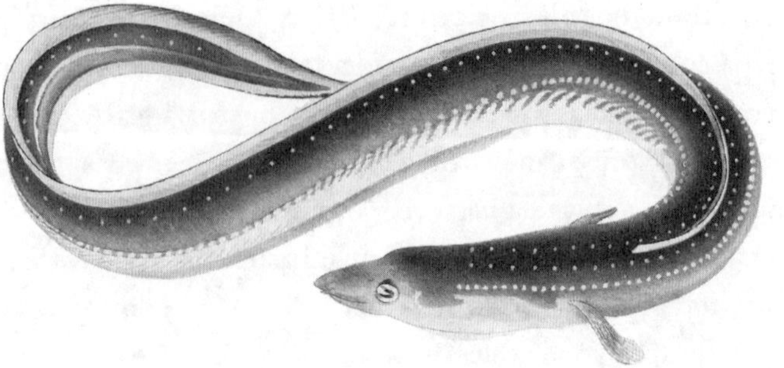

The Japanese eel, found in freshwater and coastal regions of Japan, Korea, China, and the Philippines, spawns to the west of the Mariana Islands. The Japanese consume nearly 70 percent of the world's supply of cultivated eel and often cite eel as their preference had they but one dish to eat before they died. (Wikimedia Commons)

and elvers, the higher the price, and the greater the incentive to steal them. The European eel's soaring profitability caught the attention of treasure seekers the world over, including international criminal networks and their syndicates. (Interestingly, some small-scale elver poachers quit the practice, frightened away by the perceived threat of organized crime.)

Those small-time poachers had reason to worry: eel mules are relentless. In 2021 Malaysian-born seafood trader Gilbert Khoo was convicted of smuggling 6.5 *tons* of live Spain-caught eels past multiple border agents to a barn in Gloucester, U.K., with the intent of shipping them via Hong Kong to Chinese eel farmers. Potential street value of the eels grown to full adult size: $290 million euros. Two years earlier, French customs officers at Charles de Gaulle Airport arrested a pair of dealers on their way to Kunming, China. While the pair protested and denied any wrongdoing, the police found 300,000 live elvers packed in plastic baggies (one kilo per bag) cooled with frozen water bottles wrapped in thermal blankets and packed neatly *in their suitcases*. These incidents reflect just a fraction of the underground elver trade: roughly 100 tons of European eel was seized from illegal traders in 2020 alone. And despite stronger laws, matters are not improving. In the spring of 2023, Spain's Civil Guard, in a joint operation with the French National Gendarmerie, Europol, and the European Anti-Fraud Office, seized 1.5 tons of live elvers and arrested twenty-seven suspects. As one eel scientist told me over a couple of beers: "It's a f@#king shit show."

Okay, so the European and Japanese eel are having a tough time of it. But what, you may ask, does that have to do with the American eel or, for that matter, Maine? Another excellent question with a simple answer: no eel species stands alone, as the fate of one sought-after eel species is linked inexorably to the fate of the others. Just weeks before the export ban on European eels was triggered, the river price for American elvers in Maine soared nearly nineteenfold—from less than $100 a pound in 2009 to about $1,870 a pound in 2012. For struggling fishermen, elvers were suddenly "dollars in the water." And while a dollar may not sound like a lot, consider that an American elver weighs only about 0.2 grams, or roughly 0.0004 of a pound. (That's about half of what European elvers weigh as they near shore, so there are nearly twice as many American as European elvers to a pound.) A cupful of elvers pulled out with a hand net could pay the grocery bill for a month or the electricity bill for a year. A bucketful of elvers might pay off a truck loan, or a hospital bill. And that's baby fish taken straight from the river. Eel farmers using those fry as brood stock have it even sweeter. Andrew Kerr, the UK-based chairman of the Sustainable Eel Group, was kind enough to do the math. "Think about it," he said. "A ton of elvers amounts to five thousand tons of adult eels. The profit in that just blows the mind."

These "mind-blowing" payoffs make smuggling and poaching all but inevitable. As we know, elvers are extremely difficult to count and nearly impossible to track, but the evidence is quite strong that the number of eels grown in China's aquaculture operations far exceeds the number of elvers legally imported into that country. The Chinese government reports that between the years 1995 and 2000 China generated an average of 1.5 metric tons (that's 3,300 pounds) of adult eel for every kilogram (2.2 pounds) of glass eels it grew up on its farms. This comes down to 1,500 kilograms of adult eel for each kilogram of baby eel, a truly remarkable multiple well beyond the expected forty-to-one ratio for American elvers. Yet, apparently, this was just a start. Between 2001 and 2008, China reported that its fish farms generated about 4.5 metric tons of adult eel for every kilogram of imported elvers, a ratio of 4,500 to one. Between 2009 and 2015, the multiple mysteriously jumped again to an astonishing 15 metric tons—more than *33,000 pounds*—of adult eel for every 2.2 pounds of elvers. No doubt China has mastered the art and science of elver farming, but to attribute this astonishing leap in productivity to improved technology, better feed, or other factors stretches credulity into the realm of magical thinking. A far more likely explanation for China's extraordinary eel production is that many tons of eel are grown up from elvers that have entered the country illegally. And by far the largest share of that contraband comes in the form of American eel.

In January 2024, a pair of Japanese scholars named Hiromi Shiraishi and Kenzo Kaifu published a paper titled "Early Warning of an Upsurge in International Trade of the American Eel" in the journal *Marine Policy*. In the article, they reported East Asian customs data indicating that imports of live elvers from the Americas to Hong Kong grew from 2 tons in 2004 to 53 tons in 2021 to an incredible 157 tons in 2022. Imports from the Americas—all presumably the American species—accounted for 89 percent of all live elver imports to East Asia that year. (East Asian nations and territories account for fully 98 percent of the world's Anguilla farming production.) Nearly 13 tons, 26,000 pounds, came from the United States. And while the bulk of these imports—more than 100 tons—were imported from Haiti (a nearly tenfold increase from 2021), more than 99 percent of Haitian elvers were traded via dealers in Canada and the United States. The authors concluded that "it is reasonable to conclude that currently A. rostrata [American eel] is arguably the most extensively exploited Anguilla species in the world."

Sheila Eyler, project leader with the U.S. Fish and Wildlife Conservation Office, has devoted much of her career to managing the American eel with the mission of protecting it. She's proud of her work but not convinced that it's enough. "We're very good at fishing down populations until they are gone," she sighed gloomily. Eyler and her team are doing what they can to stanch the bleeding, notably working with stakeholders to ensure eels safer passage in their upriver migration. No doubt that has helped. But as a scientist, Eyler had far less control over the demand side of the eel equation. The sudden surge in demand for the American eel, she said, came as a complete surprise to her and other regulators. "No one ever envisioned that the market would go crazy," she told me. From the vantage point of a scientist, one can understand why this market frenzy came as a calamitous surprise. But those who sought eels to make their fortunes were poised to take full advantage of the madness. And that is precisely what they did.

CHAPTER 2

THE KINGPIN

preliminary, pre-world creatures, cousins of the
moon,
who love blackness, aloofness,
always move under cover . . .

—Alice Oswald, "Eel Tail"

MY LONG-AWAITED FACE-TO-FACE WITH BILL Sheldon came on a bleak afternoon in December. We met at his family compound, a cluster of well-tended buildings strung along the Kennebec River in Woolwich, Maine. As I eased my way into his driveway, I caught a view beyond the river to Bath, the "City of Ships," and home to both Sheldon's younger brother, John, and Bath Iron Works, by far the state's largest locally based employer. There had been a flurry of snow that morning, the roads were slick, and I was a few minutes late. Sheldon stood at the door of what seemed to be his man cave, dressed for the weather in a Vineyard Vines puffer vest and Trinity tweed flat cap. Shrugging off the chill, he stepped back into the knotty-pine paneled warmth, sank heavily into the deep leather sofa, and removed neither cap nor vest. I followed him inside and looked around for a place to hang my coat and scarf. He offered no suggestions.

Half a year earlier, I had tried to reach Sheldon through his attorney, Walter McGee. While cordial, McGee informed me that his client was currently in residence at a federal penitentiary in New Hampshire. "Bill is not encouraging visitors," he said. "I suggest you wait." When at last we met, Sheldon was a scant two months out of lockup, and what I assumed were his natural suspicions had curdled into something closer to paranoia. It didn't help that I had not committed to memory the entirety of his scientific oeuvre—publications from the early 1970s that had established him as a true scholar of the American eel. He was rightfully proud of this work, and of the "Sheldon elver trap," the now outdated contraption he'd designed to jump-start a glass eel's journey from freedom to sushi plate. A net of another sort stretched unfurled across sixteen feet of the polished wood floor of his office, abutting a boat-shaped bookcase stocked with milky-green, thick-glassed bottles and other treasures coughed up by the sea. Was he a collector? I asked. He shrugged. There was a telescope aimed across the frozen river, and photos of family members backed by ocean vistas. From this I presumed he had children and grandchildren; was that right? Sheldon ignored my lame attempts at small talk and got right to the point.

"Eels are easy to stress," he blurted, instructively. "A stressed eel is a weak eel. A weak eel won't make it to China."

Prison had not cramped Sheldon's style, or at least not by much. At family gatherings and other occasions, he still donned a fabulous raccoon coat of the sort favored by entitled Ivy League undergrads in the roaring twenties. Despite his conviction, he had retained his elver fishing license and what he told me was a forty-four-pound elver quota, and his wife, Cynthia, and daughter, Melanie, had their generous quotas, too. True, he'd relinquished his legal right to deal in eels (in 2014), and the government authorities had fined him $10,000 and forced him to surrender his Ford Super Duty pickup with the vanity plate "EELWGN." And all that hurt. After all, he'd made his fortune—and his name—in eels.

I got my first glimpse of Sheldon in BuzzFeed, in an article published way back in 2013. I reached the author, journalist Peter Smith, by phone, to learn more about his experience of Sheldon's eel dealing operation. Smith told me that he'd joined Sheldon for a drive in the Eel Wagon to the city of Ellsworth, Maine, gateway to Acadia National Park. But that was more than a decade ago, and Smith's recollection was foggy. So with his help I made an attempt to re-create the experience on my own.

Arriving at Ellsworth from the south, I hung a right onto High Street, a charmless four-lane strip, and drove past the fast-food joints and bait shops to (the now defunct) Jasper's Restaurant and Motel. As Peter Smith tells it, this is where Sheldon parked his truck, grabbed a bag and an extension cord from the back seat, and strolled to the front desk to register for a room with a window facing the parking lot. He found his room, dropped his duffel on the bed, and then plugged one end of the extension cord into an outlet and snaked the other end through the window. Later he'd connect that cord to the bubbler on the water tank in the flat bed of his truck, to pump oxygen for the elvers he'd buy from fishermen on the river. But first he'd wash up and maybe smoke a joint (according to Peter Smith, he held a Maine medical marijuana card) or grab an espresso to brace for the work to come.

Several hours before sunup, Sheldon would return to the parking lot to double-check the flare gun positioned "gut height"

William Sheldon, the "Eel Godfather" of Maine, in his fabulous racoon coat. Along with a profound knowledge of the ocean, rivers, and wildlife, Sheldon has a deep appreciation for the finer things in life. (Stephen Rappaport)

from his truck's grab handle, then hoist himself into the driver's seat. He'd feel reflexively for the safe box where he kept bank-wrapped wads of $20 and $50 bills and tested the weight of the Glock 40 displayed in full view on the dash. He had faith in his fellow Mainers, and he wasn't the type to worry. Still, he took no risks: he had the flare gun and the Glock, and he had Larry Taylor, a bodyguard armed with a concealed .45, an unconcealed 9mm, and a showy 12-gauge pistol-grip shotgun.

Sheldon and Taylor would drive through the darkness to the Union River to connect with the elver fishers before another dealer got to them first. (That river, one scientist told me, is "one of the best eel spots in the United States.") The morning fog was just rolling out to reveal a riverbank thick with fishermen in headlamps, some packing up for the morning, some still fiddling with their nets. Sheldon and Taylor sat on folding lawn chairs beside the truck, waiting for the stream of fishermen to trickle over to them: strong-shouldered women in thigh-high rubber boots tugged over camouflage pants; burly, grizzled men in overalls and flannel shirts. Some came with dainty ounces of elvers barely making a ripple in five-gallon buckets, others with buckets roiling with a pound or more. Sheldon sieved the contents of each bucket through a fine mesh net into a metal bowl and weighed each dry batch to a tiny fraction of an ounce. He always paid cash—counting out hundreds, sometimes thousands of dollars in bills. When the spirit moved him, he'd round up the payoff a few bucks, urging the bleary-eyed fisherman to "have breakfast on me." Everyone, it seemed, loved the guy. Once the last elver fisher was paid and gone, Sheldon and Taylor packed up the truck and drove back to Jasper's Motel, where they'd set up in the parking lot to buy elvers from fishermen they had missed earlier, or who had dipped and trapped on other rivers. Some days were better than others. The best hauls—and the best money—came on moonless, fog-blotted nights, the nights Sheldon's suppliers were most at risk of getting clobbered and their nets cut by thieves. On nights like that, with half a million dollars in cash at hand to buy every elver he could get his hands on, Sheldon saw the true potential of his business. And like all ambitious entrepreneurs, he dreamed of having more.

SHELDON WAS NOT BORN TO a life of crime, though he has always had a taste for adventure. His father, forty-four years a welder, believed that a fellow ought to have a job with security, benefits, and a retirement fund. A dutiful son, young Sheldon went along with the plan. He enrolled at the University of Maine, earned a degree in wildlife management, and signed on as a Sea Grant–funded technician with Maine's Department of Marine Resources, where his assignment was to keep tabs on the behavior patterns of the American eel. (Maine had no glass eel fishery at the time, but Sheldon had fished grown eels in rivers and knew the animal.) The state job was steady and challenging, but paid less than what he knew he was worth. So, like so many Mainers, Sheldon got a side gig. He bought a wetsuit, completed a course in underwater diving at a nearby college, and drove to the Machias River on summer weekends to play Paul Bunyan in scuba gear, reclaiming waterlogged tree trunks that years earlier had sunk and lodged in the river-bottom mud. Sheldon told me that he got good at spotting "sinkers" that "wanted to float" and would come up easy. He'd dive to the bottom, knot an eight-foot length of float rope to the top of the submerged log, have a buddy in a nearby boat winch it to the surface and onto the beach, and then haul the monster four feet up the bank and drag it onto his truck. Muddy riverbeds lack the light, air, and microorganisms that rot wood, so sunken timber is sunken treasure. Sheldon recalled dislodging and hauling out fifty to sixty tree trunks in a day, most of them ready for the sawmill. (That number seemed a bit high to me, but we'll go with it.) "We'd get eighty dollars for every thousand board feet," Sheldon said. "Make a couple of hundred in a day. That was more than I made in a week working for the state."

Convinced that golden opportunities didn't come wrapped in a conventional job, Sheldon kept his options open. And just as he expected, opportunity—this time in the form of eels—hunted him down. This was the early 1970s, when sushi was taking off and the demand for eel had started to exceed the supply, especially in Japan, where the domestic species was already in decline. A fishery attaché at the US embassy in Tokyo contacted Sheldon's boss at DMR to ask whether the state had enough baby eels to merit the opening of a commercial glass eel fishery that might help Japan satisfy its cravings. "Do we got eels?" Sheldon recalled being asked. "Yeah, we've got tons of 'em."

Sheldon had spent the springs of 1971 and 1972 on eel duty, observing them in the Kennebec, Penobscot, and St. Croix Rivers. And in every river, brook, and stream he checked, there were plenty. He watched elvers squirt straight up waterfalls and down the face of hydroelectric dams. They were ubiquitous and, it seemed to him, indestructible. He had never eaten eel, didn't want to, and harbored no concerns for their safety. Still, he was captivated, and in 1974 he published a seminal twenty-five-page manifesto on locating, catching, and managing young eels in captivity, which boldly speculated: "It seems likely that the entire North American population (of eels) could be sustained by the spawning of adults from only a few of the freshwater population." If this were so, he reckoned, Maine had enough eels to satisfy demand the world over.

Ever the treasure hunter, Sheldon recognized the opportunity and grabbed it. He began by kludging that eponymous elver trap from a window screen, a wood frame, and a garden hose. He used the trap to scoop up a sample batch of baby eels that he shipped to potential buyers in Japan, not sure whether the elvers would survive the trip. Most did survive, but the Japanese preferred their own species, *Anguilla japonica*, and with shipping and other costs, they would not pay enough for the American species to convince Sheldon to throw in his lot with eels. So instead he quit his state job and took a leap into the lobster business. As for eels, he said, "I passed on my knowledge to Mr. Randall Livingston in South Carolina—the first-ever commercial glass eel exporter in the country."

TODAY, RANDALL LIVINGSTON, PRESIDENT AND owner of W. R. Livingston Fish Co. in Moncks Corner, South Carolina, is something of a (no-longer-living) legend in eel circles. But in the early 1950s, Livingston was just a commercial fisherman and fish seller, mining the waters of the Santee-Cooper River and Lake Moultrie for catfish that he sold to (among others) vendors at the Fulton Fish Market, two blocks of scruffy open-air stalls not far from Wall Street near the southern tip of Manhattan. (The market later upgraded to a 400,000-square-foot indoor facility in Hunts Point, the Bronx.) Like many commercial fishermen, Livingston and his employees made frequent unintended "bycatches" of yellow eels, large fish not worth the cost of trucking out of state. He tried to sell the eels locally, but the locals declined to bite—he literally could not give his eels away. A practical man, Livingston was reluctant to trash what he knew was a perfectly good eating fish, so he decided to brave the shipping costs and slip 800 pounds of eels into a catfish shipment to Fulton Market. To his relief, New Yorkers did bite, and not just the dealers at Fulton Market. Chinatown chefs, too, turned out to be eager customers; their restaurants featured eel in several preparations, including a specialty eel egg roll. The wholesale price for whole, head-on gutted adult eels started out at twenty-five cents a pound and gradually rose to forty-five cents, back then about the same price as salmon. But after a few years, Livingston found it more and more difficult to do business in New York City, where fish peddlers, he complained, began cheating him on price, sometimes offering only a few cents per pound at delivery knowing—given how quickly fish spoil—that he had little choice but to accept.

Casting a wider net, Livingston found that the foreign market for eels was strong, especially during the holiday season. By the early 1970s, Livingston was shipping 150,000 pounds of mature eel annually to buyers in the Netherlands, Belgium, and Germany.

So much did the Europeans enjoy his eel, Livingston claimed, that he could sell them "ten times more" were his fisherman able to catch them. That was only partially true: Europeans did love the succulent and fat South Carolina eel taken from Lake Moultrie. But they did not love South Carolina River eel, which was lean and tough and did not take well to the smoker. To provide foreign clients with the sort of eel for which they'd be willing to pay, Livingston needed to up his game. Rather than ship mature river eels, he decided to harvest baby eels and either grow them to market size in the controlled environment of his catfish ponds or pack them in water and ice and ship them off to be raised on eel farms in Japan. A reasonable proposition, with one caveat: neither he nor his suppliers had much experience with glass eels or elvers.

Livingston got word that "a guy up in Maine" knew something about baby eels and that guy was Bill Sheldon. An outgoing, gregarious man, Livingston had no problem cold-calling Sheldon to seek his advice. "I told him the best places to catch elvers," Sheldon said, along with tips on how to catch them and keep them alive. I asked Sheldon why he'd share his secrets with a sharp competitor like Livingston, and he told me that he had no financial interest in elvers at the time; he was making plenty in lobsters. What Sheldon didn't mention was that Livingston already had a partner in the Maine elver business: a scrappy young mother of three by the name of Pat Bryant.

IF BILL SHELDON IS, AS is often said, the Godfather of the eels of Maine, then Pat Bryant is surely the unsung Godmother. But unlike Sheldon, Bryant is an open book. When I called to arrange a meeting, she did not hesitate to invite me to her neat four-bedroom home at the end of a leafy drive in the former shipbuilding town of Nobleboro, not far from the Maine coast. The door was open when

I arrived, and I removed my shoes before padding into the kitchen, where Bryant was making chili for a church supper happening that evening. I noticed she was also nursing a margarita. "It's what I drink when I cook Mexican," she said, though I hadn't asked. "I drink wine when I cook Italian, and beer when I cook American." I was working up the nerve to ask what she drank when she cooked Chinese when her Chihuahua, Herbie, took a hard nip at my shin. Bryant barked an obscenity. "He's very protective of me," she said, with what sounded like great affection. Then Herbie had a go at my stocking feet, and to my horror she scooped up the little yapper and flung him out of the room.

With her blond highlights, neat figure, and high-octane charisma, Bryant, a great-grandmother, might be mistaken for one of her daughters, the eldest of whom is just sixteen years her junior. When those daughters were young, Pat styled hair at Mr. Louie's in Damariscotta, while her second husband, Paul, supervised electrical maintenance at Bath Iron Works. Pat loved her job, but she didn't like having a boss, so she scrimped and saved to buy her own salon. The business did well, but with three daughters to feed, clothe, and keep out of trouble, money was always tight, even with both parents working full-time. So it felt like kismet when a friend of her brother's—a retired Maine State Police officer—mentioned a side gig he thought might suit her. Seems that a Mr. Livingston, an eel dealer from South Carolina, had employed her brother's pal to investigate a pair of locals he had hired to keep an eye on his Maine elver operations. "They were just crooked, anything illegal, they would do," Pat said. "Con artists, hustlers, all these years later, one of them is still in prison!" Clearly, Mr. Livingston was in need of a new pair of eyes in Maine, and Pat was up for the challenge. She and eels went way back.

"My father used to throw off a line in Newcastle and get eels,"

Pat said, Newcastle being a town not far from where we were chatting. "There were lots of eel fishermen around then, catching larger eels. But you can't sell those; they've eaten in the wild and have a different texture, don't have the fat content. They have that muddy taste." Cultured eels, Pat said, taste like meat. So rather than fishing for wild eels, Pat and Paul tried to cultivate eels from elvers in forty clay-bottomed farm ponds they fed with river water. It wasn't easy. "We had no control," Pat said. "They'd escape, slither off, go every which way."

Still, enough eels stayed put to begin to pay back the effort. Early Saturday mornings they'd transfer five hundred to six hundred grown eels into an enormous water tank set into their box truck and speed seven hours straight down to Mott Street in New York City's Chinatown. "I damn near ran over a dozen people pushing rickshaws and whatnot," Pat told me, though, it being 1978—not 1878—I found that hard to imagine. "You're trying to park your semi and they're hollering at you and using all kinds of damn language you can't understand, waving their arms. But we'd get in there. And then we'd go to a supermarket in Queens. They took the eels, paid their money, and you were out of there. We did that for a couple of years. My daughter thought it was funny. She said, 'Mom, you cannot be the eel queen of the Waldoboro River because you have all your teeth.' You know eel fishermen didn't go to the dentist, they thought they were much better off spending their money on a [Ford F-]150 than on their teeth. They'd buy booze, cigarettes, pot, then cars and vehicles, then, if there was any money left, groceries. At least, that's what everyone thought. As far as the townspeople were concerned, when eels were cheap, we were all bucket-totin' barbarians."

Whatever eel fishermen were back then, they weren't rich: mature eel *retailed* for maybe $2.50 a pound, not terrible but—considering how tough it is to reel in an eel—not nearly enough for eel fishers to quit their day jobs. Elver prices were much higher, and catching elvers was much cleaner—they didn't fight you like a grown eel. Pat and John agreed to join with Mr. Livingston to deal elvers, caught by them and as many as 120 other Maine fishermen they recruited to the task. And rather than Mott Street in Chinatown, they'd truck the elvers down Rockaway Boulevard in Queens to John F. Kennedy Airport, where they'd meet up with Livingston and his wife. At the time, it was legal to trap and dip for elvers in most states along the eastern seaboard, so the Livingstons—who drove from their home in South Carolina—took detours to purchase elvers from dealers in Delaware and Connecticut. Arriving at the airport, the two couples would huddle on the tarmac to hand-pack a couple of hundred pounds of elvers into specially made Styrofoam containers cooled with bags of ice. When all was ready, Pat told me, they'd ship the elvers off on a midnight Flying Tigers flight to Asia.

Pat gave the chili a good stir, polished off her margarita, and left the kitchen, returning with the May/June 1975 issue of *Aquaculture & the Fish Farmer*, published in Little Rock, Arkansas. "That's Mr. Livingston's photo on the cover," she told me. "He looks like Hal Holbrook." (I agreed the likeness was remarkable.) As far as Pat knew, Livingston was the first elver exporter in the United States. "He was way ahead of his time," she said. "I just loved that man."

Fishing elvers was not a classy job back then, nor, for that matter, terribly lucrative. Still, Pat relished the freewheeling treasure hunt of it, and the way it drew people in, especially other women. "Every hairdresser that ever worked for me became an elver fisherman," she said. "We fished at night and did hair in the day—and we did that for a very long time." Pat likes to joke about the time she lost power at her home—without electricity, the pumps would stop and the elvers in her holding tanks would die. "Every stylist but one just got up and left the salon, left customers sitting under the hair dryers, and we all raced back to the house," she said. "We were all running down to the pond in heels and miniskirts, hauling buckets of water to save the eels." Pat's daughters, too, joined the elver business, which they named (what else?) PB Eel. Elvers did so well for them that in 1995 Pat sold her hair salon, Paul retired from his job at the ironworks, and they moved to South Carolina to help Mr. Livingston manage his eel farm. Unfortunately, for reasons that Pat preferred not to share, things didn't work out, and two years later she and Paul returned to Maine.

By then, Pat said, elver fishing had "gotten weird." As the price crept upward of $200 a pound, what was once a family-friendly fishery began to feel closer to a Cosa Nostra operation. "The creeps got into it," Pat said. "Damnedest thing you've ever seen. They'd cut up our gear, steal our nets, just was a whole ridiculous state of affairs." It got so bad that when Pat and Paul stepped out for the evening, Pat stashed their elver earnings in the doghouse, on the logic that no self-respecting thief would risk grappling with her mutt. She bought a Smith & Wesson revolver and a 9mm Luger. She felt threatened and alone. As for eel Godfather Bill Sheldon, well, she didn't have much use for him, and she shared with me a long list of his alleged transgressions—many tantalizing, most unverifiable. And she said he tells his eel story backward: it wasn't him who helped Livingston; it was the other way around. "Bill Sheldon loved Mr. Livingston, too," she told me. "He should, because he owes him everything."

Sheldon recalls matters differently, of course, but he does agree that Livingston helped him out when his lobster business tanked. "I had the fastest lobster boat in the world," he told me, a modest claim given that few lobster boats are built for speed. "It was a custom-made Young Brothers, fiberglass hull, with a shower and a full-sized walnut rolltop desk in the pilothouse. I named it *Lucky One*. It cost a lot of money, and I pretty much lived in it." In 1992, *Lucky One* ran out of luck, ran aground, and sank. Somehow, Sheldon had let his boat insurance lapse and owed $135,000 on the mortgage on his home. "The bank told me to sell the house to pay off the mortgage and they'd call it square," he said. "So, I lost my boat, and I lost my home." Sheldon called Livingston to ask for help getting back on his feet. Livingston did not disappoint. "The boat sank March nineteenth," Sheldon said. "On March twenty-fifth, I was in South Carolina with my traps and nets out fishing with [Livingston's] sons. We fished most states up and down the East Coast from South Carolina to Maine, caught a lot of elvers, and we made money."

What made elver fishing especially appealing was that there was no need to buy a boat or much else to break into the business—just a net and a bucket would do. And no one seemed to care how or where you trapped. Sheldon said he and Livingston's sons were "like Gypsies," skipping north up the eastern seaboard from motel to motel as the weather warmed, scooping up elvers everywhere rivers met the sea. "It was like catching mosquitoes," Sheldon said. "No one gave a hoot."

Livingston died of a heart attack in 2008, and his sons inherited the business. According to Sheldon, the sons were fishermen, not businessmen, so he graciously stepped in to take the reins. "I decided I'd buy eels from Randall's sons and ship them overseas myself," he said. "I've been buying eels ever since."

Sheldon became known as the largest elver dealer in Maine, renowned for his knowledge and skill. He lured newcomers to the fishery, teaching them how best to arrange their fyke nets and when and where to anchor them. He built an online presence and cheered on Maine elver fishermen both in and off-season, promising support and a good price. These efforts, while generous, should not be mistaken for simple acts of charity. Sheldon needed elver fishermen to be successful because he needed elvers—he procured as much as half the state's entire quota on behalf of his patron, the Delaware Valley Fish Company, then and now the largest exporter of eels in all of North America. And to a freethinking man like Sheldon, half of Maine's annual legal elver haul—just under 5,000 pounds—just wasn't enough. Those vexing quotas were holding him back, and for what? He saw no reason that fishermen shouldn't be allowed to catch more Maine elvers, or even elvers in other states, as he could see with his own eyes that baby eels were not endangered. "Every stream, every river, every lake and pond up and down the East Coast has a run of eels, that's how plentiful they are," he told me. "All fishermen in Maine would like to see a higher quota. We don't want to see it overfished, but the quota could be doubled, and it wouldn't hurt this resource."

DAVID SYKES, RESIDENT AGENT IN charge of the U.S. Fish and Wildlife Service (USFWS), has a few things in common with Bill Sheldon—an independent spirit, a love of the outdoors, and a deep knowledge of the natural world. Still, much like Pat Bryant, he keeps his distance from the man. Nothing worse, he told me, than a guy preying on the hopes of desperate people who are just trying to get by. Sheldon didn't just selflessly "mentor" novice elver fishermen as he claimed, Sykes told me; he also tutored them in the fine points of breaking the law.

Crew-cut sharp and triathlete trim, Sykes favors green tea over coffee. A former cop and Secret Service agent, he grew up on Peaks Island, a tight-knit community seventeen minutes by ferry off the coast of Portland. With its stunning views of Casco Bay and lively waterfront, Peaks Island is so popular with tourists, some call it the Coney Island of Maine. Sykes returns there regularly with his wife and four kids, and he plans to retire to Maine when the time is right. But for now his base is Boston, so that's where we met.

It seemed to me that Sykes, understated and unflappable, was fixated on one mission: saving the world from people like Bill Sheldon in general, and Bill Sheldon in particular. One might venture that this fixation stems from a certain trauma. Back in 2011 and new on the job, Sykes got a call from a Fish and Wildlife Service colleague in South Carolina, tipping him off to a massive elver-poaching operation. Sykes's superiors in Washington had also gotten word and ordered him to drop everything on his calendar and pull together a team to track down, confront, and arrest the elver thieves. On its face, this seemed like a straightforward—even routine—assignment for a man who had spent his career chasing bad guys. But at the time, Sykes had little experience of wildlife crime, and no idea what he was up against. What he assumed would be a simple matter of a few friendly conversations, stern warnings, and slaps on the wrist turned out to be a drawn-out—and potentially lethal—military-style operation.

"Eel fishing happens in the dark," Sykes reminded me. "And when people are doing hundred-thousand-dollar deals in cash in the middle of nowhere at four A.M., you expect trouble." But what happened was a lot more trouble than he imagined. "Operation Broken Glass" stretched into a multiyear undercover investigation involving sixteen state and federal agencies and scores of government operatives. Agents of the USFWS posed as fishermen and dealers of illegally caught elvers. Sykes and his team quickly learned that eel thieves do not like posers. In 2013, Tommy Water Zhou, a forty-two-year-old seafood dealer from Brooklyn, procured a one-year elver dealer's license from the state of Maine. A few months later, he bought elvers from two undercover USFWS agents posing as eel poachers from Virginia. The legal price at the time was $2,000 to $2,500 a pound, but the agents had agreed to sell their catch for the black market price of $1,500, and Zhou was more than happy to do the deal. But a few days later he warned Eric Holmes, one of the uncover agents posing as a fisherman, that while he would do business with him, were Holmes or his partner to betray him he would pay a hit man $200,000 to kill them. "I didn't blink an eye," Holmes told me when I caught up with him by phone. In April that year, Zhou, still under surveillance by law enforcement, drove to JFK International Airport and shipped eleven boxes of undeclared elvers to Hong Kong.

Operation Broken Glass agents surveilled elver thieves such as Zhou and Sheldon over a period of months, even years, before confronting them. "The case of Bill Sheldon alone would have been significant," Holmes said. "But when we infiltrated, we saw what we were in for . . . and we went after every illegal fisherman and dealer we could find." The take-down came in one precisely orchestrated, multi-state raid on April 30, 2014. "Our agents were punched, kicked," Sykes told me. "There was a helicopter chase. My biggest concern was keeping my people safe. But my men had to take the heat. In a sting like this, once you put a suspect in handcuffs, everyone knows who you are, and your cover is blown. That puts everyone at risk. You can't take the poachers and dealers down one at a time, because word gets out. You've got to hit them all at the same time."

Sykes and his team arrested 110 suspects in eight Atlantic states from South Carolina to Maine. They carefully culled the bit players, whittling down the number to twenty-two. Of these, all eventually pled guilty to wildlife trafficking, and five of those to illegal dealing. Bill Sheldon was chief among them.

By some trick of fate, Stephen Rappaport, then a fisheries reporter for the *Ellsworth American*, happened to be driving down High Street the morning Sheldon got busted at his unofficial headquarters at Jasper's Motel. "I saw Bill's trucks and maybe five Fish and Wildlife trucks, so I pulled over and grabbed my camera," Rappaport told me. A former New York City attorney and self-avowed "law and order guy," Rappaport came to Maine for the scenery and stayed for the lifestyle. He knew Sheldon well and, like a few other outdoorsmen I met, respected him. "I know a lot of fishermen who sold elvers to Sheldon, and he never shorted one of them," he told me. "He was instrumental in getting the export market organized, in dealing with the foreign buyers, mostly Chinese. He's a hard worker, a very smart guy." At the time of the bust, Sheldon was dealing elvers out of rooms 26 and 27 on the first floor of Jasper's Motel. Parked outside were his pickups, each with an aerated live fish tank in its bed. Federal wildlife and fisheries officers joined the Maine Marine Patrol in the raid, searching both motel rooms and both trucks while other agents searched Sheldon's home overlooking the Kennebec River in Woolwich. They came armed with a warrant to seize and copy every record—whether electronic or paper—related to Sheldon's elver business, as well as other items that could be linked to his illegal activities—cash, waders, nets, even the elvers themselves. According to the search warrant affidavit filed by Special Agent Holmes, Sheldon trafficked in glass eels poached in South Carolina, Maine, and Virginia, and advised an undercover agent posing as a fishermen to take glass eels from forbidden rivers. Ever the expert, Sheldon also coached the agent on how to avoid arrest if he were caught and sold elvers to an unnamed exporter without disclosing their illegal status.

Sheldon at first denied any culpability, but the evidence against him was overwhelming, including recorded conversations in which he declared he was "aware" that the elvers he was buying were illegal. Eventually, Sheldon and his co-conspirators confessed to poaching more than $5 million worth of elvers over a three-year period in violation of the Lacey Act of 1900, the federal law that prohibits the trafficking of illegally taken wildlife and plants. At his sentencing hearing in Portland on May 3, 2018, he admitted to the illegal transfer of 268 pounds of elvers, or roughly half a million dollars' worth. Though unlikely ever to be known, the actual amount was thought to be much higher. Cassandra Barnum, one of the two government attorneys prosecuting the case, stated that 268 pounds represented "only a small portion of his overall dealings." Barnum went on to declare Bill Sheldon "unique among the defendants in these cases on several vectors. Perhaps most significantly by his own pronouncement and by consensus of the community, he knows more about elver fishing than anyone . . . The bottom line . . . is that Bill Sheldon not only facilitated a black market in illegal elvers, he also encouraged it. He didn't just dodge the law himself; he told other people what to say if they got caught. And he still seems to think and wants you to think that what he did isn't a big deal and that he deserves to continue participating in the fishery he cheated."

Sykes agreed with Barnum's assessment, adding that arrogance was a common quality in wildlife criminals, who often claim a special knowledge of the creatures they exploit. "Sheldon knew eels," he told me. "Knew how to keep them alive, knew how to take care of them. That's the way it is in wildlife crime—the criminals know a lot about the thing they are stealing, and they believe they can take better care of them than anyone else. Sheldon's whole life is eels."

Standing before the sentencing judge at his hearing in 2018, Sheldon spoke of his embarrassment and shame, and cited his younger daughter's recent death by suicide as part of the price he had already paid for his mistakes. "Debbie took her own life on the last day of elver season," Sheldon testified. "Her death left a huge hole in my heart, and I will forever feel like I was responsible for it because I know Debbie was very worried and concerned about me because of my indictment." This moved the judge, who issued a (relatively light) sentence of six months in prison (delayed for thirty-five days to allow Sheldon to attend his granddaughter's high school graduation), a $10,000 fine, and three years of supervised release. But when we met, Sheldon downplayed his crimes, attacking the contention of most scientists that the American eel as a species is in danger. Sheldon seemed to believe that he held stewardship over the species he'd plundered and that, as a veteran of the elver fishery, he had earned what all evidence suggests he so brashly stole. There are plenty of eels, he told me, and anyone with eyes can see that they are not threatened.

In 2014, the year Sheldon was busted, he made the calculated decision to voluntarily forsake his license to deal eels. At his court hearing four years later, his defense attorney, Walter McKee, made much of this alleged sacrifice, insisting that Sheldon was no eel kingpin but merely a rank-and-file employee of what McKee vaguely called "the company," namely Maine Eel Trade and Aquaculture. What McKee didn't mention was that Cindy Sheldon, Bill's wife (and, impressively, a vice president of the Savings Bank of Maine), maintained executive status at the company, through which the family could legally continue to buy and sell eels openly and pretty much indefinitely. None of this sits well with the men and women who have devoted their careers to the protection of the American eel and other threatened wildlife, some risking their lives in the process.

In 2019, David Sykes and the Operation Broken Glass team won the Leadership Award from the International Association of Chiefs of Police. Sykes appreciates the recognition, but he's doubtful that his efforts will put much of a dent in elver poaching or greatly reduce the species' risk of endangerment. "Greed is a natural human trait," he told me. "There's nothing we can do about that." What we can do, he said, is learn enough about the eel to ward off its further decline. But that, too, is a very tall order. Like Sheldon, eels are masters of deception, but they are far better at keeping secrets.

CHAPTER 3

NUNS OF THE WATER

It is very strange
that men should deny a Creator and yet attribute
to themselves the power of creating eels.
—Voltaire, *Questions sur l'Encyclopédie*

"TO A PERSON NOT ACQUAINTED with the circumstances of the case it must seem astonishing, and it certainly is somewhat humiliating to men of science, that a fish which is commoner in many parts of the world than any other . . . which is daily seen in the market and on the table, has been able, in spite of the powerful aid of modern science, to shroud the manner of its propagation, its birth and its death in darkness, which even to the present day has not been completely dispelled." So wrote the German marine biologist Leopold Jacoby of the eel in 1879. Much, but not enough, has changed since then.

On the bright side, we do know a few things. We know that eels are beautiful swimmers, with muscular torsos that slip effortlessly through the water like liquid velvet. We know that they have snakelike bodies with one continuous dorsal, anal, and caudal fin and tiny embedded scales. We know that some eels rock pectoral fins that could pass for tiny Dumbo ears, and others are tarted out in colorful snowflake tattoos. And we know that unlike their parasitic imposter, the lamprey, true eels don't suck their prey dry but chomp down with proper jaws. We also know that eels range wildly in size, from an unassuming two inches, the spread of a butterfly's wings (the tiny *Monognathus*), to an intimidating fourteen feet, the standing height of an African bush elephant (the giant moray). We know that eels have air bladders that they use to regulate their depth in the ocean, much as does a submarine. And contrary to the beliefs of many natural scientists through the ages, we also know that all eels are fish.

So where to start? There are so many species of eels! Ichthyologists count 820, each with its own lifestyle and environmental niche. Fortunately for us, of these, only nineteen or so fall under the genus *Anguilla*, the so-called freshwater eels. (Some count only eighteen, or even fifteen, if one excludes subspecies from the list.) Of these, those best suited to temperate climes—the Japanese eel, and the two Atlantic eels (the European and the American)—command the most commercial attention. For those of us living north of the equator, these are the eels we think of if we ever think of eels. Understandably, not all of us do.

Anguilla first appeared in a world in which humans played no part, a world beyond imagination. Genomic analysis dates its ancestors to before the Early Jurassic, the age of giant sea reptiles, when dinosaurs ruled. That's 140 (plus or minus) million years before the rise of any primate, an era when Homo sapiens was barely a gleam in the galaxy's eye. Scientists believe that this early version of the eel first appeared in the ancient Tethys Ocean near what is today Indonesia. Even then, the eel was caught between worlds.

During the 165 million years of dinosaur existence, the supercontinent of Pangaea slowly split into the landmasses Laurasia and Gondwana, which eventually splintered into the continents we know today. Africa and the Arabian Plate moved north and collided with the Eurasian Plate, effectively closing the link between the western and eastern oceans. The eel population was parted, and going forward, the Japanese eel evolved independently from the Atlantic eel. Three million years ago the Isthmus of Panama closed the gap between North and South America and altered the eel's path once again. The Atlantic widened with the continental drift, and the Atlantic eel split into two species—the European eel in the east and the American eel in the west. The Atlantic currents settled into a pattern we now call the North Atlantic Gyre, a rotating current that flows from the east coast of North America to the west coasts of Europe and Africa.

Atlantic eels—both the European and the American species—rely on the North Atlantic Gyre to launch their migration from what is believed to be their birthplace in the Sargasso Sea toward the continental shelves of the Americas, Europe, and North Africa. As its name implies, the American eel—the only freshwater eel in the United States—typically peels off in the Americas, with a good number landing along the east coast of the United States and Canada. Along with those of a few other species—humpback whales, Arctic terns, bar-headed geese, monarch butterflies, and humans (who, after all, have found our way to the moon), the epic migration of the freshwater eel is among the most extraordinary feats of long-distance navigation in the animal kingdom. The migration of infant American eels to our pretty pond in Maine likely

A passenger grabs a club with which to defend an oarsman threatened by a giant eel. While eels are top predators that can languish for decades in freshwater environments, there is no record of an eel of any size posing a danger to humans (W. E. Wigfall [1908]. Wellcome Collection)

took a year or more, while their tiny European cousins battled the currents for an astonishing two and a half years in pursuit of their preferred freshwater inlet.

Given this peculiar and largely unobservable migration pattern, it's little wonder that the freshwater eel caught the attention of history's thought leaders, particularly in matters of sex and reproduction. It's quite possible that early Native American thinkers had their own theories as to how and from where eels swarmed to their shores, but since we have few if any written records of these we must turn to Europe—and the European eel—for enlightenment. In his exhaustive and groundbreaking *History of Animals*, written nearly 2,400 years ago, Aristotle offers this observation: "The eels that are called females are the best for the table: they look as though they were female, but they really are not so." This confusing appraisal reflects the great philosopher's belief that the eel was "neither male nor female, nor is anything produced from them." Hence it was Aristotle's view that the eel was androgenous and incapable of sexual reproduction. He reasoned that all creatures were made possible by pneuma, the "breath of life" that contained within it a vital heat that, like the sun, made things grow. When this force interacted with "elemental matter"—the stuff of which all living things are made—it caused life to emerge. Under this logic, Aristotle popularized the idea that the eel sprang spontaneously from the "entrails of the earth which are found spontaneously in mud and moist soil." Put simply, Aristotle posited that the reproductive maneuvers of the eel were irrefutable evidence of spontaneous generation, the theory that life can arise from nonliving matter.

Some scholars take Aristotle's meaning to have been that eels are born not spontaneously from mud but from eel larvae that had gotten *buried* in the mud, an interpretation somewhat closer to what we now know is true. But that interpretation, while generous, is not likely to be accurate, since Aristotle's legions of followers continued to promote the spontaneous generation theory for generations. To be fair, Aristotle's contributions to human thought were monumental, and his observations of fish and other animals astute, among them that "no eel has ever been found to contain semen or eggs; and when eels have been opened neither seminal nor ovarian ducts have been discovered." If not spontaneous generation, then, what force of nature was behind the great proliferation of eels? With this, he rested his case.

PLINY THE ELDER, THE ROMAN author and naturalist, addressed the eel question in his *Naturalis Historia*, an encyclopedic and enormously influential work of uneven accuracy completed some years before 79 CE, the year he perished soon after the eruption of Mt. Vesuvius. Never a stickler for evidence, Pliny the Elder theorized that when stung by the itch to procreate, eels rub themselves on rocks, shedding scales and other bits from which new eels emerge, a process twenty-first-century scientists might characterize as "cloning." A hundred or so years later during the reign of Emperor Marcus Aurelius, the Greco-Roman poet Oppian built on this theory with the bizarre but (at the time) credible idea that eels coiled around each other oozing a thick, foamy excretion that burst into life the moment it hit the sand. This insight seemed to provoke a series of increasingly fanciful propositions: that eels sprang fully formed from putrid matter, or leaked from the gills of other fishes, or were spawned by aquatic beetles Sardinian fishermen affectionately called the "eel mother."

The German Benedictine abbess Hildegard of Bingen (1098–1179), noted philosopher, composer, and medical practitioner, was unable to get her head around the idea of eel immaculate conception, and proposed that eels reproduced sexually, despite the apparent absence of genitalia. Each winter, she opined, the female chooses an appropriate stone and spits "seeds the size of horse beans" onto it. The male then spits "something like milk over the seeds," and after some struggle, the male and female together lie on top of the seeds, the male protecting them with his tail, the female blowing "vital air" onto them until they come alive. A primitive version of in vitro fertilization, given that this process involved eels of both genders, this is perhaps one of the more romantic tellings of the eel procreation story.

If all these theories sound wildly unlikely, they are indeed in the stark light of the Digital Age. But it's not difficult to see why our less illuminated forebears found them credible. The pre-Enlightenment worldview was dominated by a church that did not overly rely on proven fact or experimentation to support its judgments. Faith often played the lead role, as did intuition. The genitalia of the freshwater eel are nearly invisible, and as I've mentioned, great swaths of its life cycle are unobservable. Yet everywhere you looked, there were eels! How could that be? The undeniable abundance of this apparently chaste creature required, as one scholar put it, a "theory of reproduction on a grand scale."

That "grand" theory would have to wait as a parade of history's most elevated scholars continued to weigh in on the gnawing "eel question," many (if not most) of them unburdened by proof. In his *Codex Canadensis*, written and drawn between 1664 and 1675, Louis Nicolas, a Jesuit missionary sent from France to save the "savage souls" of the Canadian wilderness, refers to Aristotle in his own elaborate theory of where and how eels spawn. He wrote, "The eel is born from rotten material as worms are in earth. In my own opinion, I would suggest that the eel has on the outside a secret regenerative power that we do not understand." This summoning of a "secret regenerative power" served to buoy Aristotle's contention that a living organism can emerge unbidden from nonliving matter.

Izaak Walton (1593–1683), the English biographer and nature writer, seemed to conflate eels with fairies. In his book *The Compleat Angler*, he wrote without irony that eels "are bred of a particular dew falling in the Months of May and June on the banks of some particular Ponds or Rivers (apted by Nature for that end) which in a few days are by the Suns heat turned to Eeles." If you think about it (and I will not insist that you do), Walton may have been onto something. The philosopher Martin Heidegger once noted that the rise of modern science was rooted in the valorization of certainty and the demotion of wonder, resulting in a sort of disenchantment. In Walton's time, the world may have preferred to remain enchanted by eels, which were sometimes portrayed as magical creatures, even by the most venerated rationalists.

Sir Carl Linnaeus (1707–1778), botanist, physician, and undisputed "father of taxonomy" (as well as the father of seven children), was described by Jean-Jacques Rousseau as a "guardian angel sent from heaven." Apparently, even angels have their blind spots. Linnaeus, a great advocate of breastfeeding, railed against the use of wet nurses, asserting that human infants absorbed the personalities of the women who nursed them. More to our point, he (erroneously) described the freshwater eel as "viviparous," meaning that its eggs were fertilized internally and its young hatched fully formed. (Not that he'd ever witnessed such a thing, of course.) Linnaeus's error was built on a foundation laid by another esteemed rationalist, Antonie van Leeuwenhoek (1632–1723), the largely self-taught "father of microbiology" and inventor of the microscope who a century earlier had mistaken an eel's bladder for a womb and the parasitic worms found within it for baby eels.

While Izaak Walton fiddled with his fairies and before Linnaeus and Leeuwenhoek mistook parasites for eggs, a new breed of Italian experimentalists was treading a more enlightened path. Francesco Redi of Pisa (1626–1697), physician to the Medici family and acolyte of Galileo, was possessed by a radical idea: that science should be informed by critical judgment, experimentation, and—yes—actual evidence. Redi, later known as the father of experimental biology (by now you've noticed that there are legions of "scientific fathers" with links to eels), was one of an intrepid band of investigators working to dislodge Aristotle's sticky theory of spontaneous generation. To that end, he designed a primitive but effective experiment that proved that maggots do *not* (as was thought) arise "spontaneously" in rotten meat, but rather come courtesy of flies. Redi believed that a similar "life begetting life" strategy applied to many other (though not all) animals. Those life-begetting animals included eels, which he reckoned sprang not from scales or mud or dew, but from parents. Redi fortified his intuition with what he claimed were dutiful observations of eels descending on dark and cloudy August nights "from the lakes and rivers in compact groups, toward the sea. Here the female lays her eggs from which, after a variable time depending on the rigors of the sea, hatch elvers or young eels which then ascend the fresh waters by means of the estuaries."

Though unavoidably vague as to how and where this all happened (because, after all, it didn't happen), Redi's insight was a giant step in the right direction: that eels generate both semen and eggs and that their method of procreation does not differ significantly from that of many other fish. Still, as long as the eel's sexual organs remained elusive and its eggs invisible, the debate as to where eels came from was far from settled.

Just how eels begot other eels was a mystery aching to be solved, and there was no shortage of sleuths ready to take up the challenge. Among these was Dionisio Andrea Sancassani, a surgeon and, of all things, an expert on the treatment of wounds. One dreary evening in 1707, Sancassani was wading through the soggy streets of Comacchio, Italy, then a remote and impoverished town on the northern Adriatic coast. Enclosed within a lagoon that froze hard in the winter cold and festered malodorously in the summer heat, Comacchio would later be described by one observer as a "picture of hell," where the "souls of the damned, the eels, which lie in writhing heaps" are chopped to bits by "a fiend armed with a sharp hatchet." While this description is almost certainly overwrought, it wasn't far from the truth: late-eighteenth-century records of the town show an average annual eel catch of as much as a thousand tons. Eels and the eel fishery were Comacchio's lifeblood, employing men, women, and even young children. Why Sancassani found himself at the "eel house" that particular evening is not clear, though it's a reasonable guess that his intention was to select a succulent specimen for his dinner. Whatever his reason for being there, he was startled when a fisherman brought for his inspection an eel described as "copiously enlarged." So struck was Sancassani by this ungainly creature that he unsheathed his handy scalpel (to believe historical accounts, one must assume he was never without it) and slit the eel open to reveal what he later described as an ovary-like organ ripe with what to him looked like eggs. As a surgeon, not an anatomist, Sancassani was not in a strong position to believe his own eyes. For a second opinion he sent the (one hopes carefully preserved) corpse to his friend and colleague, the naturalist Antonio Valisneri, chair of medicine and professor at the University of Padua. Valisneri closely examined the bloated remains, and to his great pleasure confirmed that his dear friend had indeed found what so many before him had failed to find—the female genitalia of the European eel. Almost immediately, Valisneri prepared a comprehensive report of the discovery for the Academy of Bologna, published in 1710 under the title "De Ovario Anguillarium."

Antonio Maria Valsalva, professor of anatomy at the University of Bologna, was skeptical of Valisneri's claim. Inventor of surgical instruments and innovator of medical techniques, Valsalva was an ophthalmologist, rhinologist, and surgeon of such esteem that the Pope himself tried to employ him as his personal physician. (Valsalva gracefully declined the offer, as he preferred to remain at the university and at his post as president of the Bologna Academy of Science.) Renowned for many things, Valsalva is today most famous for his *Treatise of the Human Ear*, and for describing the structure and function of the now familiar Eustachian tube. It

Italian Antonio Maria Valsalva, a renowned anatomist and medical man deemed by some scholars the "father of psychiatry," was among many eighteenth-century scientists fascinated by the question of whether eels were truly sexual beings or—as Aristotle wrote and many thought—reproduced asexually through some version of spontaneous generation. (Wikimedia Commons)

is perhaps these triumphs that led him to take an interest in the common eel, the oil of which was an ancient (and wholly ineffective) remedy for deafness. That's my guess. But I'm also open to the more popular view that Valsalva, like so many wise men before him, was simply bewitched by the eel question, a puzzle he hoped to solve with the help of the disemboweled "pregnant" Comacchio eel.

Alas, after examining Sancassani's eel, Valsalva was not persuaded. Not one to mince words, he boldly proclaimed the so-called ovaries of the chunky eel as mere greasy blobs of fatty tissue. This was terribly disappointing, but no one, least of all Valisneri, felt in a position to challenge the great man's view. Still, there was progress. The involvement of a scholar of Valsalva's stature generated plenty of buzz, and the ovaries of the eel became a matter of grave importance to Bologna's scientific elite. The mutilation of many unfortunate eels ensued to no avail, and then—after several decades passed—another Italian, Pietro Molinelli, determined to settle the matter. A physician and philosopher of no great distinction, Molinelli put his money where his scientific betters put their mouths: he offered the fishermen of Comacchio a substantial reward to bring him a gravid (aka pregnant) eel. In 1752, Molinelli was grandly presented with what he was told was just such a miracle. Excitement mounted, as did the hopes of Bologna's eel-obsessed scientific community. But once again, those hopes were dashed when it was discovered that the cunning fisherman had sliced open the eel's belly and packed it with eggs of an entirely different species. There was no pregnant eel, nor would one be found in Molinelli's lifetime.

Bruised egos notwithstanding, the Italians mustered their forces and pressed on. Carlo Mondini, yet another Bolognian physician and anatomist, accepted for examination yet another presumably female Comacchio eel. Mondini applied himself with "great zeal" to the task of finding evidence of the eel's gender, and, satisfied that he had found it, presented his findings to the Bologna Academy in 1777. The paper, "De Anguillae ovariis," began on a sour note: that the "ovaries" and "eggs" that Valisneri had described more than half a century earlier were in reality a diseased swim bladder speckled with pustules. But this disappointing prologue was followed by some very good news: an accurate description, accompanied by fine illustrations, of the true ovaries of the eel as discovered by Mondini himself.

Break out the spumante!

Well, maybe not just yet. Again, a skeptic raised concerns. This time it was Lazzaro Spallanzani, renowned expert on animal reproduction at the University of Pavia, and a physicist, physiologist, and priest. (So many European scholars of the time—like so many Mainers of today—seem to have been polymaths.) So keen was Spallanzani to interrogate Mondini's finding that in October 1792, at the age of sixty-three, he took himself to the dismal lagoon of Comacchio to investigate. He spent months there observing the return of aged eels to the Adriatic, a spectacle of which he wrote quite movingly:

> The constant efforts of the eels to escape from their prison, this persistency in trying to surmount all the obstacles they meet, this obstinacy in letting themselves be caught rather than turn back, this movement of a blind instinct which carries them to a sojourn in the sea as soon as they are fully grown, can only result from a need as lively as it is imperative. And what is there more pressing, more irresistible than the propagation of the species.

Spallanzani was no fan of the theory of spontaneous generation. (He was in fact one of several scientists to disprove it.) Still, he estimated that in the past forty years, 152 million Comacchio eels had been gutted and salted in preparation for sale. How, he wondered, could it be that among all those eels, only one pregnant eel had ever been found? His awkward question for Mondini was this: If what you found in that fat old eel are ovaries, where pray tell are the eggs? Mondini had no answer. Nonetheless, Spallanzani remained surprisingly optimistic and urged his colleagues to keep up the good fight: "Our still prevailing ignorance regarding the procreation of the eel, instead of deterring us from further investigations, should spur us on to strain every nerve to dispel this dark cloud of ignorance, having ever before us the examples of seekers of truth in other fields of natural science, who by careful

After several long months observing the migration of silver eels at the lagoon of Comacchio, the distinguished physiologist and natural historian Lazzaro Spallanzani (1729–1799) concluded that the "persistency" of migrating eels to "surmount all the obstacles they meet" and even stare down death on their last-gasp struggle to return to the sea could be explained only by an innate "imperative" to keep the species alive. (Wikimedia Commons)

and preservering [*sic*] search at last succeeded in removing the seemingly impenetrable vail from many a mystery of nature."

Scientists in Italy and beyond took this stirring call to arms to heart, none more so than Martin Rathke, an eminent German embryologist. Rathke studied animals of all sorts, including worms. But it was his interest in marine life and the embryonic development of sex organs that best prepared him to tackle the eel question. In 1824, he published a portrait of female eel genitalia, described as two "cuff and collar"–shaped organs flanking the backbone. In 1838, he verified the presence of eel eggs through the lens of a microscope. To complete this trifecta, in 1853 he published a detailed if awkward description of a pregnant eel, as "the first and only specimen of such which had come up to that time into the hands of an investigator."

Rathke had simply verified Mondini's (wrongfully) discredited findings, and it is Mondini who deserves the credit for uncovering the female eel's reproductive apparatus. That said, Rathke's work was not without value: his findings made it undeniable that female eels exist. But that left at least two vital questions unanswered: What, if anything, fertilizes the female's eggs? And, more fundamentally, in the case of eels, if males exist, do they even matter?

CHAPTER 4

FREUD'S EEL ENCOUNTER

It is surely possible to throw oneself into a line of thought and to follow it wherever it leads.

—Sigmund Freud, *Beyond the Pleasure Principle*

IN A NOAH'S ARK CONCEPTION of life, a male and female mating pair dutifully represents each animal species. But this "natural order of things" seemed not to be the order of eels. The German zoologist Karl von Siebold believed that—like wasps, bees, and ants—female eels reproduced asexually, through a process for which he coined the term "parthenogenesis." Others held that so-called female eels were actually hermaphrodites that had both male and female sexual organs yet appeared female, as their testicles were somehow obscured. Under either scenario, the service of strictly male eels was not required for reproduction. And that made eels an especially interesting animal to consider—after all, what could such a creature tell us about us? From a purely biological viewpoint, were males of eels—or other species—strictly necessary?

In 1872, three noted Italian scientists—Giovanni Battista Ercolani, Giuseppe Crivelli, and Leopoldo Maggi—made the case that not even the eel had escaped Noah's Ark. Each scientist claimed to have independently discovered traces of sperm in the fatty folds of the European eel. Ercolani's public announcement of his finding opened breathlessly on these words: "The author this day appears before the academy with fear and trembling, since he intends to present something new regarding a question which has been the rock on which the vessels of so many distinguished scientists have foundered." The poor man was right to tremble, as his own vessel foundered when careful examination revealed that his so-called sperm-bearing eels bore "not the slightest trace of a testicle-like construction." Pretty much the same humiliating fate befell Crivelli and Maggi.

While they didn't know it at the time, Ercolani and his fellow seekers were doomed from the start. Assuming that bigger eels were older and therefore more likely to harbor fully developed sex organs, they had aimed their scalpels mostly at larger specimens. While this approach made good common sense, it overlooked Charles Darwin's dictum that in nearly all fishes, the female is larger than the male, and often much larger. Darwin wrote that "increased size must be in some manner of more importance to the females, than strength and size are to the males for fighting with other males." By focusing on large and therefore female eels, the Italian scientists had very little chance of unmasking male genitalia.

By contrast, the Polish zoologist Szymon Syrski took Darwin's words to heart. While director of the Civic Museum of Natural History in Trieste, Syrski had made a survey of the spawning behaviors of every fish species in the region, including eels. Noting the failure of other naturalists to find gonads in large eels, he turned his efforts to smaller ones, and found what he described as a "completely new organ." Syrski's 1874 paper, "Uber die Reproductionsorgane der Aale" (On the Reproductive Organs of Eels), was published to much excitement in the prestigious *Proceedings of the Vienna Academy*. In it, the author described what became known as the Syrski organ: a seminal duct that (when pumped full of air or—oddly—quicksilver) could be seen by the naked eye to run along the eel's entire length. Syrski wrote that in all eels equipped with this organ, the female reproductive apparatus was "entirely wanting."

Syrski's claims of having found the testes of the eel had significant implications: it offered very strong evidence of maleness and therefore that the mature eel was *not* a hermaphrodite. Not surprisingly, this came as a crushing disappointment to those scholars who had banked heavily on the idea that the eel was essentially self-sufficient in its reproductive habits. Among these was the biologist Carl Friedrich Wilhelm Claus (1835–1899), director of the Vienna Institute of Comparative Anatomy, and the first to take public umbrage with Syrski's claim. A staunch Darwinist, Claus had a long-standing fascination with hermaphroditism, a condition that Darwin deemed a remnant from an early stage of vertebrate development. In *The Descent of Man, and Selection in Relation to Sex*, Darwin wrote that "some remote progenitor of the whole vertebrate kingdom appears to have been hermaphrodite or androgynous," and that "we have to look at fishes, the lowest of all classes, to find any still existent androgynous forms." While Darwin agreed that humans have a "god-like intellect," he believed that it was also the case that every man and woman carries the "indelible stamp of his lowly origin." The eel, Claus believed, was the living embodiment of that stamp.

Darwin wisely abstained from making direct public comment on the eel's mating habits, but he seemed convinced that eels were hermaphrodites, noting that "it has now been recorded by too many good observers to be any longer disputed." Claus harbored hopes that the eel represented Darwin's "remote progenitor," and this inclined him to agree that eels were hermaphrodites. This hope also disinclined him to accept Syrski's finding of a true male organ unaccompanied by a female organ in an actual eel. But this was all conjecture, and Claus was an empiricist: what was needed was physical proof. Claus maintained a second laboratory in Trieste, where he directed the oceanographic research station and had access to plenty of eels. But as a widely recognized "great man" of science, he had no intention of rummaging through steaming mounds of eel innards to search for telltale clues of hermaphrodism. For this, he enlisted the efforts of a faithful protégé, a gifted overachiever by the name of Sigmund Freud.

Why Freud? Fair question, as we know him today not as an eel man but as the father of psychoanalysis. But at age twenty Freud's research focus was on animals, and centered on the nervous systems of fish. Brainy and ambitious, he was thrilled with the offer of an all-expenses-paid trip to Italy to tackle a mystery that throughout history august minds could not solve. Dispatched to Trieste, he was issued a laboratory bench, a microscope, and a steady supply of mature eels fresh from the harbor markets just a few blocks away. In his letters to friends back home, he sounds mildly amused with the setup. Though perhaps thinking himself above the lowly task to which Claus had assigned him, his writings reflect a robust schoolboy optimism spiced with just a dash of snark. To his childhood chum Eduard Silberstein he wrote in 1876: "Seeing that eels keep no diaries from whose orthography one can make inferences to their sex," he had no choice but to slice and dice them. The search was both tedious and annoying, made no less so by Syrski, who, Freud carped, claimed to "have discovered testicles, and hence the male eel, but since he apparently doesn't know what a microscope is, he failed to provide an accurate description."

Ouch.

One can only imagine Freud perched at his solitary laboratory bench, a leather apron belted snugly around his slim waist, his delicate neurologist-to-be hands covered in eel slime and guts. "I have been tormenting myself and the eels in a vain effort to rediscover his male eels," he whined to Silberstein, ". . . but all of the eels I cut open are of the gentler sex." He signed off with a cartoon sketch of an eel slithering through the text, its jaws fixed in an enigmatic Mona Lisa grin. As summer waned, Freud went home to Vienna for a well-earned break, but he soon returned to Trieste to resume his gruesome labors. This time, he changed his tactics. Having learned Darwin's lesson on the link between fish size and gender (the males of many fish species tending to be smaller than the females), he restricted his study to eels of less than 500 millimeters (about nineteen and a half inches), with most of them in the 250-to-480-millimeter range. He disemboweled four hundred eels in total, and, at last, in one managed to locate what looked like a remarkably small teste. Or maybe not. Regardless, he'd had enough, and it was time to go home.

Observation on the Form and the Fine Structure of the Looped Organs of the Eel, Organs Considered Testes was Freud's first published work. But for him, it was a mixed blessing. On the one hand, he may have confirmed the findings of the distinguished zoologist Syrski, a good thing for a young scientist on the make. On the other hand, to locate actual eel testes would be to undermine the Darwinist theories of his powerful and influential mentor, Claus. A bad thing for a young scientist on the make. Stuck between a rock and a hard place, Freud downplayed the discovery and quietly took a step back from questions of animal procreation. As one scholar mused: "Is it just . . . that the discoverer of the castration complex wrote his very first paper on the missing testes of the eel, and let almost twenty years go by before he gave sexuality another scientific thought?"

So, what motivated Freud and his mentor and the legion of other mighty men of science to concern themselves with the technicalities of eel propagation rather than be content with the knowledge that somehow eels manage to do so in spades? Fishermen and epicures had no trouble procuring and profiting from eels: by value the fish made up a third of Europe's nineteenth-century freshwater catch. Eels were abundant and everywhere; didn't that pretty much sum it up? Was it not unnatural to probe so deeply into matters that nature herself preferred to keep secret? Isn't not knowing sometimes for the best?

Perhaps. But appeals to reason are no match for obsession. Modern scholars remained fixed on the question of eel reproduction for the very reason that it had vexed their predecessors. Divining eel sex was the brass ring of biology—a mystery for the ages that serious scholars of natural history believed should be well within their grasp. The Germans, building on the work of Syrski, were determined to settle the matter. After Freud published his iffy sighting of a wee gonad in 1877, it was said that every German-language journal and periodical ran at least one article on the eel, accompanied by the following notice: "In spite of our modern aids, science has not yet succeeded in clearing up the mystery of the propagation of the eel. The German Fishery Association of Berlin, will, therefore, pay a reward of 50 marks to anyone who will send Professor Virchow, at Berlin, an eel in a state of pregnancy sufficiently advanced to throw some light on the propagation of eels." Germany's royal superintendent of fisheries, known to history only as a "Mr. Dallmer," volunteered to forward the pregnant eels to Berlin, and to cover the cost of the postage. At first, Dallmer was thrilled by the overwhelming response. Packages arrived from every corner of the German-speaking world. But as the boxes and eels mounted higher, his delight turned to bewilderment and then to horror. "Most of the senders have sent me only intestines, or also the supposed young of the eel, which invariably turned out to be intestinal worms," he groaned. "Most of the senders had eaten the eel, and nevertheless requested to have the 50 marks forwarded to them." Sick eels, shredded eels, cooked eels, mostly eaten eels, even fake eels flooded his office. One can only imagine the mess, and the cost. And while the fishery association tottered dangerously on the edge of bankruptcy, not one pregnant eel had crossed its threshold.

Alarmed, German biologist Leopold Jacoby decided to take matters into his own quite capable hands, declaring "I arrived at the conviction that the problem can be solved only by employing extraordinary means." And employ them he did, by traveling to Comacchio himself and tagging along with the fishermen in hopes of being the first man on record to spot a sexually mature eel—or for that matter, any eel—in the open ocean. "I have gone to sea in Chioggia fishing vessels . . . I have fished with them, and by offering them rewards I have urged them to catch eels out at sea," he wrote. Jacoby came to the belief that much could be learned from the fishermen, who "year after year . . . by day and night think and talk of nothing else but of the eel on which their prosperity depends, which was fished by their ancestors centuries ago, so that their power of observation of the mode of life of this fish has naturally been sharpened . . ." Still, he also described "no lack of attempts to deceive me; fishermen would take eels along from the shore, and on their return exhibit them to me as having been caught at the sea." Eel fishermen, while knowledgeable, were apparently as slippery as the eels themselves.

Jacoby never did locate an ocean-swimming eel, though he claimed he would have had he been endowed with the proper equipment. (As every well-bred athlete knows, it's unsportsmanlike to blame one's failures on one's gear, but apparently Jacoby simply could not contain himself.) "To catch a river eel in the open sea, which is an essential condition of solving the most perplexing question of the eel problem, will therefore remain an impossibility as long as we do not possess vessels and apparatus specially adapted to the purpose."

As it happened, one lucky man possessed both.

CHAPTER 5

OH, WHAT A LUCKY MAN

Altogether, the whole story of the eel and its spawning has come to read almost like a romance, wherein reality has far exceeded the dreams of phantasy.

—Johannes Schmidt, "The Reproduction and Spawning-Places of the Fresh-Water Eel"

THE EELS THAT SPARKED A frenzy in twenty-first-century Maine, the eels that landed Bill Sheldon and his co-conspirators in the clink and linked the rural state to international appetites and crime syndicates—the secrets of their origin and life cycle mystified scientists well into the twentieth century. While it was agreed that "river eels" spawned somewhere out to sea, the much sought-after pregnant eel remained elusive, as did eel eggs or other signs of eel procreation. And try as they may, no one had ever managed to track down the eel's spawning ground. But thanks to the obsessive efforts of one wildly ambitious young Dane, that was about to change.

Ernst Johannes Schmidt was born in 1877, to a middle-class family indebted to both science and beer. His father, also Ernst, was the estate manager of Jaegerpris Slot, a royal palace fifty kilometers northwest of Copenhagen resplendent with fine gardens and ancient oaks. His paternal great-grandfather Christian Schmidt was a botanist, and an inspector at the Royal Gardens. When Johannes was seven years old, his father died and his mother, Camilla, moved with him and his two younger brothers, Alfred and Jorgen, to Copenhagen, where she opened a boardinghouse. The little family settled in just a short walk's distance from Camilla's brother, Johan Kjeldahl, a celebrated chemist and, as luck would have it, head of chemistry at the Carlsberg Brewery Laboratories.

Like his father and grandfather before him, Schmidt was

Danish biologist Ernst Johannes Schmidt, blessed by both birth and marriage, was the first adventurer to track the course of Atlantic eels back to their presumed breeding ground in the Sargasso Sea. Despite this triumph, Schmidt never witnessed this spawning nor spotted an adult eel—or a single egg—in the open sea. (Wikimedia Commons)

fascinated by the natural world. As an undergraduate at the University of Copenhagen, he trained as a botanist under the tutelage of no less than Eugen Warming, the "father of ecology." While writing his PhD thesis on the shoot architecture of mangroves in what is now Thailand, he took a part-time job at Denmark's Commission for the Investigation of the Sea. From there forward, marine life was his passion.

In 1904, Schmidt was tapped to lead an expedition to Iceland and the Faroe Islands aboard the research steamer *Thor*, aimed at the study of commercially important fishes—cod, flounder, haddock, herring, plaice, and eel. On the voyage he captured a seven-and-a-half-centimeter-long European eel larva, a so-called thin head. This finding came as a surprise to all on board, as at the time eel larvae were thought to exist only in the Strait of Messina between Sicily and Calabria, off the coast of Italy. Schmidt's fortuitous find catapulted him into the thick of the ancient quest for the eel's birthplace. He wrote, "I had little idea, at the time, of the extraordinary difficulties which the task was to present, both in regard to procuring the most necessary observations and in respect to their interpretation."

If Schmidt had a deep interest in eels prior to his North Atlantic encounter, there is no mention of it in the historical record. It seems that he was introduced to the complexities of the fish by his mentor, C. G. Johannes Petersen, then the most illustrious marine scientist in Denmark. Petersen had instructed his protégé to keep a lookout for eel larvae on the *Thor* voyage, and Schmidt, quick to recognize the significance of the discovery, brandished it like a sword to carve out a starring role for himself in scientific circles. "Owning to various circumstances," he wrote, "it came about that Denmark, a country where eel fishing is an especially important industry, was accorded the task of prosecuting the investigations further, and it fell to my lot to take charge of the work." Somehow, Schmidt sensed that eels would be his ticket.

Schmidt was an adventurer, not one to slash open eel bellies or pay fishermen to bring him pregnant specimens. His vision was much grander: to trace the trail of eel larvae like so many breadcrumbs back to their breeding ground. His logic was simple—the smaller the eel larva (leptocephali), the younger it must be, and the closer to its birthplace. Finding the eel breeding grounds, he reasoned, was simply a matter of tracking down the tiniest possible larva, a challenge he believed was well within his reach. As it turned out, that challenge consumed the better part of twenty-five years of Schmidt's not terribly long life. As a colleague rather grimly characterized it: "One notices . . . that the [eel] problem increasingly captures and enamors Professor Schmidt, depriving him of peace of the soul."

As I've mentioned, Schmidt was lucky in many things, and especially in love. In 1903 he married Ingeborg Kuhle, the lovely, gracious daughter of the CEO of the Carlsberg Brewery, his uncle's employer and the largest and most prestigious brewery in Denmark. Seven years later, Schmidt was appointed director of the physiological institute funded by the Carlsberg Foundation. For Schmidt, these events led to quite pleasing outcomes—both his income and his status in the business world grew dramatically. He became a well-known public figure and a rising star in the scientific community blessed with the rare good fortune to pursue his passions with the support of public and private investors who expected only good science in return.

Schmidt's intention was to scour the entire North Atlantic for eel larvae, a task for which he pronounced the *Thor* "useless." The generosity of Vendsyssel Packing Company of Copenhagen (a purveyor of frozen fish) brought him *Margrethe*, an aged but fundamentally trustworthy schooner equipped with everything he needed for his eel survey. He sailed from the Faroe Islands and made his way south past the Azores to the edge of the Sargasso Sea. It was there that his crew netted 714 European and 24 American eel larvae. The larvae were too large (and therefore presumed too old) to suggest a recent spawning, but no matter. Convinced that he had found the eel's breeding grounds, Schmidt eagerly pursued a search for smaller specimens.

In December 1913, *Margrethe* ran aground and was wrecked off the coral island of Anegada, in the British Virgin Islands. A less lucky man might have seen this as a bad omen and gone home. But not Schmidt. He treated the setback as an opportunity. While shipless, he procured smaller and smaller—hence younger and younger—larvae from the crews of commercial vessels armed with pelagic trawls, cone-shaped nets that they towed behind their ships. He was getting closer.

The outbreak of the Great War in 1914 forced Schmidt to retreat from his ocean adventures for half a decade. The break was not welcome, but it did offer one advantage—it gave him time to expand his research vision. When he began his search for eel larvae in the eastern Atlantic and the Mediterranean, he had not concerned himself with the American eel. Interestingly, some scientists of the time believed that the European and American eel were essentially the same species. Schmidt wasn't sure, but as he ventured farther west, he began to note critical differences between the species. American and European larvae, identical to the naked eye, could be distinguished by their blocks of muscle fibers—or myomeres—visible only with the aid of a microscope. (European larvae have 112 to 119 myomeres, while the smaller American larvae have fewer, 103 to 111, all numbers that correlate with the number of vertebrae in adult eels.) The meticulous, monotonous process of counting myomeres might have pushed even Freud beyond the boundaries of patience. But Schmidt was unfazed, perhaps even energized by the work. And on the basis of his counts, Schmidt firmly established that the American and European eels were distinct species. "These [American] larvae were taken in the same area as those of the European species, even, indeed . . . in the same haul," he wrote. "It was with mingled feelings that we noted this fact, since it involved a further complication of the eel question, which at this point seemed more intricate than ever."

Eager to return to his ocean quests but unsure as to how to arrange it, Schmidt got lucky yet again. About a year after the Great War ended, the 550-ton, four-masted schooner *Dana*—property of the East Asiatic Company of Copenhagen—set sail under his direction from Gibraltar to the Sargasso Sea. On June 8, 1920, he and his team caught more than thirteen hundred thin heads, a few as small as seven millimeters, about one-quarter of an inch. On June 27, they captured nearly eight hundred with a single dip of the net. Schmidt reports that this "cruise" caused him to look at the American eel in a new light. "True, the technical difficulties have not diminished," he writes. "But the comparison of the life history of the two species which our investigations have enabled us to make is, to my thinking, one of the most interesting chapters in the history of the eel. Indeed, it is hardly too much to say that the life-history of the European eel can only be properly understood at all by comparison with that of the American." (Ah, the eels of Maine, perhaps feeling rather neglected in the face of all this European history, would be delighted to hear that.)

The following year, the *Dana* set sail again, cruising past French Guiana to Barbados, St. Vincent, St. Lucia, Guadeloupe, and Martinique. There were forays to the Gulf of Panama, where a steel wire pulley was employed to scavenge larvae from depths of up to 10,000 meters. April brought a five-millimeter specimen, the puniest—and presumably youngest—yet. Schmidt and his team speculated that they had missed its hatching by a day or two at most, and possibly by mere hours. They were so very, very close.

In 1923, Schmidt published the *The Breeding Places of the Eel*, a lengthy treatise prepared for the Royal Society in which he announced to the world that he had found the Atlantic eel's natural spawning ground. "Given the many difficulties we have faced," he wrote, "there is every reason to be pleased with the accomplishment, which, to put it in English, ends every discussion about the breeding place of the Eel."

Monumental at the time, this "accomplishment" remains influential today. Yet even Schmidt was well aware that the "discussion" had not truly ended. A brilliant and charismatic advocate for Danish science, he had promised much, delivered something less, and proudly proclaimed victory. He knew the risks of overstating his case, but also that for him the risks were worth taking. "One must always take the chance while it is there," he had said to his colleague the ichthyologist Anton Bruun, "because it most often will not come back." Again and again, Schmidt took that chance, completing twenty-six ocean expeditions, including the largest privately funded research cruise on record. He had traced the path and development of the Atlantic eel from the Sargasso to continental rivers and back and identified hydrographic parameters—water salinity and temperature—that influenced their survival. So influential was Schmidt's work that the German geologist and polar explorer Alfred Wegener relied heavily on it when he developed his theory of continental drift and linked the movement of eels to that of tectonic plates. Eels, it seemed, were at the bottom of countless scientific questions.

Schmidt relished the world's attention. A master promoter of Denmark, science, and himself, he made frequent appearances on the radio and in periodicals and engaged a wireless telegraph to broadcast updates and good wishes. When possible on his voyages he packed a movie camera with which to document his adventures, for the public and especially for his funders. When *Dana* docked at the Danish port of Helsingør (the city immortalized as Elsinore in Shakespeare's *Hamlet*), Schmidt and his crew were hailed like conquering heroes by a cheering squad of thousands.

According to his biographer Bo Poulsen, on Schmidt's return from a two-year oceanographic circumnavigation of the world in 1930, he became "an uncontrollable force in the 'Carlsberg family,' a sort of cuckoo in a warbler's nest." But if one were to build on that metaphor, one would be forced to say that Schmidt's nest was empty. For after sailing the globe collecting specimens in five thousand locations over 65,000 nautical miles, Schmidt had failed to find a single eel egg.

Schmidt was indeed a fortunate man, but not as fortunate as some make him out to be. While it's fair to say he set science on the right track to the eel's breeding grounds, he offered no proof that he himself had found it. While Schmidt claimed to have solved the mystery of the eel's birthplace, nearly a hundred years after his death that mystery remains: neither he nor anyone else has documented proof of spotting mature eels in the Sargasso Sea.

As the ancient Greeks well knew, our species is plagued with a gnawing curiosity, and it seems that nature custom-made eels to prey on that affliction. In 1874, the German anatomist Max Schultze confessed on his deathbed that everything was known to science with the notable exception of the "eel question." Here in the twenty-first century, it's in some ways soothing to consider how much of that question remains unanswered. It's a leap—but not a big one—to say that eels evolved to elude human understanding. But they have not eluded our grasp.

CHAPTER 6

TALES FROM THE UNCANNY

All the rest is hypothesis and dream
—Louise Glück, "Theory of Memory"

THE FRENCH CHEF ADRIEN FERRAND grew up with eels, which he caught with his father while on summer visits to his grandparents' home in Burgundy. His grandmother prepared them, but not to her grandson's liking. "They were no good," he told me. At fourteen, Ferrand determined to do Grand-mère one better and attend culinary school. Fifteen years later, his Restaurant Eels was lauded by critics as among the best bistros in Paris, even in the world. Intrigued, I agreed to meet Ferrand at his workplace and taste for myself.

Tucked into a stark first-floor corner space flanked by a motorcycle stand on one side and a barbershop on the other, Restaurant Eels had a laid-back, Scandinavian vibe and a youthful clientele who clearly knew a thing or two about food. And Ferrand's food was worth the trip—including his signature smoked eel with Granny

Sampling the signature dish of smoked cultivated eel with licorice root, apple, and hazelnuts at Restaurant Eels in Paris. Chef Adrien Ferrand's remarkable preparation would make an eel lover of the harshest skeptic. (Ellen Ruppel Shell)

Smith apple, licorice root, and hazelnuts made with European eel cultivated on a small farm in Greece. Each plate was beautifully composed, essentially a work of art. But I'll admit to a pang of disappointment. For once the dinner crowd thinned and we had a chance to talk, Ferrand confessed he had not given eels a lot of thought.

So why name your restaurant Eels, I asked?

"Ah, that," he said. "Of course. Eels are something very special. They speak to me of something I can't explain, something beyond words, perhaps beyond memory. I'm sorry I can't say more, but I am a chef, not a poet. Maybe you would like a dessert?"

Something beyond memory? Not a poet, perhaps, but certainly of a poetic sensibility. What is it about the eel that brings out the poet in us? Nothing like us or what we hope to be, the eel is nearly impossible to anthropomorphize. It has neither the brainy quirks of an octopus nor the childlike playfulness of a dolphin. It's not fierce like the shark, nor majestic like the tuna. And yet, it drew in Ferrand, as it did so many other artists.

My first literary encounter with the eel came by way of the German novelist Günter Grass and his chilling bildungsroman *The Tin Drum*. Given the reach of that remarkable novel it would not surprise me to hear that it was your introduction, too. If so, you surely recall the shocking role eels play in the book. The story opens abruptly in an insane asylum in what was then Gdansk, Poland. There we meet Oskar Matzerath, the thirty-year-old protagonist who has confessed to a murder he did not commit. Oskar, who identifies as a dwarf, is grandiose, salacious, and a thoroughly unreliable narrator. When on his third birthday his mother gifts him with the titular tin drum, he throws himself headfirst down the cellar stairs to fend off adulthood and the horrors it brings. (Significantly, the scene is set in the 1930s and the Holocaust looms.) From there, the larger-than-life story unfolds in a series of harrowing vignettes. The one I'm thinking of places Oskar in the company of his stepfather, Alfred; his mother, Agnes; and his mother's cousin and paramour, Jan. It's Good Friday, and the little family marks the holiday with a stroll along the Baltic coast. They come to a jetty and scramble from granite block to granite block all the way to the breakwater. There they stare in fascination as an old man tugs at his fishing line, pulling hand over hand against the pounding surf. Time passes, and a severed horse's head surfaces above the waves, so fresh its mane gleams black in the sun. The family watches in horror as the fisherman, grinning demonically, yanks the ghastly skull to shore and pulls eel after eel from its gaping mouth, nose, and eye sockets. Agnes, who is pregnant, bends from the waist and pukes her guts out. Oskar stands by, robotically banging his drum while his stepfather, impervious to his wife's distress, bargains with the fisherman for four eels to boil up for their Lenten supper.

Later that evening, Agnes refuses to eat the eel, and vows to never again eat fish of any kind. A few weeks later, Agnes reverses herself and gorges compulsively on fish of several varieties, notably eel. After a month or so, she and her unborn child die of what a doctor diagnoses as "fish poisoning." At her funeral, Oskar imagines his mother bolting up from the open coffin and vomiting white bits of eel. To our great relief, she stays put in her casket, "to bury the eel beneath the earth, so there might at last be peace."

There are many interpretations of this passage, some involving sex, and few convincing. No matter. For readers like me, the memory of Grass's eels is indelible. We are horrified by the fisherman and the horse's skull squirming with eels, but also mesmerized: eels have an uncanny knack for grabbing our attention and sticking in our minds. It's doubtful that many other creatures—let alone another (freshwater) fish—would evoke such a powerful and lasting image. Nor was *The Tin Drum* unique. The 2017 film *A Cure for Wellness* bombed with many critics and at the box office, but movie buffs brave enough to see it were unlikely to forget the film's protagonist floating in an isolation tank, where he is swarmed by a posse of three-hundred-year-old "therapeutic" eels and nearly drowns. In this film the eels steal the show: as one critic opined, "I think you need to start with the eels. The eels are everything in *A Cure for Wellness*. They are what I am going to remember from this oddly forgettable movie, and they are a metaphor for the film's promise and failure to live up to that promise." Which leads one to wonder: What exactly did the eels promise? More questions are raised by the 1984 blockbuster *Indiana Jones and the Temple of Doom*, with its gluttonous "eel eater" digging into copious platters of "snake surprise," a banquet dish of juvenile eels oozing from the guts of a casually coiled boa constrictor. Marvel Comics had its own very special take in the form of "the Eel," an alias used by two slimy supervillains, the first appearing in 1963, the second in 1983.

In his 2017 essay on animal metaphors, the American literary scholar Ryan J. Stark calls eels "weird" and "creepy," both common descriptors, especially among those who have not spent much time with them. Those who *have* spent much time with them, by contrast, tend to take a more nuanced view. The British author Graham Swift, an avid fisherman, has had more than a few close encounters with the eel. In *Waterland*, his tragic masterpiece of doomed love, betrayal, and madness, Swift does for the metaphorical eel something like what Herman Melville did for the metaphorical whale. His novel centers on Tom Crick, a history teacher on the verge of (involuntary) retirement who strives to awaken the flagging interest of his students with stories of his troubled and traumatic childhood. He says that his father was a superstitious man, "and since my mother's death, which was six months before we lay by the eel traps under the stars, my father's yen for the dark, his nocturnal restlessness, had grown more besetting." Through Crick, Swift describes the eel as "not an unhandsome creature. It's sleek and smooth-skinned. It has little glimmering amber eyes which, for all one knows, could be the windows of a tiny eel-soul. It has little panting gills and, behind them, delicate whirring pectoral fins." As was Oscar in *The Tin Drum*, Tom is an unreliable narrator—one of his students accuses him of telling self-serving fairy tales. But that's the point. For Swift, the mystery of the eel represents the option of not-knowing, and of trading off the very human demand for certainty in exchange for a sort of peace. He writes that the eel possesses an "instinctual mechanism more mysterious, more impenetrable perhaps than the composition of the atom . . . there is much the eel can tell us about curiosity—rather more indeed than curiosity can inform us of the eel."

The Swedish journalist Patrik Svensson touched on similar themes in his memoir *The Book of Eels*, in which he recalls fishing for eels with his father in a stream near his childhood home. His eel memories are fond, but he acknowledges that others feel less comfortable and traces this discomfort to what Freud (who you'll recall had his own eel encounters) called "unheimlich": the unease and uncertainty that overcome us when what we see is at once familiar and contains an element of strangeness. There is merit to this argument. We often fear what we don't know, and the eel, while familiar, is not easy to know. (Graham Swift implies in *Waterland* that the eel is not knowable at all.) But I'm not sure we need to invoke Freud to explain the eel's uncanniness.

Like most primates, humans evolved to fear snakelike objects, of which the eel is an obvious example. Perhaps that explains why the word "Anguilla" takes its root from the Latin "ango," or "to strangle." So the real question is not whether or why eels are frightening. Of course they are! The real question is why a legion of scientists, historians, anthropologists, entrepreneurs, artists, and—yes—authors are so utterly bewitched by them. To begin to answer that question, one might turn to the work of the Hungarian philosopher Aurel Kolnai, who points to the paradox that things that disgust us also hold a "curious enticement." (If you doubt this, consider the popularity of reality shows such as *Fear Factor*, a TV series in which contestants compete by gulping slurries of pureed rat and bedding down in coffins stuffed with cow intestines.) In the case of eels, I concede that disgust may play a role for some readers, moviegoers, and reality TV fans, and perhaps also for some authors and filmmakers. But like me, these are interlopers, or, at best, bystanders. For the scores of actual eel people I've come to know, it is something else altogether. Naturally, they are captivated by the eel and its ways, but it's more than that. For them, it seems, the pursuit of the age-old "eel question" is something closer to a religious quest.

CHAPTER 7

DON'T CALL HIM AHAB

It is not down in any map; true places never are.
—Herman Melville, *Moby-Dick*

REINHOLD HANEL, CODIRECTOR OF FISHERIES Ecology at Germany's Heinrich von Thünen Institute, wasn't born to be an eel man. A native of Austria, he grew up not far from the Tyrolean Alps, many miles from the sea. His father, a telecom engineer, was not an angler, a practice Hanel has always considered distasteful. Over six feet tall, bearded and burly, he's no snowflake, but hunting fish for sport does not sit comfortably with him. "I prefer to observe them," he told me.

Hanel shared cherished memories of spending time with his grandfather, a hunter and forager who taught him a good deal about nature and the part humans play in it, for good and for ill. Their mountain hikes together spanned rivers and streams and sparked his interest in freshwater life. But despite its distance, he managed to keep one eye on the sea. "This Austrian guy [marine biologist and noted evolutionary theorist] Rupert Riedl, his TV documentary *Gardens of Poseidon* was very influential," Hanel told me. But it was much more than that: Riedl's graduate students, many of them marine biologists in the making, were literally Hanel's teachers at the University of Vienna. "I wanted to go on their marine excursions, and I begged them to take me," he told me. "I practically kneeled in front of them. Finally, in 1992, they took me along. After that, I went every year, and it was great. But it wasn't until 2007, when I got my professorship at Kiel University, that I got involved with eel larvae." Since then, he reckons he's devoted a full year of his life—both days and nights—trawling the oceans in pursuit of the elusive creatures. A Captain Ahab of the Atlantic eel? "Oh, please," he said, looking pained. "Let's not go there."

To allow me a close glimpse of his work, Hanel agreed to meet me in Bermuda, where he and his research team had plans to launch their next voyage. Rimmed with pastel-painted bungalows and all-inclusive resorts buffered by acres of golf courses, Bermuda's coral-pink beaches are among the finest in the world. But even before the Bermuda Triangle was a thing, the island was a frightening place—alarmed by the humanlike squawks of the local seabirds, adventurers dubbed it Devil's Island. With a maximum elevation of less than 300 feet, Bermuda is mostly flat, which makes it easy to miss that it's essentially a volcanic mountaintop jutting up some 6,560 feet from the ocean floor. Topographical maps show steep drop-offs at every twist and turn of coast, and many square miles of coral reefs of the sort ancient mariners were wise to avoid. And like the eel, Bermuda is unique, the only significant landmass in all the vast Sargasso Sea.

The Sargasso Sea is as much idea as place—a two-million-square-mile ellipse of dazzling cyan-blue water floating like an oil slick in the western heart of the Atlantic Ocean. Roughly the size of

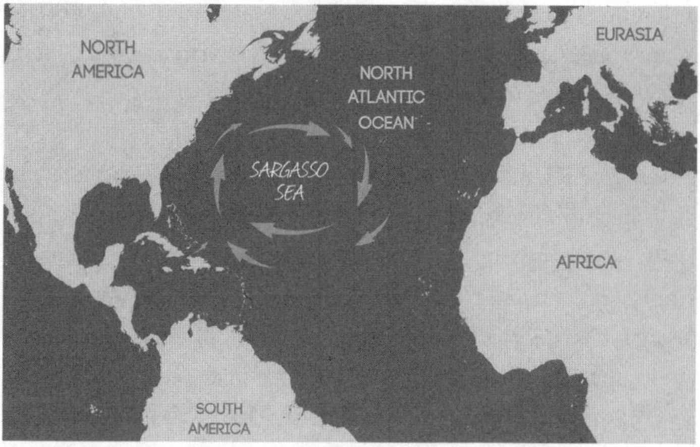

The Sargasso Sea is the only sea in the world with no coastline and is bounded by four ocean currents that form a clockwise circulating gyre that makes for outstanding visibility—with warm deep-blue water transparent for up to two hundred feet. The Sargasso's calm seas are thought to be the sole birthplace of all Atlantic eels. (The Sargasso Sea Commission)

the continental United States, it is a sea within a sea, bounded not by land but by a quartet of ocean currents lapping at its perimeter: the North Equatorial Current to the south, the North Atlantic Current to the north, the Canaries Current to the east, and to the west the familiar Gulf Stream that runs up the east coast of North America. These currents are quite powerful, but tucked safely within them, the Sargasso has the luxury of stillness. The sea takes its name from sargassum seaweed, great bobbing rafts of which lurk so abundant on its surface that Christopher Columbus mistook the tangled mats for solid ground. From a distance, sargassum looks inert and lifeless. But a closer look reveals leafy appendages and round, berry-like structures filled mostly with oxygen that—like miniature PFDs—keep the plant and its tiny passengers afloat. Portuguese sailors likened these structures to "salgazo," the small wine grapes they knew from home, hence the name. Sargassum is unique, a plant that can reproduce by fragmentation while floating unanchored in the water. Under the right conditions, a small chunk can metastasize into acres of the stuff.

Columbus is credited with the first written account of sargassum, which he experienced on his voyage to America in 1492. His flagship, the *Santa María*, and its sister ships, the *Nina* and *Pinta*, were becalmed in the Sargasso for three days, and his understandably terrified crew feared they would run aground. They urged Columbus to allow them to turn back to avoid getting forever tangled in the weeds. Apparently unfazed, he ignored them, and they made the crossing in a mere ten days. Later, he compared the mild conditions he encountered on the voyage as "wanting nothing but the melody of nightingales." His crew members did not agree, and grave myths of the Sargasso's dangers grew only graver over time.

In *Twenty Thousand Leagues Under the Sea*, first published in book form in 1870, Jules Verne portrays the Sargasso as something like a marine graveyard: "a perfect meadow, a close carpet of seaweed, fucus, and tropical berries, so thick and so compact that the stern of a vessel could hardly tear its way through it." Verne's protagonist, Captain Nemo, navigated the mess by diving "some depth" below the surface in his submarine, the *Nautilus*. In 1897, the *Chambers Journal for Popular Literature, Science and Arts* warned prudent seaman against crossing the Sargasso "for it certainly will not be long before tangling weeds would altogether choke up his screw and render it useless." Captain C. C. Dixon, an experienced seaman writing for the Royal Geographic Society in 1925, asked, "Who could know whether this weed got thicker and thicker till there was no turning back? Its changing tints and shadows as daylight faded and at the approach of dawn needed but little help from the imagination to be wrought into fearsome monsters that inhabited its depth and whose very appearance would steal away one's sanity."

Looking out to the Sargasso from the shore, it's hard to imagine what provoked such Sturm und Drang: the water is dazzlingly beautiful. This description by the French artist Yves Klein (notable for his "Klein blue" monochromes) rings true: "I do not like the nothing, and it is thus that I met the empty, the deep empty, the depth of the blue." Sunlight penetrates deep below its surface, because other than salt, the Sargasso harbors few minerals or plankton. The sea is so spare of nutrients that were it not for the great clots of seaweed on its surface, it might pass for an ocean desert. But sargassum thrives where other plants falter, upward of eleven million tons of it congealed into a floating rainforest that serves as sanctuary for some 140 species of fish, at least 40 of them endangered or threatened. It seems somehow fitting that it is here—deep below this labyrinth—that the Atlantic eel both begins and ends its life.

On my first morning in Bermuda, I rose early to walk Tobacco Bay Beach in the company of Fae Sapsford, Marine Research Fellow of the Sargasso Sea Commission. A storm was blowing in, and the winds were gusting. Fae, who was twenty-five, was dressed for the weather in black jeans, an orange baseball cap, and a dark blue sweatshirt with the logo BERMUDA ISLANDS, EST. 1609. Cars are hard to come by on the island, and she had borrowed her father's Ford compact sedan to fetch me from my hotel. Fae had a busy morning ahead and did her best to push through the island's idea of rush hour. The coastal route took us past several public schools, and I noticed that all the children thronging the playgrounds were Black. A Bermuda native, Fae agreed, and mentioned that she was a not-so-proud graduate of all-white private schools, as were most of her white friends and neighbors. "I'm

Tobacco Bay, Bermuda, on a blustery day in March. Note both the conspicuous absence of people and the two layers of sargassum—a newly deposited golden layer, and an older rusty brown layer—both of which serve as habitat for a variety of tiny creatures and a snare for tons of colorful plastic refuse. (Ellen Ruppel Shell)

ashamed to admit that Bermuda has a lot of catching up to do," she told me.

Fae attended university in England and held a freshly minted master's degree in medieval studies from the University of Cambridge. Fortunately for me, she was also a tireless citizen scientist. In addition to her duties with the Sargasso Sea Commission, she volunteered as a student coordinator in the laboratory of Rebecca Helm, a professor at Georgetown University who specialized in, among other things, the biology of jellyfish. A relentless beachcomber, and a self-taught expert on sargassum, Fae's Instagram handle is @sargassogirl.

When we finally reached the beach, Fae leapt from the car to point out two distinct layers of the sulphureous algae—a fresher, golden layer and an older, rusty-brown layer—that had swept in from the sea and formed a thick, smothering blanket on the sandy shore. I mentioned that sargassum was making headlines at the time as a notorious "seaweed blob" threatening to swamp 1,350 miles of Florida shoreline. But on Tobacco Bay, it was neither new nor threatening. Here sargassum was an oasis of biodiversity, a nursery for scores of sea creatures of which Fae could not get enough—snails, barnacles, starfish, shrimp, sand hoppers, sea anemone trailing long threads of tentacles, and especially the bloated, translucent, red, green, and blue jellyfish. We kicked off our sneakers and waded barefoot into the shaggy tangles to treasure-hunt for the tiny beasts sequestered in the tendrils. "So many rafting animals that wash up," she said, gleeful. "They seem too fragile to survive, but here they are!" Zipping open her orange belt bag, she removed a collection cup and carefully dropped in each precious find for future study. The Sargasso is also a trash trap, especially for plastic, evidence of which was everywhere we waded. The good news, Fae said, was that sea dwellers cling to the bits of man-made detritus to buoy themselves, thereby extending both their life span and their range. A more optimistic person might have thought this trade-off cheering, but ankle-deep in pink and blue plastic bits, it seemed to me a devil's bargain.

Later that afternoon, the weather blew up into a gale, and Hanel's research vessel—already behind schedule—was further delayed in Europe. When at last I caught up with him and his team in their informal headquarters at the Bermuda Institute of Ocean Science, they were circling nervously like a shoal of salmon trapped in a kiddie pool. Three years earlier the COVID-19 pandemic had canceled their survey, so they were determined to make up for lost time, and patience was running thin. Everyone was anxious to get on the boat, and with every passing day, that anxiety grew deeper.

These expeditions never go smoothly, Hanel said with a sigh. We were perched side by side on a solid cement bench overlooking the Institute's sprawling lawns. The bench was frigid, and I was nursing a hacking cough, but Hanel, dressed in a baggy white T-shirt, sweatpants, and slip-on Crocs, seemed not to notice either annoyance. His mind was fixed firmly on the mission, a mission he had pursued for a decade and a half. When I asked how he got started in the larva hunting business, he told me that his introduction involved a Canadian trawler crewed by commercial fishermen from Newfoundland with accents so thick he could barely understand them. The accompanying research vessel, on loan from the Danish government, carried four scientists who, with zero culinary skills between them and no cook on board, were condemned to eating canned food for a month. Two of the four, both geneticists, got violently seasick just hours after leaving shore and struggled with nausea for the entire voyage. One memorable day, the research vessel lost its trolling line. "None of us had an explanation for that," Hanel said, laughing. One memorable night, the team was startled awake by the guttural roar of humpback whales tangling in another trolling line. The whales all but destroyed the trawler, and it took five precious days to repair the damage. (Research expeditions are costly: a single day and night at sea can cost upward of $100,000.)

"That trip," he said, "was a complete failure for us." And yet that failure did nothing to diminish his resolve to take up Johannes Schmidt's mantle. "We have so many questions," Hanel said, casting a wistful glance past the lawn and out to the ocean. "How do the larvae get into the Gulf Stream? Why do some European eels go to Spain, and others to Norway or Egypt? At what point does the American eel diverge and how does it know when to do so? And of course, an important focus of our survey will be narrowing down the eel spawning area . . . Finding a sexually mature eel in the spawning area would be a very important discovery."

It was March 2023, and Hanel addressed these questions with

a renewed sense of urgency. Three years earlier—at the height of the pandemic—the very foundations of his assumptions had been shaken by Eric Feunteun, a noted marine ecologist and director of the Marine Biology Station of Dinard of the French Museum of Natural History. Feunteun claimed to have found evidence that not all Atlantic eels breed in the Sargasso Sea, a rebuke of Schmidt that Hanel and many other European and American scientists found unconvincing but could not ignore. And yet there they were, stranded on land, struggling with infections and lockdowns, unable to prove him wrong.

Feunteun is a celebrated scientist who, unlike Hanel, grew up with eels. "The eel has always been a family question," he told me. "My grandmother owned a café, and she was sometimes paid in glass eels—buckets of them. She dumped them in the garbage. My grandfather used glass eels in carpenter's glue. They were so abundant in France then, they were considered pests, full of mischief, sneaky. My grandmother told me the eels came from the Sargasso Sea, and I wondered, what's that? Why do they go there? They became my life's passion."

In 2020, Feunteun and three coauthors published evidence in the influential journal *Scientific Reports* suggesting that at least some Atlantic eels breed outside the Sargasso Sea, in the seamounts of the Mid-Atlantic Ridge. They noted a chemical "signature" in the eel otoliths (a series of small bone-like calcium carbonate particles lodged just behind the eel's brain) that hinted that the larvae had been exposed to a volcanic environment. This finding underlay their hypothesis that some subset of eels was lured by odors and other signals generated by the volcanic activity of the Mid-Atlantic Ridge, an undulating and mostly underwater mountain range that juts as much as 10,000 feet up from the ocean floor. "We know that eels have huge olfactory bulbs in the back of their brains and are keenly attune to odors," he told me. "And we know that silver eels dive thousands of feet below the surface every day and rise toward the surface at night. They scan the entire water column, but why? They don't eat, so it's not about finding food. Maybe [this vertical migration] is a clue to their orientation. European eels, regardless of their origin, seem to converge in the Azores, which is not the closest path to the Sargasso Sea. So what is the reason for silver eels to take a longer route? Our hypothesis is that the Azores acts as a landmark for eels, and from there they turn southwest and follow the Mid-Atlantic Ridge." Feunteun made the point that male and female eels do not synchronize their migrations, but rather leave at different times of the year—in Europe males return to the sea in August and September, females in November and December. Males are generally about half the size of females, and much slower swimmers. The idea that all silver eels somehow come together simultaneously to find their mates in the vast Sargasso Sea, he said, is highly unlikely. This doesn't mean that all eels spawn in the same place, however, or that no eels spawn in the Sargasso Sea. "Eels have survived millions of years," Feunteun continued. "They are such a plastic species they may well have more than one spawning place."

When we spoke, Feunteun sounded exhausted and almost apologetic. "I am sixty years old, and I started this work when I was twenty-five," he told me. "I've spent thirty-five years really focused on the eel. So naturally, I expected [the paper would generate] controversy. But I did not expect people getting so upset."

Hanel was more than upset—he considered Feunteun's proposal an outrage. The theory that the Atlantic eel spawned anywhere but the Sargasso was for him a dangerous idea that if pursued could set science back decades. "There are serious errors in that paper," he snapped. "Those volcanoes could not reach the eel larvae, and there are so many other problems. We wrote the journal [*Scientific Reports*] to object, and it took two years to get a response—they tried to calm us down! I'm not saying that other researchers shouldn't look for an alternative hypothesis. But the Mid-Atlantic Ridge theory is built on a misinterpretation of the data. I find it weird, but if a journal feels that a hypothesis without data is important for readers, okay."

Clearly, for him this was anything but okay, and he was determined to prove it wrong.

A DAY OR TWO AFTER we first met, Hanel's research vessel—the *Walther Herwig III*—arrived in Bermuda, nearly a week late. A sixty-three-meter stern trawler with an ocean-blue hull, it was a sturdy, if aging, craft. The weather finally clear and the ship readied, Hanel and his ten-member scientific team set off in the general direction of the assumed eel spawning grounds. (Like Schmidt, Hanel invited a filmmaker on board, this time in the form of the Dutch documentarian Hans Dortman.) The ship came equipped with the latest in DNA sampling technology and assorted high-tech apparatus of which Schmidt could only dream. Despite some additional delays and some technical difficulties, this hunting expedition was far more successful than Hanel's first: among other things, the team found plenty of eel larvae, some of them quite small. They also located what they now believe might be the southern limits of the eel's ocean range. But not all went well. "We brought a net to catch larvae at five different depths," Hanel said, on return to his lab in Germany. "It didn't work."

More to the point, much like Schmidt, Hanel and his team failed to locate an adult eel or a single egg. Nor, in all likelihood, will anyone else anytime soon. That's because locating the eel spawning ground is no mere matter of finding a needle in a haystack, it's a matter of finding a needle in a haystack that blows with the wind.

"We assume a regular distribution [of larvae], but that does not exist," Hanel told me. "Density [of larvae] varies with conditions. So that's a huge challenge. It's also very important that eels spawn in a place where their larvae can drift in the right direction, so there are also currents to consider." Spawning depends not strictly on geographic location, but on oceanographic conditions—currents, water temperature, salinity—all largely unpredictable factors.

Hanel insisted that he differed from Schmidt, in that finding eel eggs or adult eels or even the spawning grounds was not his personal priority. "Our purpose is to scientifically monitor the changes in larval abundance in the Sargasso Sea to learn more about the species, and how better to manage it," he said. "I'm not Indiana Jones searching for the holy grail."

Still, he could not hide his frustration. As Fish and Wildlife's David Sykes made clear in an earlier chapter, it's nearly impossible to protect the eel without having a better understanding of its breeding habits and life cycle. Hanel is painfully aware of this: in a recent analysis, he and a team of other scientists concluded that data modelers had overestimated the number of eels in one German river by more than a factor of five. Such errors are common, he said, and "obscure the necessity" for conservation measures. Given such uncertainty, an international consortium in which Hanel took part in 2023 advised that all European eel fisheries be closed until glass eel stocks recovered, advice that was overruled by pretty much every EU nation. "Should we wait until it is less than one percent of its previous numbers to close the fishery?" Hanel asked, his voice rising. "Would we do that if it were any other commercially important fish? I'm not an economist, and I'm not speaking for fisheries. My obligations are only to science. And as a scientist, I know that the freshwater eel is something we need to worry about. We don't even know for sure what it eats in the larval stage, or how it finds its way in the sea. We don't fully understand the impacts of pollution or climate change on its life cycle. So how can we know how to help it survive? Until we get that basic knowledge, it's impossible to know what steps to take to save it. And I fear that it could already be too late."

CHAPTER 8

SHAPESHIFTERS

> You're all a bunch of Melun eels: you squeal even before they put you in a pot!
>
> —François Rabelais

EELS ARE SHAPESHIFTERS, BUT IN this they are not unique. Caterpillars turn into butterflies, and tadpoles into frogs, in a process called metamorphosis, an awkward developmental interlude during which animals transform dramatically. But the eel elevates metamorphosis to the stuff of myth: from birth to death, it enters and leaves five distinct anatomical stages, each correlated with specific environmental cues encountered along its extraordinary migratory path.

The two Atlantic species are thought to breed in overlapping circles—a sort of Venn diagram with the American eel spawning somewhat farther to the west, the European eel somewhat farther to the east. (Occasional interbreeding of the European and American species results in "hybrid" eels that split the difference genetically and complete their growth stage midway between east and west, notably on the coast of Iceland.) After the eels spawn, the resulting larvae hatch after two days at a size of roughly three millimeters (about a tenth of an inch). The larvae grow until their yolk sac is exhausted, about six days, doubling in length and gathering their strength. Eel larvae, or leptocephali (Latin for "flat head"), bear so little resemblance to adult eels that until the late nineteenth century they were mistaken for an unrelated species. In fact, leptocephali look less like fish of any sort than they do dainty willow leaves, transparent, gelatinous ribbons tapering at both ends, like tiny sails engineered deliberately to catch the currents. The larva's pointy head comes equipped with a tiny brain that orients it vertically within the water column—ascending hundreds of meters at night, possibly to save energy in warmer surface water; descending hundreds of meters at dawn, presumably to avoid predators. With their vacant, lump-of-coal eyes and jaws armed with needle-sharp teeth, eel larvae appear poised to puncture. But that's just a bluff. Larvae are anything but menacing and (though it's not certain) appear to subsist on a diet of soft "marine snow," organic detritus that drifts through the water like so much fairy dust. The ghoulish teeth might be vestigial, that is, perhaps they served some unknown purpose long ago. Or they may be a calcium reservoir that nourishes larvae as they grow. Or perhaps they are just there for show, to scare off predators. No one really knows.

Freshwater eels linger in the larval stage far longer than do most other fish, and just how long is one of the few metrics in which the European and American eel differ. (Genetically the cousins are quite similar, save for a few inborn disparities affecting growth, metabolism, and the number of vertebrae.) For American eels, the larval stage lasts six to nine months, while European eel larvae can linger in that state for as long as three years. During this

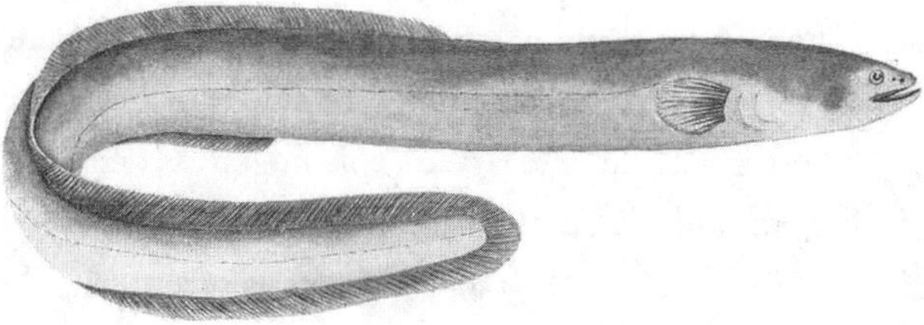

The American eel (*Anguilla rostrata*) is the only freshwater eel in the Western Hemisphere. Due to their nearly identical appearance, it was long assumed that the American and European eel were the same species, but they are not, and differ in various genetic markers, and in the number of vertebrae. Interestingly, a hybrid of the American and European eel does exist and is generally found in Iceland. (Wikimedia Commons)

time, larvae can grow surprisingly large: my first encounter with a glistening five-inch-long specimen came as a shock.

Since American eel larvae have no way of knowing where they will end their first migration—whether Greenland, Venezuela, or someplace in between—each aspiring eel is biologically equipped to endure the full range of weather conditions, from subtropical to arctic. (This makes it all the more curious that the American eel seems not to have splintered into a number of subspecies, each suited to a different climate.) The manner in which eels are propelled toward their respective destinations is a matter of heated debate. Scientists long assumed that larvae drifted passively at the whim of the currents, and until recently most transport models were built around that assumption. But in 2014, computer simulations published in the journal *Limnology and Oceanography* challenged that theory, offering evidence that the larvae have minds of their own. When we spoke, the biologist Joel Llopiz of the Woods Hole Oceanographic Institute, an author on the paper, could not hide his delight over this discovery. "These little guys can actually swim," he told me, as though these "little guys" were his nephews. Even at a glacial speed of 0.13 miles per hour, Llopiz said, this skill plays an essential role. The larvae's epic migration demands inconceivable amounts of energy and dooms most to certain death—scientists estimate that less than 0.3 percent ever reach shore. By almost any measure, those are lousy odds, and without the ability to self-propel, those odds would be even worse.

American eel larvae proceed instinctively from their spawning grounds by way of the Gulf Stream, the mighty flow of balmy water that curls around the North American coast and across the Atlantic toward Europe. (Scientists suggest that the larvae are imprinted with a characteristic pattern of gene expression that helps guide them on their journey, though again, this is not certain.) As the larva crosses the topographical border of the continental shelf, it enters its first metamorphosis, transforming from a flat, transparent ribbon to a translucent and tightly packed cylinder responsive to variations in electric and magnetic fields, light, and temperature. No longer a floundering blob of ichthyoplankton struggling in the sea, this "glass eel" has what appears to be a tiny red heart, dark threads of nerves running down its spine, and gills. It's also a strong enough swimmer to break free of the prevailing currents.

Glass eels are significantly smaller than eel larvae, certainly less than three inches, and appear far more eel-like in appearance. The naturalist Rachel Carson, very much an eel person, described them, politely, as "curiously shaped." I'm not sure I agree, as to my untutored eye their shape resembles nothing more curious than strands of bucatini softening at a rolling boil. What they certainly are is ethereal. (Dipping a hand into a river-rush of glass eels not far from Carson's salt pond reserve in mid-coast Maine, I found they slipped imperceptibly through my fingers, like stardust.) In the ocean, salt is the enemy, and eel larvae do what they can to rid themselves of it, quivering as their every cell strives to maintain a critical electrolyte balance. Close to shore and fresh water, the glass eel must recalibrate physiologically to retain salt, a critical transformation in its cellular machinery that demands huge expenditures of energy. It's just a hunch, but I would not be surprised if glass eels in saline transition require more calories per gram of body weight than do most any other living creature. And acquiring and metabolizing those calories is an energy sink unto itself.

As glass eels near coastal estuaries, they darken with pigment and thicken into elvers. So subtle is this change that the terms "glass eel" and "elver" are used interchangeably even by those who should and do know better. (In Maine, "elver season" is essentially glass eel season, as older, larger, pigmented elvers are generally less desirable than are their younger, smaller, transparent selves.) Sometimes, the two stages are distinguished by their behaviors: glass eels migrate from open seas to estuaries (where saltwater meets fresh), and elvers migrate from estuaries to the upper reaches of rivers. But this distinction doesn't quite hold. Though classified as a freshwater fish, many Atlantic eels (nobody knows what percentage) never set fin in fresh water, but rather spend the growth stage of their lives in brackish coastal rivers and estuaries. In fact, recently scientists have found that some freshwater eels never leave the ocean at all.

Any number of factors might direct some elvers to hunker down in the first tidal marsh or estuary they encounter and others to forge bravely upstream battling currents, squirting over concrete dams, wriggling through wetlands, to settle into a freshwater lake, stream, or pond. Marko Freese, a marine scientist at the Thünen Institute of Fisheries Ecology in Germany and a member of Hanel's research team, offered two possible explanations for this disparity:

natural selection or human disruption. The natural selection theory would suggest that some eels are genetically directed to avoid fresh water, and while there is some early evidence of this, Freese isn't buying it. "Natural selection takes a very long time, so that's unlikely," he cautioned. "It's more likely that eels sense that the freshwater systems are not passable." In other words, that something human-related—a dam, a power plant, polluted waters, predators—foiled the elver's intentions to leave the relative safety of saltwater.

Once settled into their habitat of choice—be it fresh, brackish, or salt water—elvers transform once again. Their skin goes slick, their backs shade to a murky yellow/olive green, and their bellies fade to a creamy off-white. Also, their tiny scales embed further into their slime-coated skin. In this prolonged "yellow" stage, eels tend to stay put, spending the daylight hours in burrows and tree snags, eluding predators, and their nights trolling for prey. It's for this reason that we never spotted a grown eel in our Maine pond—though had we ventured out on a moonlit night in scuba gear, we might well have encountered one or two foraging for food. Perennially ravenous, yellow eels eat any living thing that doesn't eat them first—insects, finfish, crustaceans, snails, and, if need be, each other. Yellow eels can swim both backward and forward, and their snakelike bodies can burrow deep into crevasses to grab crabs, worms, clams, and other creatures out of reach to less dexterous fish. If a desired critter gets stuck or resists, the eel will simply spread its jaws, chomp down, and spin to tear off a bite-sized chunk of flesh. Cold weather (and cold water) makes them sluggish, but to be honest, sluggish is the yellow eel's natural state: they are eating machines, and their job is not to move quickly but to grow.

Eels are neither male nor female at birth, and, as I will soon

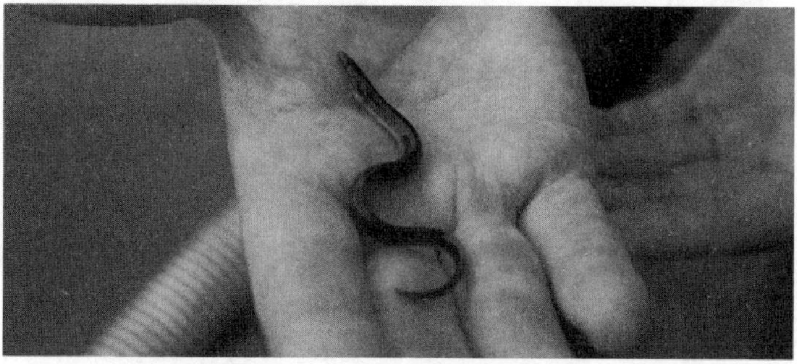

A juvenile eel in the elver stage. Often conflated with the nearly transparent "glass eel" stage, elvers are pigmented and slightly larger—four to six inches—and are generally found either in freshwater inlets or in estuaries. A significant number of "freshwater" eels—especially males—never leave salt water. (U.S. Fish and Wildlife Service)

explain, environment—not genetics—plays a larger role in their sexual determination. Do eels go through a hermaphroditic phase in which they display both male and female characteristics but are as yet incapable of reproduction? As we know, that's a question that has plagued scientists since ancient times. The current view is that some males undergo this "intersex" stage, while females make the leap from ungendered to gendered directly. Males differentiate and reach sexual maturity far earlier than do females, and at the smallest size possible, possibly to make them less visible to predators on their return to the spawning grounds. Females, as is so often the case, have a more complicated trade-off to make—weighing the risk of death by predators against the need to maximize their own fertility. It's a no-win proposition: the older and larger the female, the more eggs she produces and the more likely to pass on her genes, but the greater risk she takes of dying before she can mate. (This is rather like the uncomfortable calculation women make when trying to decide when to get pregnant: either wait until you are established in a career and—in theory—better able to support a family, or move quickly to avoid forfeiting the opportunity to conceive at all.)

As mentioned above, an eel's sex is determined less by genes than by environmental conditions. Eels tend to become male in crowded estuaries and eel farms, and to become female in wide-open spaces, like lakes and ponds. (Scientists have also considered latitude, water temperature, and salinity as potential drivers of eel sexual differentiation, but so far have failed to confirm the influence of any of these factors.) One theory for this surprising correlation between population density and gender (popular with Maine fishermen) is that males enjoy each other's company more than do females. Pretty much no scientist with whom I spoke (from Maine or anywhere else) buys this idea. Another theory (favored by scientists) is that males return to the breeding grounds far sooner than do females, and in that shorter time period are better able to survive the competition of other males. Pretty much no fisherman I spoke with buys that idea. Since neither these nor any other theory is beyond a reasonable doubt, let's stick with what we do know: that freshwater eels offer a remarkably powerful illustration of the power of non-genetic factors to shape sexual differentiation.

SHORTLY BEFORE REACHING SEXUAL MATURITY (precisely why and when remain a mystery), eels brace to leave on their epic return to their birthplace. Male eels are typically three to eight years old when they depart, while females wait longer, some growing in forgotten pools for forty years, and occasionally even longer. How much longer depends on many factors, including whether they've landed in commodious digs. I could find no stories of geriatric freshwater eels in Maine, but in Europe, long-lived eels wear the mantle of myth. In 2014, an eel named Ale (Swedish for "eel") was found dead, floating in a well outside a residence in the tiny fishing town of Brantevik, Sweden. Ale's human keepers believed that their ancestors had dumped Ale in the well deliberately, knowing that the ravenous eel would make quick work of the flies and other intruders in their water supply. By the family's reckoning, Ale had provided this service for 155 years. A team from the Swedish University of Agriculture Science Institute of Freshwater Research was enlisted to verify the claim, which they hoped to do by counting the rings on the eel's otoliths. (Otoliths first appear in the larval stage and grow like rings on a tree, reflecting changes across the eel's entire life.) But when the scientists arrived on the scene, Ale's headless body had deteriorated into a pulpy mess. After a search, the eel's head was found in a nearby freezer. "There were only rotten parts of the flesh left and some pieces of back bone," the lead scientist, Håkan Wickström, wrote me in an email. "When the head subsequently was found, the otoliths had fallen out, i.e., there was nothing to age!"

A tragedy.

Nonetheless, the scientists agreed that from all evidence, Ale had lived a very long life indeed (though perhaps not 155 years). Part of the reason for this is that Ale was not a wild creature but a pampered pet, fed regularly by her owners and untroubled by predators. Indeed, it's known that females can live eighty years and more in captivity, where they have no need to fight for food or, for that matter, go through the grueling process of readying themselves for migration and procreation.

Rachel Carson, forever empathetic, wrote beautifully of the aging eel's transition from sedentary yellow to migrating silver, which she imagined well before taking residence at her summer cottage on Southport Island, in her adopted state of Maine. "Now it was autumn again, and the water was chilling to the cold rains shed off the hard backbones of the hills. A strange restiveness was growing in Anguilla the eel. For the first time in her adult life, the food hunger was forgotten. In its place was a strange, new hunger, formless and ill-defined. Its dimly perceived object was a place of warmth and darkness . . . She had known such a place once—in the dim beginnings of life, before memory began."

When eels get the call to return to the place "before memory began," their bellies silver and their back skin turns black and glossy, as if baptized in motor oil. Their eyes—already large—double in size and attune to the color blue, the better to distinguish ocean predators. Their gonads increase in size, their alimentary tracts regress, their intestinal functions cease and their bodies brace for the crushing deep ocean pressures to come. For most of their lives, eels live by one rule: eat and don't be eaten. As they move from the yellow to silver stage, their fat stores balloon to 28 percent of their body weight. But throughout thousands of miles on their final odyssey to their ancestral home, they eat no more, consuming their own bodies—bones and all—for fuel. The rule has changed: from now on their purpose on earth is not to eat, but to reproduce.

As do eel larvae, silver eels rise toward the surface in the evening and dive deep into the depths in the morning, adding many miles of "vertical migration" to a horizontal journey of as many as 6,000 miles or more for the European eel, something on the order of 3,000 miles for the American species. By the time they reach their birthplace, they have shriveled to puckered husks, yet somehow muster the energy for a last push toward life. Males spew out a cloud of sperm and females release their eggs. A day or two later, they may or may not repeat this process in the same or a nearby location. Mission accomplished and their life circle complete, the eels perish in what one hopes is a surge of ecstatic relief. But relief or not, we have no direct evidence of this dramatic *l'amour et la mort*.

Like criminals perpetrating the perfect crime, the dying eels leave no trace, and no human has caught them in the act.

If the story I've just told of the eel's life trajectory sounds like a fairy tale, some parts of it almost certainly are: not everything we believe we know about eels is rooted in demonstrable fact. This is especially true in matters of reproduction. The fish ecologist Julian Dodson, professor emeritus at the University of Laval, was a member of the first scientific team to attempt to track American eels from the Canadian coast to their assumed breeding ground in the Sargasso with the help of satellite technology. "The satellite transmitting tags we used were $4,500 each," he recalled, adding that their first attempt ended in the consumption of those pricy tags by sharks. (To be specific, data from the tags revealed temperatures consistent with the bellies of porbeagles, a subspecies of the mackerel shark.) Only 4 percent of tagged eels were traced into the North Atlantic, and not one made it anywhere near the Sargasso before losing contact. Four years later, in 2016, Dodson's team tried again, this time trucking thirty-eight large female eels to Nova Scotia and dumping them directly into the Cabot Strait, in hopes of avoiding the sharks. They managed to track eight eels to the open ocean, and one a bit farther out to sea. "But the signal died, it crapped out on the edge of the Sargasso," Dodson said, laughing. "The only thing that could improve matters is a major change in technology. Our group no longer exists, we're all retired. But I believe there is a group working on new tags and new satellites."

Allow me a moment to step back and explain what is meant by a "pop-up tag." Properly called pop-up satellite archival tags (PSAT), these ingenious devices record the behaviors and habitats of marine species in the wild. Once implanted or otherwise attached to the animal, they act autonomously, collecting and storing data on ocean pressure (depth), temperature, and light levels in a time series format. A release mechanism allows the tag to detach from the animal and ascend to the surface, where the archived information is transmitted to a satellite. (The release happens automatically when the tag reaches its programmed pop-up date, or if it registers a constant depth that suggests the fish is dead, or if the fish dives too deep, to ensure the tag isn't crushed under pressure.) Scientists can then download the data at will.

Rosalind Wright, a senior specialist at the National Fisheries Services in the UK, is one among the new generation of scientists applying this technology in a search for clues to the eel's migratory habits. She led the scientific team reputed to have followed adult European eels all the way to their presumed breeding ground in the Sargasso. To do so, Wright and her colleagues surgically implanted PSATs equipped with seven-inch antennas onto the bodies of twenty-six eels that had been taken from freshwater rivers in the islands of San Miguel and Flores, in the Azores, where European eels are thought to congregate before their final trip south. Given the relatively large size of these eels—twenty-eight to forty inches—it was assumed that they were all females. Once tagged, the eels were returned to their respective rivers and tracked as they swam at speeds ranging from less than 2 miles a day to roughly 7.5 miles a day. (Quite slow compared with large American eels, whose speeds in the open ocean range from 24 to 31 miles per day, so perhaps, as some scientists have demonstrated in the laboratory, the satellite tags slowed them down.) Of the twenty-six eels, the tags on five were tracked to within the Sargasso's boundaries, and one to the breeding ground.

Wright and her team claimed to have found the "first direct evidence of migrating adult European eels reaching the presumed breeding place in the Sargasso Sea." But other scholars aren't so sure. Since Julian Dodson had attempted a similar feat with the American eel, I asked him to comment. "This is a very poor paper, and I am not sure that I have much faith in any of the conclusions," he responded in an email. "I don't know where to begin." The calculations, he wrote were "full of biases," and "none of the eels tagged in this study migrated fast enough—greater than 12 km per day—to arrive at the spawning area in time to spawn . . . the authors speculate that European eels may make long, slow migrations at depth (no evidence of this is presented) to conserve energy and avoid predation (speculation). The timing would enable the completion of their maturation before they arrive on the spawning grounds in time for the peak of the *second* spawning period. I do not know where this idea of a second spawning period comes from!!"

When I called Wright to comment, she seemed to take a step back from the paper's conclusions. "We were able to extend the life of our satellite tags to eighteen months" and therefore follow the eels farther than did scientists on previous attempts, she told me. "We know they dive down as far as 2,000 meters [1.25 miles] during the day and navigate there in darkness. And we know that there are no great balls of eels spawning together in the same place—they come together in different places. But we don't know how on earth silver eels know how to return to their birthing place, or how they synchronize their return. These are the sorts of mysteries that obsess us, and why so many of us consider the search (for answers) our life mission."

What is certain is that announcements of "ancient eel migration mystery unraveled" by the BBC and other media outlets were wild oversteps. The eels of Maine, as do all Atlantic eels, breed and perish at some point on their final trek home, but descriptions of this death march—no matter how convincing, moving, or poetic—remain mostly conjecture. The ancient quest to understand the creature's migratory behavior stretches back to well before Schmidt first identified the presumed spawning area in the Sargasso Sea, but his presumption was built on assumptions that have never been verified. In the final decade of his life, Schmidt revealed his disappointment in this agonized and bluntly honest admission: "The solution of the [eel] problem seemed wrapped in deeper darkness than ever." One hundred years later, science is not yet out of the dark, but a dawn of an unexpected sort does seem to be on the horizon.

CHAPTER 9

ANIMAL MAGNETISM, OR SNORKELING WITH EELS

her sweat,
her tears,
her ancient years.

—Irate Watcher, "eel in the ocean"

PARISIAN BY BIRTH IF NOT by temperament, Caroline Durif suffers fools gladly. When I awkwardly asked whether she grew up fishing eels with her father, she arched a brow yet remained composed. "My [last] name comes from Auvergne and means 'from the stream,'" she said. (A "rif" is a stream in the old local dialect.) "That is the closest I've ever come to fishing."

I should have known.

For the first half of her life, Durif did not once set eyes on eel, nor did she wish to. "I thought they were scary," she said. So why chose eels as the subject of her PhD thesis? Was it concern over their loss of habitat, exposure to disease, or their general decline? Ah . . . no, nothing so lofty. "I got funding," she said.

France is highly dependent on hydroelectric power, and as we know, water turbines and eels do not mix. Durif's money came by way of a power company intent on finding ways not to pulverize eels in its hydroelectric plants. The assigned mission was to find ways to save the eels without putting the electric company out of business. She didn't know—or care—anything about eels, but it did strike her as an interesting challenge.

Durif and her team tagged sixteen eels with surgically implanted radio transmitters and released them upstream of a power station to see whether and how they would proceed under real-world pressures. Rather than risk the turbines, most eels switched direction and swam upstream, reversing direction only after a heavy rainfall made it possible for them to pass over the overflowing dam unharmed. Pretty amazing. "Salmon and smolts go directly into turbines, but eels find their way around them," Durif said, with an almost motherly pride. Eels, then, were clever animals, or at least they acted that way. Clearly, this finding merited a second look. In a follow-up study, Durif and her colleagues tracked silver eels over a period of three years to learn what variety of bypass best allowed them safe passage over dams. The team concluded that different environmental conditions at the dam site demanded different approaches, and custom-built a fish pass specific to each power plant. The eels were not only clever, but also not misled by groupthink.

Through these and related observations, Durif's feelings about the eel ripened from fear to wonder to affection. "I remember very well the first time I saw an eel," she said. "We had gone for my first sampling trip in the lake of Grand-Lieu in France. I was fascinated. I thought the eels were very beautiful. I noticed their nice, shiny skin, their tiny scales in beautiful patterns, their gorgeous eyes. They were like pets."

How so, I asked.

"They like contact, like dogs," she explained. "And did you know eel are the only fish that can swim backwards?"

The only fish? Later I learned that other fish do swim in reverse, but imagining a backward-swimming eel made me smile.

Durif snorkeled with eels that were close enough to flirt with the GoPro camera strapped to her wrist. "They are so curious, and they don't flap around like other fish," she said. I found this surprising, as eels are photophobic, meaning they avoid light and also humans frolicking close to the water's surface. I asked Durif to explain, and she smiled conspiratorially. "Eels break rules," she said. Why, of course they do.

Durif and I spoke several times over Skype, then arranged to meet at her home about fifteen miles from the Instagram-perfect port city of Bergen, Norway. My flight was delayed for hours in Amsterdam, and I arrived jet-lagged, stiff, and cranky. Durif collected me at the airport and drove me to her charming home, where her son and daughter, both teenagers, politely blew me off in perfect English. (They also speak French.) While my host polished off some last-minute paperwork, I took a stroll around the neighborhood to check out the scene. Everywhere there was the screech of seagulls and a dazzling view of the sea. The air smelled of salt. I could not imagine a more fish-forward location.

At dinner that evening, Durif and her husband, Morten Kismul, a petroleum engineer, served some sort of delicious white fish proceeded by an elegant appetizer of smoked wild eel on digestive biscuits. (As I mentioned earlier, wild eel is not my cup of tea, and I'm a tad ashamed to admit that I sequestered most of my portion in a paper napkin.) The eel, over a foot long, had been caught and

Eel scientist Caroline Durif and her husband, Morten Kismul, preparing an eel appetizer in their kitchen on the west coast of Norway. The endangered European eel, caught and smoked by a local fisherman, was a special treat available only to researchers. (Ellen Ruppel Shell)

smoked by their neighbor, the fisherman Alte Nilsen. Mr. Nilsen was the proud owner of what Durif called a "man cave," a basement lair equipped with an eel aquarium and the necessary apparatus for smoking them. Years ago, he may well have sold live catch to fish brokers trolling the harbors in dual-masted barges, or "eelfisching-boats," in which eels were exported to Denmark, where eel meat was—and is—quite popular. But today Norway forbids the export of freshwater eel, and the eel fishery is closed. Norwegians have never eaten much eel, so Nilsen and his fellow eel fishers make do by selling what they can to scientists like Durif for use in research. Or, as in my case, to share with the odd houseguest doing research.

After dinner, Durif and I retired to her family room to talk politics, culture, and eels. It being June in the west of Norway, the sun was reluctant to set and Durif, erudite and ebullient, made lively company. I would have gladly battered her with questions well into the night, had we not a boat to catch early the next morning.

THE CAR-FERRY RIDE TO DURIF'S laboratory on the island of Austevoll featured spectacular scenery—pine forests, rock formations, pastel-painted homes—and was followed by a stunning drive through ancient farmlands alive with squawking geese and ducks, and silently grazing livestock. This spectacle was Durif's daily commute, and I couldn't help but think how much it all reminded me of a good day in Maine. "Those are wild sheep from the Viking era," she said, pointing to a flock just yards off the dirt road. "Every year I buy a lamb from the farmer who lends us the use of this field." I was about to ask her what she did with the lamb when we came to a stop at a gaggle of bright orange painted buildings. This was the Institute of Marine Research's Austevoll Station, her workplace. Durif first ventured here in 2004 as a young postdoctoral fellow, speaking no Norwegian and accompanied by her first (native French-speaking) husband. She arrived with the audacious (and perhaps naive) goal of unlocking the secret of how eels orient and navigate in the ocean.

"It's so strange that silver eels in the south [perhaps Spain or North Africa] leave coastal waters and return to the sea at just four years old, while silver eels in northern regions [perhaps Norway or the UK] wait until they are twenty-five or thirty years," she said. "How do these old ladies know when to go, and how do they know how to get there? Everyone had the same question: How do eels navigate?"

Most fish are excellent navigators and, like other animals, rely on their senses to find their way. But what senses are we talking about? From childhood we are taught of five: sight, smell, hearing, touch, and taste. Humans have evolved to make the most of these, and we assume that other creatures do the same. But that assumption overlooks that the sensory apparatus of other species differs significantly from ours. And that is especially true of fish.

Consider the flounder. Flounders are born with what we think of as properly spaced eyes, one on each side of its face. But as the flounder approaches adulthood, one eye sneaks around its head to join the other, a maneuver that happens surprisingly quickly, perhaps in a day or two. To anyone who has seen a flounder, this seems a cruel mistake—what's the point of both eyes pointing in the same direction, looking at the same thing? For humans this double vision makes no sense, but for flounders the purpose is quite clear. A flounder's eyes don't lie flush against the face as do ours. Rather, they protrude gawkishly and swivel independently of each other while its body remains camouflaged and inert flat against the ocean floor. The flounder's freakish (to us) facial configuration endows it with outstanding binocular vision that equips it to snatch passing prey while hunkered down on the seafloor, hidden away from predators. A triumph of evolutionary bioengineering, for sure.

Unlike the sharp-eyed flounder, eels have rather poor vision. But they do possess a strong sense of touch and an outstanding sense of smell. Among fishes, the Atlantic eel has been called a "champion sniffer," capable of distinguishing the scent of a few drops of rose water diluted in a pool the size of a Great Lake. But while this keen olfactory sense helps eels locate prey throughout their ravenous and sedentary yellow eel phase, it's not at all clear how heavily silver eels rely on smell to guide them back to their breeding grounds, a phase during which they do not eat. For this, eels likely depend on a form of perception that humans are thought not to possess: a "sixth sense" that links them to the earth's ever shifting magnetic field.

My middle-school understanding of magnetic fields being suspect, I asked a scientist friend to help me sort it out. She explained that the earth's core is a solid iron ball surrounded by molten iron and nickel, a sort of "planet within the planet" where physical processes take place that ultimately protect the earth from cosmic radiation and makes possible life as we know it. The cooling and crystallization of this iron core perturbs the surrounding liquid metal and creates powerful electric currents that generate a magnetic field stretching far out into space. This field shifts with time, but over the short term remains stable, unaffected by weather or changing seasons. This makes magnetic signals a reliable aid for human travelers equipped with compasses, an exquisitely sensitive instrument invented by the Chinese sometime between 200 BCE and 100 CE. It's thought that other animals, too, rely on the earth's magnetic field for navigation—notably birds, but also turtles, lobsters, and insects. Naturally, neither these creatures nor any other animal has access to an external compass. But some do possess an internal, biological compass so accurate as to be considered superior to early human-made navigational aids. This "magnetic sense," or magnetoreception, equips these animals to navigate over vast distances, even when celestial bodies and other guideposts are blotted out by fog, clouds, or storms. (As a directionally challenged human beholden to directionally gifted friends myself, I often contemplate the possibility that some lucky humans, too, possess an internal compass.)

The idea that animals orient and navigate using a magnetic sense is not new—in 1859, the Russian zoologist Alexander von Middendorff theorized that birds were guided by "an inner magnetic feeling." But very few scientists agreed. As recently as 1944, the biologist Donald Griffin, who codiscovered the sonar of bats, opined that the magnetic sense was "biophysically impossible." For one thing, no one had found a magnetic sensor in birds or other animals, so it seemed that the magnetic "sense" lacked a sensing organ. For another, the earth's magnetic field is weak, so weak it seemed unlikely that any animal (with cells composed mainly of molecules of oxygen, carbon, and nitrogen, all of low magnetic susceptibility) would be able to make sense of it.

Still, von Middendorff's "magnetic feeling" remained a compelling concept, one some scientists thought worth further investigation. In the 1960s, the German ornithologist Friedrich Merkel and his student Wolfgang Wiltschko grew interested in the question of how the European robin knows when and where to migrate each autumn, a mystery they believed had some link to this elusive magnetic sense. To test the theory, they designed a series of experiments. One experiment involved positioning the birds in cages surrounded by a Helmholtz coil, a contraption comprised of two circular wire coils carrying the same electric current that together generate a nearly uniform magnetic field. When Wiltschko shifted the coils to rotate the magnetic field, the robin shifted along with it, suggesting that the bird possessed some sort of biological compass. Wiltschko and his wife, the animal physiologist Roswitha Wiltschko, repeated the experiment with other birds, and found that the robin was not unique. Other scientists have since found similar behavior in fish, turtles, mammals, birds, insects, and even bacteria.

Usually, sense organs are easy to spot. Their job is to reach out and gather information from the environment, which typically involves an obvious entry point—a nostril or eye or taste bud or fingertip. Visible rows of sensors called "lateral lines" suggest a sense of feel that helps eels and other fish locate their prey. Unfortunately, magnetoreception offers us no such clues, as the magnetic sensing organ—or even a clump of magnetic sensing cells—has yet to be located in any animal. Magnetic fields can pass effortlessly through tissue, so the cells that detect them could be anywhere on the body—in an eye, an ear, a gut, or a fin. Unlike sense organs that rely on exposure to the external environment, magnetic-sensitive cells may even be hidden deep in the flesh. Yet while no one has found a particular organ sensitive to magnetic pull, it is widely agreed that many animals have magnetic receptors of some sort, and there are several theories on the ways these receptors might work. The theory scientists think most likely to apply to eels involves an oxidized iron crystal called magnetite.

In *An Immense World*, his majestic interrogation of how animals make sense of things, the science writer Ed Yong recounts how scientists working in the 1970s discovered a variety of bacteria able to turn themselves into "living compass needles." It is thought that certain proteins in these so-called magnetotactic bacteria synthesize nanoparticles of magnetite and rely on them to sense their planetary location and guide them to their desired habitats. Magnetite and similar magnetic compounds have since been found in fish, birds, insects, and humans. So theoretically, other animals, too, could build this sort of compass, by tethering a magnetite needle to a sensory cell. As the animal moves, the needle yanks this tether, generating a signal picked up by its nervous system. Again, this is a theory: there are debates as to whether the magnetite found in animals is even functional, or just an incidental byproduct of the animal's metabolic machinery. And it bears repeating that no one has located a magnetic sensory cell in an animal—let alone a magnetic-sensitive organ.

Nonetheless, recent findings suggest that a magnetic compass may well be a driver of animal behavior. In 2022, a team of American and European scientists published a study in the *Proceedings of the National Academy of Sciences* describing magnetite found in salmon noses. As noted in an earlier chapter, salmon are famous for their dramatic migrations, and scientific interest in a magnetic component guiding that migration has been strong for decades. The study in question looked at proteins in the magnetite structures of salmon and found a genetic link between these and the proteins found in certain bacteria. Some scientists believe that this link is likely to apply to other animals with specialized magnetite structures. These include the American eel, which, like the salmon, has magnetite crystals in and around its head.

The so-called magnetic maps used by animals for navigation appear to have an important limitation—namely that while generally reliable over long distances, they are far less so over short distances. For this reason, most species thought to depend on magnetic reception for navigation use it to guide them only during lengthy migrations: to pick one nonrandom example, an infant eel traveling from the Sargasso Sea to our little pond on the coast of Maine.

As I've mentioned, scientists have posited that glass eels may rely on smell, water temperature, and tides to make their way to the continental shelf, and also that they respond to the electrical "shadow" of the new moon. But while these and other factors may function as orientation clues over limited distances, the gradients in these variables over thousands of nautical miles are inconsistent and small. This limitation is especially profound for the eel, which made it ripe for being tested for magnetic orientation. But early studies failed to show consistent orientation of eels relative to a magnetic field. While some involvement of a magnetic sense in their migration seemed probable, just how eels accessed and used that sense to navigate was a matter of heated debate.

We know that European and American eels—the Atlantic eels—are widely distributed. And yet many assume that all Atlantic eels spawn at (very roughly) the same time and (very roughly) the same place. The orientation mechanisms necessary for the European and American eels to synchronize their migration to enable this congregation in time and space, Durif understood, was both a terribly important question and a mystery for another day. The question she and her group hoped to answer was far simpler: How do eels find their way home? The team's working hypothesis was that the geomagnetic field worked as an environmental cue to set eels on a direction relative to magnetic north, like a compass, and later provided more specific positional information, like a biological GPS. True navigation required that the eel first form a "mental grid" in relation to the target destination and adjust the "compass" as it moved closer to that destination.

Durif and her team compared the migratory routes of all five species of temperate freshwater eels with the geomagnetic field of each of their spawning areas. They found that the larvae of every species drifted along paths of increasing magnetic intensity, while adult eels of every species followed paths of decreasing magnetic intensity. This finding was consistent with the theory that eel larvae have a mechanism by which they "imprint" the path of their outward migration, and years later as adults retrace that magnetic route by following the gradient of decreasing intensity. To be clear, eels are not thought to be imprinted with the exact location of their breeding grounds, but rather to follow a magnetic "isoline"—a line of constant magnetic intensity in the ocean similar to a highway or river on land—that together with the compass orientation leads them to the spawning area.

While elegant, this compass and GPS theory of eel navigation remained controversial. Yes, larval and adult eels appeared to be following some geomagnetic signal, but where was the proof? Although fifty years had passed since the seminal experiments of the Wiltschkos and colleagues, understanding of magnetoreception was still primitive, at best at an early stage. The fact that (as far as we know) humans lack the capacity to sense the earth's magnetic field complicated matters and made it difficult to design experiments. Durif and her team returned to the Wiltschkos' approach: generate an artificial magnetic field in the laboratory and see whether it guided the eel's movements, and if so, how.

To make that happen, Durif's advisers got in touch with John Phillips, a biologist at Virginia Tech who had long experience in creating artificial magnetic fields to study magnetic reception in fruit flies, newts, frogs, and other animals. But when Durif asked Phillips to help build a magnetic apparatus to study eels, he wasn't sure just how to approach it. Phillips's work had been on insects and small terrestrial animals whose magnetic compass orientation was light dependent. Eels spend their daytime deep underwater, where light is scarce. And eels are relatively large animals so tracking their behavior required a grander apparatus than Phillips had built in the past. "My previous experiments didn't involve such large Helmholtz coils," he told me.

Still, Phillips is not the type to shrink from a challenge: his controversial work on salamanders was the very first to prove the impact of light on the magnetic compass system in an animal. And he was a true believer in the power of magnetic fields. "I'm probably an extreme, but I think all animals have a magnetic compass," Phillips told me. "Including humans." He flew to Norway to help Durif build her experiment.

By Phillips's standards, Durif's "MagLab" was enormous, but to my eyes it was an elven two-room hut, maybe a third of the size of a Manhattan studio apartment. Custom built without steel, iron, or other magnetic materials, it sat adrift in a grassy field, far from any possible magnetic interference. (The lab was carefully shielded from other orientation cues as well, including odors, light, and sound, and sunk into a hole filled with cement to minimize vibrations.) One room of the shack was crammed nearly wall-to-wall with a 1,400-liter test tank (fed by a seawater reservoir) balanced between a pair of giant coils. "When I built it, it was winter, and dark the entire day," Phillips told me. "The coils were three meters in diameter. I was walking in circles in the dark, winding wire around the frames. It was fifteen kilometers of wire, and many kilometers of walking." Together, the coils are designed to cancel out the ambient magnetic field and generate an artificial one that can be manipulated to study whether and how the magnetic field steers the orientation of fish circling the tanks.

Durif and her team captured specimens for study at two locations: using traps on the River Imsa where silver eels were headed out to sea, and basket-shaped eel pots along the Skagerrak coast. (Most of the Skagerrak eels were at the yellow stage, though some showed signs of silvering.) The captured eels were chauffeured by car in tanks of oxygenated water to the research station and divided into two groups. Each group was put into one of two "training tanks" that differed from each other only in the direction of their water inflow: the seawater in the first training tank was supplied by a pipe situated 30 degrees relative to magnetic north, the seawater in the second tank supplied by a pipe situated at 300 degrees south. The eels remained in the training tanks for a minimum of two days, to give them time to settle into a directional pattern before being transferred into the testing tank. Once placed into the testing tank, each eel was exposed to four altered conditions, with magnetic direction preset inside the tank at geographic north, south, east, and west. The scientists found that no matter where they set the

Set in an isolated patch of farmland peppered with sheep on the west coast of Norway, the magnetoreception test facility ("MagLab") is equipped with a 370-gallon test tank fed by a seawater reservoir. (Note the pair of "drifting in situ" chambers.) The tank is surrounded by sets of coiled wires that both cancel the ambient magnetic field and can generate an artificial, manipulatable magnetic field to study the magnetic orientation and reception capabilities of eels and other fish. (Ellen Ruppel Shell)

geographic compass, eels displayed a consistent direction of orientation relative to the magnetic field, and the direction was specific to the orientation of the eel's training tank. As they had theorized, the directional response was stronger when the water temperature in the testing tank was lower, the colder water corresponding to the "environmental window" in which eels migrate.

The critical finding was this: despite the manipulation of the artificial magnetic field, the migrating eels stayed their predetermined course. This led the researchers to conclude that silver and yellow eels do indeed have a "magnetic compass" that, when integrated with other cues—like variations in water temperature and odors—orients them to their fated migratory path. From an evolutionary standpoint, this system might well confer an adaptive advantage: when an eel's migration is impeded by low water flow, dams, or other obstacles (as is so frequently the case), it is prepared to resume its migration on its original path if and when environmental conditions improve.

Of course, eels live many lives, the adult stage being only the final one. What of the larval and glass eels' epic migration from deep in the ocean into estuaries and other coastal inlets? Yes, other creatures migrate over astonishing distances, each demonstrating an impressive display of grit and evolutionary adaptation. But that a transparent, gelatinous wisp of a thing could survive let alone navigate such an odyssey seemed a biological miracle. Alessandro Cressi, a young Italian scientist on Durif's team, took the lead on testing the theory that an internal compass might guide their paths, too.

You can't tag glass eels with satellite receivers like you can adult eels; they are far too small. So instead, Cressi and his team placed the infant eels into a specially designed semi-enclosed circular aquarium submerged in a North Sea fjord. The scientists noted each eel's orientation, and then transferred it from the holding chamber to a testing tank in the MagLab. There the eels were exposed to a magnetic field that had been artificially manipulated to shift the north/south and east/west axes by ninety degrees. Although deprived of all other environmental cues—light, odors, sounds—the glass eels consistently oriented south, the same direction that they were headed during ebb tide in the holding chamber.

"We thought it incredible that these tiny, transparent eels can detect the earth's magnetic field," Cressi said. "The eel is always surprising us, opening a new chapter in our understanding of fish behavior. It teaches us that fish can do incredible things."

On my final evening in Bergen, I met Durif and her husband, Morten, for dinner at a small café known for its fish soup and reindeer stew garnished with juniper berries. It was a noisy place popular with students. Norway has draconian drunk driving laws, so to enjoy the evening Caroline and Morten had arrived by public transportation. After a few pleasantries about our kids and the (predictably unpredictable) Norwegian weather, Caroline returned to what she graciously sensed was the subject at hand. I gathered my courage and mentioned that not every scientist I'd spoken to is convinced that eels—or any animal—can be guided by magnetic signals. Smiling slyly, she took a careful sip of wine. "Once I delivered a talk on this, and after I finished, a geophysicist came up to speak with me," she said. "He'd been working with magnetic fields his entire career, and he said that he didn't believe me." The physicist pointed out that for the magnetic theory of navigation to work, eels would require some mechanism for measuring both the intensity and magnitude of the field, which are extremely difficult to measure. He had reason to be skeptical: while all science proceeds in fits and starts, as Ed Yong made note, magnetoreception "has been plagued by an unusual number of splashy studies that later prove incorrect," and some animals said to possess it probably don't.

While all that is true, it's also true that debunked theories often turn out to be correct. For example, in 1999 an American team reported that monarch butterflies have a compass sense, only to shamefully retract the paper when they realized that the insects had actually been orienting to light reflected off of their shirts. Five years later, another team of scientists found very strong evidence that monarchs do in fact use a light-dependent magnetic compass to navigate their migrations. Studies in humans are equally lumpy—while many scientists swear that humans have no magnetic sense, others insist they have evidence that it does exist in at least some people, although it's not clear how it's used. Still, we were talking about eels, not butterflies or humans, and I wondered how Durif would respond to the physicist's critique.

"We tested our theory, worked very hard on it, and we found patterns that show that [eels] do use magnetic orientation," she assured me. "The mechanism is not very precise, and the eels probably are not looking for a specific location. They just need to find a [magnetic] isoline and follow it to stay on target. When we follow a tagged [European] eel, we see that it doesn't head straight for the Sargasso Sea. It goes straight south until it hits an isoline, and then follows that line to the Sargasso."

It bears repeating that no one has actually set eyes on a mature eel anywhere in the open ocean. Hence, the magnetic orientation theory is based not on direct observation of eels in the wild, but on indirect evidence, much of it gathered in laboratories. Scientists have found that tagging an eel changes its behavior and slows its migration, so even satellite data might be misleading. Put bluntly, as with so many theories of eel mechanics and behavior—no matter how well argued—buying into the magnetic theory of eel orientation demands a leap of faith. When I raised this caveat with Durif, she smiled again, this time in agreement. "With eels," she said, raising her glass, "there's always a little bit of voodoo."

CHAPTER 10

DR. EEL AND THE LOVELY MAIDENS

We are two eels. Famished. Our black cloud
awaits . . .

—Mary Rokonadravu, "Famished Eels"

"FACT AND TRUTH," WILLIAM FAULKNER is credited with having said, "don't really have much to do with each other." Michael Miller, a seasoned eel biologist of my acquaintance, seems to share this outlook. A decades-long resident of Japan, Miller is not fluent in Japanese, a failing that he admits has held him back: though a recognized eminence in his field, he has never held a permanent academic post. And yet he is married to a Japanese woman and considers Japan his home. A bighearted, soulful fellow, I found him to be nearly as enigmatic as the eels to which he has devoted his career. "If you know eels, you can only be amazed by them," he told me.

Miller descends from a distinguished line of all-American fish fanciers. His father, Rudy, an expert on fish ecology and behavior, coauthored the classic *Fishes of Oklahoma*. His mother, Helen, a zoologist, wrote her doctoral thesis on the behavior of sunfishes. "I grew up with everything fishes and fishing and fish tanks in my room and in the house," he told me. "I have fishing lures hanging here in my room and fishing rods in sight . . . I got lucky to be in the right places at the right times to end up being part of the eel story." Only a true eel person, I thought, would consider himself lucky to be part of *that* story.

Miller once quipped that Poseidon, the king of the seas, swore an oath to keep the eel's secrets under wraps. The eel's behavior, he told me, is baked into its DNA. The real puzzler is what that code means, and why it matters. The quest to settle this and related questions pulled Miller from his childhood home in Stillwater, Oklahoma, to graduate school in Orono, Maine, where he came under the tutelage of James McCleave (the noted eel expert we met earlier over Egg McMuffins at McDonald's). After postdoctoral work in New Jersey and New Zealand, Miller was drawn to Tokyo and the laboratory of Katsumi Tsukamoto.

In Japan, Tsukamoto is known as Unagi Sensei, or Dr. Eel. The French scientist Eric Feunteun told me he preferred to call him Eel Pope, and while Tsukamoto would blush to hear this, somehow the nickname seems fitting. In 1992, Tsukamoto achieved for the Japanese eel what so many American and European scientists had over centuries failed do for their native species: mark its breeding ground, in his case at 15 degrees north, 140 degrees east, in the territorial waters of the Northern Mariana Islands. This monumental achievement entailed twenty years of hard labor, much of it dragging a fifteen-meter-long plankton net across the North Pacific, from south of Okinawa in southwestern Japan to east of Taiwan and the Philippines in pursuit of ever smaller Japanese eel larvae, just as Johannes Schmidt and Reinhold Hanel pursued the larvae of Atlantic eel in the North Atlantic. The difference is that Tsukamoto managed to clinch the deal. His article, "Discovery of the Spawning Area of the Japanese Eel," graced the cover of the influential scientific journal *Nature* and made headlines around the globe.

Miller was not an author on that paper, but he did join Tsukamoto on several ocean expeditions before moving to Japan, where together they embarked on a succession of what he called "unagi cruises" from 2001 to 2021. Miller has a collection of 13,855 photos taken on those voyages, a small selection of which he shared with me: they picture him towering over Tsukamoto as they stand shoulder to shoulder, all broad smiles and hope. "We came to say we shared everything but our wives," Miller said. Each new finding pulled them deeper into the mystery. In the summers of 2008 and 2009, he, Tsukamoto, and their scientific team found and photographed Japanese larvae, mature Japanese eels, and thirty-one Japanese eel eggs, the last at a depth of 150 to 200 meters in the open ocean. The collection of the eggs, the first ever for any species of anguillid eel, was made late into the night two days before a new moon. They found evidence that the eels may spawn more than once, though always during the nights of the new moon. Importantly, they also found conclusive evidence of a recent shift south in the spawning location, a change that is thought to play a major role in the drastic decline of the Japanese eel.

Tragically, Tsukamoto suffered a stroke in 2019 and stepped back from his research. While I was not able to speak with him in Japan, his work continues to speak for itself. In 2022, he won the International Prize in Biology, one of the world's highest honors for scholarship in natural science. The selection committee wrote, "The story of his amazing quest, which made innovative use of research vessels to strategically survey the vast North Pacific, has done more than anything in recent memory to convey to lay people the vision and passion that drives researchers in oceanography and biology."

Tsukamoto made eels matter. As an advocate and spokesperson, his devotion to the creature is absolute, as is his generosity in sharing what he has learned over a lifetime of study and exploration. Perusing his text *Eels on the Move: Mysterious Creatures over Millions of Years*, co-authored with the marine ecologist Mari Kuroki, I was moved by the stunning illustrations, and the warm, embracing prose. But the chapter "Revering" stumped me. What, I wondered, could that chapter title possibly imply? The Japanese people eat as much as 70 percent of the world's commercial supply of freshwater eel. That's 160,000 tons—320,000,000 pounds—a year, much of it served up in one of 950 restaurants that specialize in eel cooked in the traditional way. Gorging on the object of one's devotion struck me as an odd way to show respect. But then I thought back to the reverence that indigenous people of Maine held for the eel that once provided them such an important protein source, and I began to understand. As one scholar explained when I raised the issue, "Eels have an importance in Japanese culture bordering on the totemic."

For centuries, the Japanese have sung the eel's praises in art, poetry, literature, and song. The Man'yōshū, or The Collection of Ten Thousand Leaves, the oldest-known anthology of classical Japanese poetry, dating to the Nara period (710–784 CE), honors the eel for its culinary and (supposed) medicinal qualities. Eels have found their way into countless Japanese woodblock prints, netsuke fasteners, and obi sash grips, and in rakugo (traditional storytelling), novels, and movies. There are statues of eels in market squares and temples dedicated to the eel. In Toshima, a ward in the north of Tokyo, a large stone monument topped by a bronze image of Kannon, the bodhisattva of compassion, is carved with the phrase UNAGI MEMORIAL. The Buddhist and Shinto faithful regularly arrange special services to pray for the eel's soul. And for many Japanese, the eel is a fish with benefits: it represents fertility and vitality. Eating kabayaki (grilled eel) is said to build stamina and potency, and ward off malaise. Doyo-no Ushi-no Hi, the midsummer "Day of the Ox," devoted to the eating of eel (perhaps because it makes one as strong as an ox), is an unofficial national holiday.

Such ardent displays of eel veneration may seem excessive, even overwrought. But they are mild compared to the dramas played out further west by the ancients. According to Alexandre Dumas's *Le Grand Dictionnaire de Cuisine*, the Egyptians "placed eels on a par with the gods . . . They raised them in aquariums, whose priests were charged with feeding them with cheese and entrails." In the tombs of Egyptian nobility, archaeologists have unearthed the mummified remains of eels positioned daintily in tiny bronze coffins. The Greeks decreed Jupiter, father to all children of unknown parentage, the progenitor of all eels. When gifted a basket of fifty eels, Dicaeopolis, the farmer/hero who works a deal with the Spartans in Aristophanes's comedy *The Acharnians*, exalts: "O my sweetest, my long-awaited desire." The Romans not only desired eels but fetishized them. The great orator Lucius Licinius Crassus (140–91 BCE), mentor to Cicero, adorned his pet eel with earrings and necklaces "like so many lovely maidens." Quintus Hortensias, rival of Cicero, is said to have wept bitterly at the death of his favorite eel, "which he kept long, and loved exceedingly." For those of less sentimental natures, eels embodied the best of both worlds, a pet you could eat. In his epic poem *The Life of Luxury*, made public in 330 BCE, the gourmet and food writer Archestratus raves: "All in all I think the eel rules over everything else at the feast and commands the field of pleasure."

YES, THE ANCIENTS WERE EXTREME, but it's a rare society on which the eel has not left its mark. I learned this from John Wyatt Greenlee, an independent medieval scholar, cartographer, and born-again eel man, as well as a former magazine editor and collegiate volleyball coach. Greenlee's first encounter with the fish came serendipitously, while writing his master's thesis on seventeenth-century maps of London. "I was curious about maps before and after the 1666 fire, curious about what changed," he told me. "People put on maps what they prioritize. I noticed that before the fire, the maps included drawings of Dutch 'eel' ships clearly labeled as such. On these maps, these were the only ships with labels. After the fire, the eel boats were no more, and I wondered why." Greenlee learned that the Dutch traded salted eels to England from the fourteenth century on, and from the mid-fifteenth century they traded in live eels, selling them in the middle of the Thames from boats they called water ships, basically floating aquariums. As it happened, in 1666 the eel ships were banned, not because of the fire, but because England was at war with the Dutch Republic, and Parliament refused to rely on the nation's enemies for food. The resulting eel shortage led to a public outcry that persuaded Parliament to rescind the law, and the Dutch eel ships returned, to remain in England until 1938. "Eels brought a little bit of the medieval world into the twentieth century," Greenlee said. "I knew nothing about them before I first saw that map. And then I realized: it's the eels that are interesting. They bring a sort of horrifying fascination."

A self-branded Surprised Eel Historian, Greenlee wears the mantle lightly and with equal parts humor and unquestioned authority: thousands of scholars and assorted other fans follow

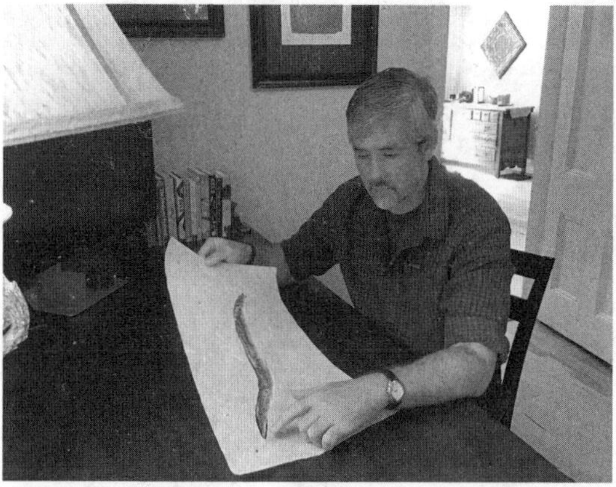

Medievalist and "Surprised Eel Historian" John Wyatt Greenlee discovered his passion while scrutinizing seventeenth-century maps that pictured Dutch "eel" ships, essentially floating aquariums with holds stocked with live eels headed to fishmongers in England, where eels were an extremely popular street food. (Vanessa Greenlee)

him on what he jokes is the "world's premier eel history" social media account. When we spoke, I asked him why he prefaced "Eel Historian" with the word "Surprised," and he explained that both his own fascination with the eel and its nearly universal cultural relevance surprised him.

"For example, for much of their history, the English have been an eel people," he told me. "Since at least the Roman occupation eels were a major food source, and in the tenth century they were by far the most eaten freshwater fish in the country—archaeologists point to eel remains as the most common thing found in food waste. Through the seventeenth century, there was a very strong eel culture—kings, peasants, everyone ate a lot of eels." So many, in fact, that eel comprised as much as 50 percent of the total protein in English diets. This was partly because eels were common in a landscape that had not yet been drained for agricultural use, and partly because marine fish did not travel well over what were then very poor roads. For these and perhaps other reasons, it is thought that people in medieval England ate more eels than all other fresh- and saltwater fish combined.

Eels were more than food; they were a form of currency in a barter economy. In medieval times (circa 1000–1300), ordinary people sometimes paid their rent in grain, eggs, ale, honey, and, notably, eels. The Domesday Survey of 1086, a registry of ancient landholdings and their owners, has more records of rents paid in eels than in any other in-kind medium of exchange. The fish were dried and threaded on twine and, like most currencies, came in dominations: twenty-five to a "stick" (apparently, the greatest number of eels one could smoke at once), ten sticks to a "bind." In 1273, King Edward I decreed price controls for certain foods, including eels, the value of which he set at what today would be $8.75 a stick. A bind—250 smoked or salted eels—was worth about $140 in today's dollars, roughly the price of an annual Amazon Prime membership. Toward the end of the eleventh century, more than a half million eels were paid in rent every year. The largest payment came from the village of Harmston, where residents tithed Earl Hugh of Chester 75,000 eels. One shudders to think what he did with them, though Greenlee has unearthed medieval recipes for eel broth, eel flan, and minced eel pie, and evidence that wallets, clothing, and even wedding bands were made from eel skin. Monasteries, at the time England's wealthiest institutions holding more than a quarter of the country's cultivated land, welcomed eels in exchange for rent, especially during Lent and other designated holy days that forbade the eating of meat. Greely said that for the Church, eels were even better than other fish because they appeared to have no sexual organs, and therefore lacked any hint of carnality.

The Bayeaux Tapestry portrays a half-dozen eels beneath an early scene depicting the Norman campaign in Brittany, where King Harold Godwinson rescues some Normans from drowning in quicksand near the River Couesnon. (Harold is the central figure with one man on his back and another whom he seems to be tugging out by the hand.) (Wikimedia Commons)

The Bayeux Tapestry, a 270-foot-long work depicting the Norman conquest of England by William the Conqueror in the eleventh century, portrays Anglo-Saxon king Harold Godwinson on a battlefield bordered by eels. In Celtic Brittany, holy wells were protected by "fairies" who appeared in the form of eels. Nobles had eels embroidered on their family crests. It's been written that King Henry I suffered a wretched death after dining on "a surfeit of eels of which he was inordinately fond." (Modern scholars suggest that the culprit was more likely contaminated lamprey, though this does not diminish the fact that Henry I was terribly fond of eel, as by no coincidence was his maternal grandson Henry II.) King Richard III, whose death in 1485 marked the end of the Middle Ages in England, stopped eel tariffs to encourage the import of eel from merchants "over seas, where they are abundant to London where they are dear." (As mentioned earlier, what today is called the Netherlands, a low-lying land hovering just above sea level, was for centuries a haven for eels.) Chaucer and Shakespeare both mention eels in their writings, Shakespeare more frequently than he did any other fish. Italian writers and artists also made much of the eel: Leonardo da Vinci, who by all evidence was a vegetarian, nonetheless could not resist positioning a succulent dish of eels with orange slices in his immortal masterpiece *The Last Supper*.

In Europe, the demand for eel, always significant, grew further in the late nineteenth century due in part to the popularity of "hot smoking," suspending eel over a smoky fire to flavor and preserve it. Hot smoking was no culinary newcomer—it traces back to the cavemen of the Paleolithic Era. But a renewed interest in the practice not only prompted a major expansion of the eel fishery but also elevated the eel's status as a luxury food. As one observer wrote in 1908, "The eel, formerly a cheap folk food, has in general become a table fish, and smoked a delicacy, which can only be obtained for expensive money." The introduction of trawlers equipped with wide, cone-shaped nets also boosted eel landings. This was true for both yellow and silver eels, and for glass eels and elvers, a fishery that started in France. Elvers were especially popular in Basque Country, where, sautéed in olive oil, garlic, and dried chilis, they remain today a traditional celebratory food, especially around the Christmas holidays.

In the Americas, it seems that eel was for those living east of the Mississippi what the buffalo was for those living in the west: the archaeological record shows that eel sustained large populations of indigenous people long before the advent of agriculture. Eel features prominently in folktales of the Algonquian and Haudenosaunee, and the Iroquois thought enough of the fish to name a clan in its honor. In what later would become Maine, the native Wabanaki people trapped eels in weirs and woven baskets, and speared them from canoes, luring them in with torches. Eel skin, composed mainly of collagen fibers that tighten as they dry, was rolled into "babiche," sturdy leather strips used to make snowshoes, moccasins, and animal snares. The skin was also used for making bandages and splints, and for lashing spearheads to harpoon shafts. Eel oil was mixed with milk and fed by drops to infants, for added nutrition and to set their taste for the years of eel eating to come.

Tisquantum, known to history by his European-given name, Squanto, was an eel aficionado. There are many accounts of his exploits, few if any of them reliable, but I've done my best to piece together a credible—and brief—synopsis. Born into the Pawtuxet band that lived mostly in present-day Massachusetts, Tisquantum was kidnapped, forced onto an English merchant ship, and sold as a slave in the port of Málaga, Spain. From there he escaped to England, where he learned the language. In 1619, he returned to his home village in America to find every member of his community dead, possibly due to smallpox care of the European invaders. In March of that year, he offered his services to the *Mayflower* colonists, who, by all accounts, were a helpless bunch—unschooled in fishing, hunting, farming, soldiering, and other survival skills. Tisquantum taught them to hunt, forage, and plant corn. More to our point, he taught them to eel. In one account, he "went at noon to fish for eels; at night he came home with as many as he could well lift in one hand . . . They were fat and sweet, he trod them out with his feet, and so caught them with his hands without any other instrument." Eel was (possibly) served at the first Thanksgiving feast in 1621, and (certainly) smoked or salted to preserve through the heartless New England winters. Why that tough old bird—turkey—beat out eel as Thanksgiving's signature dish is anyone's guess.

Cloaked in the moniker "Derryfield beef" (after a river town in New Hampshire), American eel became a favorite on colonial tables, especially in what was to become the state of Maine. John Josselyn, a British nobleman appointed lieutenant governor of the

Province of Maine, gushed: "I never eat better Eals in no part of the world that I have been in, than are here." Centuries later, another British admirer enthused that the American eel was adored for its "form and colouring, elegant gyrations, its social and even as we are told, affectionate disposition."

Elegant gyrations? Affectionate disposition? Not many other wild animals, let alone other fish, evoke such ardor. Or, it must be said, such disdain.

CHAPTER II

THE NIGHT MIND OF WATER

Like a sprat in a pickle jug.
A creel of eels, all ripples.

—Sylvia Plath, "You're"

ON THE SUBJECT OF EELS, no one is neutral. If you doubt this, try mentioning them over a beer with a friend or a coffee with colleagues. Just blurt it out: "So what do we all think of eels?" And then stand back and brace for an earful.

"The eel has ever occupied an extreme position," proclaimed the U.S. Fisheries commissioner M. C. Marsh in 1902. "He is apt to be loathed or loved. In his contact with the human race, he ingratiated himself into affections of a whole nation, or was rejected utterly."

As I've said, the eel is nature's Rorschach test.

Because they were thought not to have scales, the Hebrews disdained eels as "unclean," and condemned the eating of eel as an "abomination." Norwegians have a thing for many fatty

Jellied eel is thought to have originated in East London in the eighteenth century as a cheap, nutritious street food made from eel boiled in a stock of salted vinegar, sliced onion, peppercorns, and bay leaves, and often served with a hand pie and mashed potatoes. Rationing during World War II brought a peak in jellied eel consumption, and by the war's end, London boasted more than one hundred eel-and-pie shops. In Denmark jellied eel is known as ål i gele; in France as aspic d'anguille; in Germany as Aal in Aspik; and in Poland as węgorz w galarecie. (Wikimedia Commons)

fish—salmon, herring, mackerel. But Norwegians do not have a thing for fatty eels. In Ireland the eels of Lough Neagh are said to be the finest in the world, enjoyed by locals since the Bronze Age. And yet throughout history the Irish also feared eels as harbingers of famine, especially when the eels whistled, as they are prone to do in myth. Even in England, home of the jolly jellied eel, the fish has not always been welcome. One Brit went so far as to whine that he "would sooner eat [sea]gulls than eels."

Seagull may have seemed the safer bet, for in its unadulterated form eel was thought to be toxic to most mammals, including humans. The Italian physician and physiologist Angelo Mosso found evidence of this in the late nineteenth century, a time when poison was all the rage. Grace Coleridge Frankland, an English microbiologist, captured the mood in an essay she published in *Nature* in 1888. She wrote, "The investigation of poisons, both bacterial and animal, has been pursued with such enthusiasm in so many parts of the world during the past decade, and the public have been brought into such close touch with some of the practical applications which have followed in the track of these investigations, that the term toxin and anti-toxin, unknown in the days of Dr. Johnson's colossal dictionary, may now without exaggeration be said to form part of the vocabulary of every well-ordered household." In these "well-ordered households," cyanide and strychnine were not a bug but a feature, found in paint, wallpaper, and daguerreotypes. These products were dangerous, of course, but at least they were not designed to be eaten. The same could not always be said of arsenic, the undisputed king of poisons found in flypaper, hair dye, hats, and fibers, and also in edibles such as food coloring, flour, and sugar. With no taste or odor, arsenic was nearly undetectable: one-third of criminal poisonings of the time were traced to arsenic, and this represents only those poisonings that *could* be traced.

Mosso knew the blood of eels to be an equally stealthy killer, but he had no stomach for putting that knowledge to the test in human subjects. On the contrary, he was a staunch and dedicated advocate of public health and a brilliant medical innovator. At his Istituto Angelo Mosso, perched 9,000 feet above sea level on the peak of Monte Rosa, he observed the impact of high altitude on the brain directly through the cracked skull of a brave volunteer. Among his many inventions was the human circulation balance, a device used to measure the redistribution of blood in the thinking brain that today is considered a worthy forerunner to the fMRI. For this and related contributions, Mosso is sometimes referred to as the da Vinci of modern brain science. On top of all this, he was a skilled archaeologist, a gifted teacher, a thoughtful politician, an intrepid mountaineer, and a founder of soccer clubs. An apostle of sport and an authority on fatigue, he was an acknowledged expert on the physiology of fear. In his spare time he wrote lyrically on poetry, history, and the philosophy of science.

A brilliant polymath and consummate Renaissance man, for sure. But alas, not an eel man.

I have no idea what brought Mosso to inject a fourteen-pound dog with a scant half cubic centimeter of eel serum (eel blood minus the red blood cells). Surely he had his reasons, and one might speculate that they were honorable. One may also assume that Mosso was alarmed when the dog's heart stopped beating seven minutes after the injection. Though perhaps not overly alarmed, as he proceeded to elicit a similarly tragic response by injecting eel blood into rabbits, guinea pigs, frogs, and pigeons. For Mosso, who from all evidence had little interest in the eel, this carnage must have been incidental. So we'll leave his story here. But to those of us who enjoy the occasional plate of unagi, his experiments evoke a chilling question: Why don't the hearts of human and other eel eaters stop as well? The answer is that Mosso did not *feed* dogs, rabbits, and guinea pigs eel serum. Rather, he injected them, thereby circumventing the digestive tract, where enzymes and acids denature the lethal protein—the neurotoxin ichthyotoxin—and render it harmless. Heating also destroys the protein. That's why mammals—including humans—can gorge on smoked, broiled, steamed, and jellied eel to no demonstrated ill effect. (Theoretically, the human digestive tract should denature the protein and make the eating of raw eel safe, but having found no data to back this up, I do not recommend the practice.)

As I've mentioned, wild eels eat and are eaten in harmony with whatever environment they inhabit, be it a lake in Greenland, an estuary on the coast of North Africa, or a remote pond in mid-coast Maine. Eel is said to be the sea otter's favorite food, and raccoons seem to love it, as do many birds, turtles, sharks, and other fish. In return, eels make quick work of frogs and other amphibians, crustaceans like crab, crayfish, and lobsters, bivalves like mussels and clams, and fish. When packed together too closely, or simply famished, eels will eat each other. It's a balance of predator and prey, and to borrow Albert Einstein's immortal phrase, to disrupt that balance is to "play dice with the universe." I wondered, what did that toss of the dice mean for my beloved Maine, where for some fishermen the annual elver catch meant the difference between poverty and the good life? Bill Sheldon, an expert on eels, had told me repeatedly that elvers were if anything underfished, and that those that didn't end up in nets were likely to get eaten by raccoons or get pulverized in a turbine or perish by other means. And it wasn't just Sheldon—I'd stood at the river's edge and witnessed the elver rush, and their abundance was undeniable. I'd spoken to single mothers who caught elvers to put food on the table, and young people who fished elvers to help with their family's medical bills. If elvers could help hardworking Mainers escape a life of destitution, what harm was there in harvesting a few more before the raccoons got to them?

I put that question to the population ecologist Desmond Kahn. Before answering, he had a few things to explain. Kahn is a former president of the Northeastern Division of the American Fisheries Society and served on the society's national governing board. Since earning his PhD in 1981, he's monitored the ebb and flow of fish in rivers up and down the East Coast, including Maine. Depending on the river, those fish did not always include eels. For example, when he checked the Susquehanna, the oldest and longest river on the East Coast of the United States and once a paradise for eels, he found it was all but devoid of them, and had been for nearly a century. But was this really a problem? Why, I asked Kahn, should we care that a river has no eels? In response, Kahn steered the discussion to another Susquehanna native, a humble freshwater mussel called the eastern elliptio. Sedentary by nature, mussels rely on fish—especially eels—to transport and distribute their spawn. Some mussel species lure eels with wagging flaps of tissue, just as we might flap a hand to hail a passing cab. But the eastern elliptio takes no chances and squirts its larvae out in a mucus cloud that eels can hardly avoid. The mussel larvae cling to the eel's gills and tag along for the ride. As the larvae mature into full-grown mussels, they drop off and descend into the riverbed, where they remain for up to eighty years.

If mussels seem like boring animals, well, of course they are: What interesting animal stays put for eighty years? But mussels have a secret life: they play a key role in maintaining the health of freshwater ecosystems. Prolific filter feeders, they suck water through their gills to extract oxygen and food, along with toxins, bacteria, viruses, and other crud. A single eastern elliptio can purify ten gallons of water a day, a million mussels ten million gallons a day. This clears the way for sunlight to penetrate deep below the river surface, good news for bottom-dwelling flora and fauna (including eels). On the rivers near my Maine home, robust beds of freshwater mussels ward off erosion and stabilize the shoreline. Without mussels, the water would turn murky and the shorelines crumble, and without eels, mussels would grow fewer if at all. As Kahn told it, the Susquehanna offered a frightening glimpse of what eels mean for the health of a river.

For eons, the Susquehanna roiled with a seasonal wave of eels swarming in from the Chesapeake Bay, many with mussel larvae latched to their gills. Ospreys, raccoons, herons, and striped bass fed on both mussels and eels. Eventually, humans joined them, and fishermen pulled in hundreds of thousands of pounds of eel annually. The practice went on for maybe six thousand years, during which eels made up an estimated 25 percent of the river's animal biomass. But in 1928, the ninety-four-foot-high Conowingo Dam—the first and largest of what came to be four hydroelectric dams on the river—was installed nine miles north of the Chesapeake. Eel migration was blocked, and the eels were killed, injured, or at best obstructed. Without eel predators, populations of rusty crayfish, a troublesome nonnative invader, crept higher. Without their eel ride share, the mussels died off. Devoid of mussel beds, upriver streams grew so barren of life they were nicknamed "ghost creeks." Shorelines eroded, the water clouded, and in 2005, the environmental advocacy group American Rivers pronounced the Susquehanna America's Most Endangered River. But all that was soon to change.

In 2016, the federal government collaborated with the owner of the Conowingo Dam in a drive to trap wayward eels and transport them upstream to safety. Five years later, more than a million eels had been reintroduced to the river. With the eels came the baby mussels, as did the prospect of a Susquehanna far more welcoming to humans and other creatures. The media made much of this success story, as the media is wont to do: these days every scrap of positive news on the environment is unexpected, a much-sought-after "man-bites-dog" story. But the truth is that there's no guarantee that transporting eels upstream will restore their numbers overall, as there's no telling whether the relocated eels will survive their yellow stage in the river, let alone a several-thousand-mile return to their spawning grounds. Yes, as I've said, grown eels are incredibly tenacious, but like most wild creatures they don't take well to human interference—manhandling American eels back to their rightful place in the river might not be the best way to preserve the species. Indeed, recent studies suggest that overall, translocated eels do not fare all that well. Those studies not being conclusive, only time will tell.

An avid angler, Kahn is no fan of eels. On the contrary, he nurses sour memories of landing them as bycatch when in pursuit of higher-status fish, like trout or bass. "They'd be two, maybe three feet long," he said, his voice tightening. "They'd wrap themselves around our arms, and we'd have a battle on our hands." Personally, he could live without American eels, as, he assumes, could the world at large. But, he says, it would be a far less hospitable world. Kahn said that he didn't see evidence that American eels were on the brink of extinction, but nor could we ignore their obvious decline: not even he, an eel agnostic, would dare to play dice with the eel universe.

WE HUMANS PREFER TO HAVE our cake and eat it, too—in this case, to have an abundance of eels protecting our rivers while at the same time enjoying a side dish of unagi with our sushi platters. Given nature's reluctance to give us both, some argue that humans take the reins, and breed eels as we do livestock. Somehow, we might coax eggs and sperm from the creatures themselves and merge them into an embryo. We can do it with tilapia, carp, catfish, and oysters, right, so why not eels? Well, we can, sort of . . . but not in a way that makes sense. Eel scientist Sylvie Dufour, whom we met earlier in Paris, reminded me of the difficulties. "We have never seen a single eel egg in the wild," she said. "Nor sperm." Nor a pregnant eel, nor even a sexually mature one. That means scientists must begin the process by maturing the eels in the laboratory to procure these gametes artificially. In human terms, we're talking in vitro insemination, a tricky, complicated business. That said, it was

Dufour's own mentor, the animal physiologist Maurice Fontaine, who was the first to make this happen in eels.

Maurice Fontaine lived a very long life—104 years—and devoted a good chunk of it to addressing the "eel question." He was among the first scientists to recognize that sexual maturity in the freshwater eel comes thanks to a spurt of pituitary hormones triggered not by genes but by environmental factors, perhaps water temperature or pressure, a process that he thought might be mimicked in the lab. In 1936, he induced maturation in male European eels using a most unlikely technique: injections of the hormone-rich urine of pregnant women. Eight years later, he did something similar for female eels, this time with repeated injections of carp pituitary extract followed by a shot of another hormone, deoxycorticosterone. Much to his disappointment, these sexually mature eels did not beget more eels. Nonetheless, Fontaine had blazed a path that a new generation of eel scientists was grateful to follow. Half a century later, in 2008, Kenneth Oliveira, a biologist at the University of Massachusetts, Dartmouth, took that path toward what no one before him had done: generating an American eel in the laboratory.

Oliveira, who speaks in a hearty Boston brogue, makes no secret of his infatuation: his forearm sports a tattoo of an eel twisted into a question mark. Yet it's hard to imagine anyone less grandiose: he favors T-shirts in monotones he jokes match his hair as it fades from black to gray. Oliveira told me it costs millions to mount an ocean expedition, an amount well out of line with his budget. So rather than go to sea to search for signs of eel procreation, he set out to breed American eels in vivo.

Oliveira struck me very much as a frugal, DIY type: the fact that the American eel had never before been bred in captivity seemed to matter less to him than the low cost of giving it a try.

The first step was to capture a bunch of silver eels. For males, he went to the nearby Paskamanset River and caught them himself. For females, he sought the services of Canadian fishermen and drove hundreds of miles to retrieve them. "We got really big ones," he told me. "They cost us fifty dollars apiece."

As we know from Freud's frustrating experience, eels are too cagey to casually reveal their gender. So Oliveira took a shortcut: eels longer than fifteen inches (forty centimeters) were presumed female, and eels of lesser length presumed male. "Trust me, that works," he told me. Oliveira knew that any attempt to wait out the natural process of sexual maturation was doomed to fail, so like Fontaine he turned to hormones. In males, this meant four weeks of injections with a serum derived from human placentas. In females, it meant two months of biweekly injections of salmon pituitary extract. This chemical onslaught changed the males' appearance very little but had a visible impact on females, which swelled to as much as 140 percent of their original size. "Footballs with eyes," Oliveira called them. These footballs could ovulate at any time, so his team checked them every day, including Christmas. The process required extracting sample eggs from the fish and scrutinizing them under a microscope for a sign that the nucleus had shifted to the edge of the cell membrane, a signal that ovulation was imminent. When the moment of truth arrived, they injected the females with another hormone to trigger the release of eggs, which they mixed with sperm. (Both the sperm and the eggs were squeezed manually from the fish, a tricky process that the females in particular resisted.) Roughly forty-eight hours later, tiny white larvae—no more than three millimeters in length—pushed through the egg surface and swam free. For the first time in history, an American eel was hatched in captivity. "We got lucky," Oliveira said, with characteristic humility.

But not as lucky as he'd hoped: the larvae died in a few days. Oliveira ascribed a large part of the problem to the larvae's notoriously picky eating habits. "I literally had one postdoc full-time trying to get the darn things to eat," he told me. "Supposedly shark [egg yolk] powder is the thing, but that means killing sharks to grow eels, and I'm not crazy about that. (Most shark species are viviparous, meaning the eggs develop inside the mother.) If there was a Nobel Prize for ichthyology it would go to whoever figures out how to feed these little guys." So far, while others have tried, no one has come forward to claim the prize. "We continued the fertilization work for a few years but without funding we could not move on to the next step," Oliveira told me. In fact, the funding for eel research is so sparse that of his current graduate students only one has an eel project.

Scientists outside the United States have followed in Oliveira's footsteps, some even willing to ply eel larvae with powdered shark egg yolk to keep them alive. But no one has succeeded in producing a reliably viable Atlantic eel in the laboratory. Efforts with the Japanese eel over several decades have met with more success, but not so much success that the process is practical on a commercial scale. To a modern mind, the failure seems preposterous: after all, we can manufacture humans in vitro! How is it that we can track Higgs bosons and black holes in outer space, program machines to think, cure cancer of various sorts, yet—despite our best efforts—not find a way to breed the American eel? An unanswerable question, of course, but one that has left us with only one realistic alternative: to wrangle, contain, and cultivate a creature born to live its life free.

CHAPTER 12

THIS RIVER IS FULL OF MONEY

Oh beloved eel, you! I've loved you for so long!
—Aristophanes, *Acharnians*

DARRELL YOUNG, FOUNDER AND CODIRECTOR of the Maine Elver Fishermen Association, splits his life script into two acts. Act I, which for clarity I'll title "Before Eels," opens dramatically on a ramshackle cabin with no plumbing or electricity in the backwoods of Waltham, Maine. Young keeps a photo on hand for documentation, and believe me, it's bleak. He bought the place to live with his wife and young son in 1989, when he was making maybe $230 a week mostly chopping timber. When the big lumber companies changed their ways and didn't need him anymore, he switched to fishing herring and sea urchins. And then the sea urchins dried up. "I was poor," he told me. "Poor as a crow."

Act II of Young's life script, which for clarity I'll title "After Eels," opens on a spacious, fully renovated home with heat, plumbing, and a massive, well-appointed kitchen, its ceiling hung with a riot of wicker baskets in all sizes and shapes. In the driveway, among other vehicles, is a Dodge Power Wagon emblazoned with a custom-painted burst of flames. In winter, Young and his wife, Angela, leave their cozy rural haven for a three-month fishing vacation in the Florida Keys, hauling behind them a forty-foot luxury motorcoach that could pass for a five-star hotel suite on wheels.

"Elvers changed my life," Young told me. Yes, I could see that: his, and many others'.

Maine has hosted an elver fishery since the mid-1970s, but back then, not many fishermen signed on. A handful of people fished elvers, but there wasn't enough money involved to spark a lot of interest. When Young first tried his hand in 1990, fishing for elvers was maybe one bump up from digging worms. "We could catch as many as we wanted back then, there were no licenses, and no limits," Young said. "But the price was so low, I couldn't afford to buy a fyke net" (large and elaborate funnel-shaped rigs that cost something like $2,500). On cold, moonless nights he'd layer on the long underwear, sweatshirt, and parka and dip with a simple hand net. It was the best that he could do. "I started with my father," he said. "Then my wife joined me, and we'd make maybe thirty or forty dollars a night. Enough to put food in the fridge."

Over the years, the price of Maine-caught elvers ebbed and flowed like the tides, soaring to $230 a pound in 1995, when licenses became mandatory, crashing to $30 a pound in 1999 when pretty much no one cared whether fishers had a license or not. The price reflected several factors, notably supply at home and demand abroad. When the recession took hold in 2001, the average river price stood at $24.14 per pound, not the sort of money that sends many fishermen out on a stormy night. That year, only 1,687 pounds of Maine elvers were sold to dealers, at least officially. In 2010, when elver exports in the EU were banned, the price leapt thirty-five-fold, to $845.20. By then, fishermen all over the state had a hankering to dip a net, as they figured the price could go no higher. They were wrong.

On March 11, 2011, Japan was rocked with the most powerful earthquake in its history. The Great Tōhoku erupted eighty miles off the northeast corner of Honshu, Japan's largest and most populous island, and triggered a tsunami that ravaged the coast. Seawalls were breached, and towns and villages swamped with 130-foot tides. Cars, buildings, and square miles of pavement were swept into a lethal tsunami soup, and the pummeling cascade forced a meltdown at the Fukushima Daiichi nuclear power plant. Videos of the carnage are almost unbearable to watch: twenty thousand people lost their lives, and hundreds of thousands lost their homes.

Coastal fishing in Japan came to a standstill, and Japanese eel, the nation's most valuable inland fishery, teetered under the strain. But none of this had much impact on the public appetite for eel. Demand continued to climb as if nothing had changed, and Maine was poised to help fill the orders. The state's (official) elver harvest surged from 8,585 pounds that year to a record (official) 26,611 pounds in 2012—well over ten tons. The landing price soared, too, to $1,866.72 per pound. Almost overnight, the sleepy, creepy elver fishery burst into a gold rush.

Bill Trotter, a veteran reporter for the *Bangor Daily News*, has followed Maine's fisheries for more than two decades, so I contacted him to get a better idea of what the elver business meant for the state over the years. "Before the ban on EU exports and the tsunami in Japan, elvers were a source of supplemental income for carpenters or stern men in lobster boats," he told me. "It's a hefty expense to fish for lobster, but elvers were considered a poor man's fishery. You didn't need a boat, all you needed was a fyke net or a dip net and technically a license, and at first those were easy to get, and cheap, because not many people wanted one. March, April, May are slow months for lobsters, and fishing elvers was a way to pass the time. But then the elver market went haywire, and things went nuts—people could make years of income in just two months. The 2012 to 2013 season, the weather was really good, it was a warm spring, the slow melted early. There were flowers everywhere, people were walking down the beach in shorts and barefoot. Then the elvers showed up. There was no cap [on the amount of elvers licensed fishermen could catch]. Dealers ran around with hundreds of thousands of dollars in cash in duffel bags. It was a free-for-all."

Darrell Young has fond memories of that season, which in his telling was something like Christmas morning on steroids. "Me and my wife ended up at the Bangor River, and we caught a hundred and twenty pounds," he told me, and he sold that haul to dealers for an astonishing $224,247. In a couple of months, Young had caught elvers worth roughly five times Maine's median household income. A guaranteed win that could happen every spring, fishing elvers was better than winning the lottery. Suddenly, Young, his wife, and their young-adult son had options of the sort they thought they'd never have. Life-changing options. I asked him what this meant for his family, and he fell uncharacteristically pensive. Lots of folks from "away" assume without evidence that elver fishermen squander their profits on boats and booze. I might well have been one of those folks, especially since Pat Bryant, an eel fisher herself, had told me so. Young was not overly perturbed by this; he knew that it was human nature to jump to conclusions. Still, he failed to mention the head-on collision I'd read about in the paper, the one his wife had barely survived. Nor did he note what I later learned was the family's lack of health insurance and the million-plus-dollar hospital bills. Elvers brought Darrell and his family some luxuries, sure, but more importantly they brought him middle-class peace of mind. "We don't need money to be happy," he told me. "But we paid off our mortgage, helped our boy buy a house. We bought some land. It feels good to be able to take care of your family."

Elvers were the best luck to strike Darrell Young in some time. And he wasn't the only one getting lucky. Fishermen up and down the Maine coast were on high alert. Eel dealers set up shop anywhere they could—bait shops, gas stations, backyard sheds, garages, their own homes. The competition was crazy. No one would trust a check, and dealers paid with fat wads of bills. When the ATMs ran dry of cash, dealers switched to handing out IOUs until the banks got a chance to replenish. Poachers dipped and trapped elvers on coasts from Massachusetts to Georgia, trucked them to Maine, where the fishery was legal, and sold them to anyone with money. At least four tons of American elvers were stolen from the nation's rivers that year, much of it laundered through the Maine elver fishery. "I'll tell you, it was the Wild West," Young said, with what sounded like a hint of nostalgia.

Kristen Steele knows Darrell Young well—she'd spent long nights on the river with him and other Maine elver fishers. She did not join them to fish but to research her doctoral thesis on eel fisheries as global drivers of species loss and exploitation. She chose eels as a "demonstration subject" for interrogating the ecological, economic, and social dynamics influencing the protection of threatened species. But on the river, she keeps all that to herself. "I'm just there to observe and learn," she said. "Not to judge."

Steele, who was born and raised in upstate New York, was introduced to eels while doing field research in natural science at the Royal Veterinary College in London. "I was a vegetarian back then, so I'd never eaten one, let alone touched a live one," she told me. She was more curious than squeamish. "It was March and we were standing in brackish water. I wasn't wearing a dry suit because there wasn't one in my size. (I'm small boned, and the dry suits they had would bunch up.) I had no idea what to expect. But when the first eel came into my net—it was super slimy, gray, brown, and bronze—I nearly cried with happiness. I touched it. It was an amazing experience. It was like the ambivalence you have about having a kid, and then you have a baby, and you fall in love."

In Maine, Steele said, veteran elver fishers are fearless, skipping over wet, slippery rocks in the dark "like goats." Since childhood they have developed instincts to see things differently from other people—they can "see below the surface" to measure the tides and have a gut sense of where to set their nets. "What's so great about fishermen is, they'd chew off handcuffs to fish," Steele said. "You're out all night working no matter how cold or wet. Some nights, you catch nothing, but that doesn't stop you. There's just something about the eel that instantly captures your imagination. It's about money, of course, but also about love." Still, she admits that love sometimes takes a back seat to greed. "If you step away even for a few minutes, people might cut off the end of your net, and all the eels are gone," she said. "Not to mention that every elver fisher in Maine has a gun."

Steele has studied Buddhism, and it shows in her gentle nature and her instinct to reserve judgment of others. To my surprise, these "others" included eel poachers. By coincidence, she happened to find herself in town the day Bill Sheldon had his sentencing hearing at the Edward T. Gignoux U.S. Courthouse in Portland. Curious, she made time to sit in on the proceedings. Sheldon had behaved badly, she agreed, but unlike most other eel people I spoke with, she also saw things his way. "He got greedy and made a mistake, but he believes in this fishery," she told me. Elver fishermen, she said, are stuck in a "duality," between their respect for the dodgy, mysterious fish and their need and desire for cold, hard cash. To her chagrin—and alarm—she sometimes felt torn herself. "On those long, cold nights in Maine I'd stand in the dealer sheds and watch people bring buckets of elvers to be weighed," she told me. "The dealer would write out $5,000 checks for a couple of pounds, and I couldn't get that out of my mind. I was a poor graduate student, I needed money. And there was the river chock full of elvers, each one worth a dollar. I finally got it, not theoretically, but for real. You think, *This river is full of money, these elvers could solve all my financial woes*. I love baby eels, if I look at them too long, I cry. But I now also eat them."

The eel "gold rush" of 2012, in which Sheldon, Young, and other Maine fishermen and dealers pocketed a total of $40 million, brought a flood of challenges. Captain Colin MacDonald of the Maine Marine Patrol recalls that time with horror. "There was so much illegal activity going on, it was like pushing water with a broom," he told me. "It got to the point where my family was threatened. Just a nightmare." Back then, the penalty for illegally fishing or selling elvers—fines not less than $100 nor more than $500—armed law enforcement with what pretty much amounted to a butter knife. As poaching spiraled out of control, the Maine legislature made a show of getting serious: elver violations were reclassified as "strict liability crimes" (meaning that perpetrators were judged purely on their actions, and not on their state of mind) and the fine was raised to $2,000, the price of less than a pound of elvers. Neither measure made a dent in elver thefts. Sensing trouble and worried the fishery might be closed, in March 2013 Darrell Young took preemptive action: he assembled fifty elver fishers at the Elks Club meeting hall in Ellsworth to form the Maine Elver Fishermen Association. Since then the membership has grown, as have its lobbying efforts. Members have a "pull up the gangplank" strategy: rather than fight to increase the number of licensees (and hence increase the competition for elvers), they want to see larger individual quotas for themselves. "Maine is big," Young said in 2018. "We've got three thousand five hundred miles of shore frontage, there's over two hundred and fifty rivers, there's six thousand streams, there's an ungodly amount of brooks we don't even fish . . . there's just a phenomenal amount of glass eels."

Environmentalists see matters a bit differently: in 2014, the International Union for Conservation of Nature (IUCN) added the American eel to its endangered list. But while generally respected, the IUCN is a voluntary organization of governments and non-profits with no regulatory authority, and the American eel is not protected under any global treaties or conventions. The Atlantic States Marine Fisheries Commission (ASMFC), a deliberative body of states on the eastern seaboard of the United States, does have regulatory authority and sharply limited Maine's legal elver catch to an annual yield of 11,749 pounds, and later to 9,688 pounds, where it stands today. (In 2019, the ante was upped to allow an additional 200 pounds of elvers for use in aquaculture.) The agency also capped the number of elver fishing licenses in Maine to 425 for non–tribal members. Critically, and to much resistance, Maine's Department of Marine Resources issued individual quotas, limiting what each licensed elver fisherman was allowed to catch. Exact allotments were not made public, but fishermen were issued quotas of roughly half the poundage they had averaged over the previous three seasons. Darrell Young told me that fourteen lucky veterans were granted quotas of more than fifty pounds. (Together, Young and his wife have a sixty-pound quota.) Apparently, seven even luckier veterans were granted quotas of one hundred pounds or more. (Though he denies it, it's rumored that Bill Sheldon is among these fortunate few.) Rookie license holders with little or no history of elver fishing are issued a standard four-pound quota when and if a license becomes available. A separate system was put in place for fishermen in the state's four federally sanctioned Native American tribes, with a limit of 2,121 pounds (21.9 percent of the total quota) to be shared jointly by all interested tribal members. "State fishermen" (meaning those of non-Native heritage) objected loudly to what they considered this "overly generous" quota, a position to which many state fishermen I spoke with continue to cling.

Quotas mean nothing if they are not enforced, and license holders are required to carry identification along with a plastic swipe card encoded with their individual quotas. Dealers are legally obliged to deduct the weight of each batch of elvers from each fisherman's swipe card at the point of purchase. When a fisherman's quota is filled, he or she cannot legally sell elvers, and dealers cannot legally purchase elvers from them. It's a strong, well-thought-out

Patrol Officer Keegan Nelligan of the Maine Department of Marine Resources checks the tag of a fyke net on the opening day of elver season at Pemaquid Falls in Bristol, Maine. Officer Nelligan was armed but assured me that his preference was to use reasoning rather than threats when enforcing state fishing regulations. (Ellen Ruppel Shell)

system that authorities believe has much reduced casual poaching. But it has not stopped determined renegades from dealing illegal catch.

The ASMFC officially deems the poaching and unlicensed fishing of American elvers as a matter of "serious concern." But when we spoke, Shane Waller, a former Environmental Crimes Section attorney at the Department of Justice, snickered at that bland understatement. With his jug ears and faded crew cut, Waller bears some physical resemblance to a thirtysomething Barack Obama. And like Obama, he began his career in public service, in his case prosecuting drug crimes and later wildlife crimes, with a special focus on elvers. Waller was co-prosecuting attorney on Operation Broken Glass, the yearslong federal investigation that brought down Bill Sheldon and nearly two dozen other poachers and dealers. He'd seen the worst of it, and I asked him whether he agreed with U.S. Fish and Wildlife agent David Sykes that wildlife thieves are of a kind with drug dealers. He coughed a bark of disgust. "Anyone who runs a successful con scheme is smart in some way," he told me. "In the case of crack, you've got to know how to make it, or know someone who does. In the case of elvers, you've got to know where to find them, how to keep them alive, and how to get them to market. Both crimes involve huge sums of money, and both require skill. But there's a difference. A lot of drug dealers come from nothing, and some are feeding addictions. They are desperate, out of options. Wildlife traffickers, especially in the US, have options to make money honestly. But they chose to steal. In my opinion, that makes them worse."

It's not easy to catch a drug dealer, but it can be even harder to catch an elver thief posing as a hardworking fisherman under the cover of night. Further complicating matters is that the American eel, while red-listed by international agencies, is not protected under the U.S. Endangered Species Act (ESA). Enacted in 1973, the ESA prohibits the taking of any species of endangered wildlife and makes illegal its import or export. Since it is not technically endangered, these rules do not apply to the American eel. In the case of Operation Broken Glass and similar busts, agents must find poachers guilty of violations of the Lacey Act, the federal law that prohibits trade in wildlife illegally taken, possessed, transported, or sold. While breaches of the ESA are instantly recognizable (mere possession of the endangered plant or animal is illegal), violations of the Lacey Act are typically litigated only when criminals are caught in the act of poaching or dealing illegally—a far higher standard.

In Europe and Japan, where freshwater eels have declined in number by as much as 98 percent, responsible authorities agree on the importance of federal protections. But in the United States, where the eel has declined by at least half since the 1980s, authorities see matters differently. The U.S. Fish and Wildlife service has characterized the eel's decline as "localized" and therefore not threatening to the species overall. In 2023, the American Eel Management Board—a branch of the Atlantic States Marine Fisheries Commission—reinforced that ruling. American elver fishermen and dealers applaud these decisions on the logic that unlike the European and Japanese species, the American eel *seems* to be plentiful and therefore must *be* plentiful.

"Humans will go extinct before eels," one such fisherman told me. He reasoned that while only a tiny fraction of elvers survive to sexual maturity (less than one-tenth of 1 percent), those that do possess an unbeatable reproductive capacity. In this, he was correct: a sexually mature female releases up to twenty million eggs at a go. But unfortunately, the American eel's impressive fecundity does not automatically presage its survival as a species. The scary reality of the American eel is that it may be simultaneously abundant and doomed to extinction.

To make sense of this seeming paradox, one might consider the case of a similarly robust species: the passenger pigeon. Not to be confused with the carrier pigeon, its doughy domesticated cousin, the passenger pigeon was a freewheeling North American native and quite possibly the most abundant bird on earth. In 1806, Alexander Wilson, a Scottish American ornithologist, naturalist, and illustrator, looked up at what he claimed to be 2.2 billion passenger pigeons swarming overhead in a single flock. (He was certain that he had lowballed the count.) Not to be outdone, Wilson's rival—the painter and ornithologist John James Audubon—boasted of watching 300 million passenger pigeons pass overhead *every hour* for *three full days*. As Audubon described it: "The light of noonday was obscured as by an eclipse; the dung fell in spots, not unlike melting flakes of snow; and the continued buzz of wings had a tendency to lull my senses to repose."

Audubon shot and stuffed the birds he used as models for his prints, so it may come as no surprise that the plunder of the passenger pigeon did not overly concern him. "Persons unacquainted with these birds might naturally conclude that such dreadful havoc would soon put an end to the species," he wrote. "But I have satisfied myself, by long observation, that nothing but the gradual diminution of our forests can accomplish their decrease, as they not unfrequently quadruple their numbers yearly, and always at least double it." Audubon had every right to his beliefs, of course. But not everyone thought it prudent to allow the passenger pigeon's unregulated slaughter by hunters and sporting men. In 1857, a bill put before the Ohio State Legislature sought protections for the bird, but to no avail. A select committee of the Senate concluded,

"The passenger pigeon needs no protection. Wonderfully prolific, having the vast forests of the North as its breeding grounds, traveling hundreds of miles in search of food, it is here today and elsewhere tomorrow, and no ordinary destruction can lessen them, or be missed from the myriads that are yearly produced." What the select committee perhaps did not know is that the passenger pigeon was a gregarious creature that bred best when gathered in very large numbers. Nor, perhaps, did it anticipate the relentless pressure from hunters and sportsmen that would shrink those numbers below a critical mass and condemn the bird to oblivion. On September 1, 1914, Martha, age twenty-nine and the last passenger pigeon on earth, toppled dead from her perch at the Cincinnati Zoo. Her mate, George, had perished four years earlier.

CHARLES DARWIN BELIEVED THAT CHANGE in the natural world was a gradual process that rewarded the fit at the expense of the weak, writing: "The complete extinction of the species of a group is generally a slower process than their production." But by the time he published this insight in 1859, the people of North America were keenly aware of their power to eradicate a species. Already, the once abundant Carolina parakeet, the eastern elk, the ivory-billed woodpecker, and the great auk were gone, or nearly so. Yet while it was common knowledge that some creatures—birds in particular—were vulnerable to extinction, respected scholars insisted that marine animals were the exception. In 1882, a year after Darwin's death, the great International Fisheries Exhibition of London hosted more than two thousand exhibitors from around the world. There were displays of fishing gear, ships, seaworthy attire, and sea creatures themselves, including a man-made pond stocked with crocodiles and other "monsters." The zoologist Thomas Huxley, the president of the Royal Society known as Darwin's Bulldog, delivered the inaugural address focused on the following question: "Are fisheries exhaustible?" The answer, he said, depends.

In the case of freshwater fish in a particular river or stream, the answer was yes, of course. Huxley explained, "It needs no argument to convince anyone who is familiar with the facts of the case that it is possible to net the main stream, in such a manner, as to catch every salmon that tries to go up and every smolt that tries to go down. Not only is this true, but daily experience in this country unfortunately proves that pollutions may be poured into the upper waters of a salmon river of such a character and in such quantity as to destroy every fish in it." However, Huxley cautioned, the same rules do not apply to creatures of the sea. "I believe that it may be affirmed with confidence that, in relation to our present modes of fishing, a number of the most important sea fisheries, such as the cod fishery, the herring fishery, and the mackerel fishery, are *inexhaustible*. And I base this conviction on two grounds, first, that the multitude of these fishes is so inconceivably great that the number we catch is relatively insignificant; and, secondly, that the magnitude of the destructive agencies at work upon them is so prodigious, that the destruction effected by the fisherman cannot sensibly increase the death-rate." As we now know, Huxley's assessment did not hold. Today, the "inexhaustible" Atlantic cod is one of twenty-two species on the Greenpeace "red list" of threatened saltwater fish.

The decision not to list the eel as endangered seems built on the following premise: that plenty of individual members of a species gathered in some places foretells that the species overall will remain plentiful. And it is true that the American eel enjoys odd pockets of abundance, especially in far southernly regions of its range. But as we saw in the case of the passenger pigeon, this does not ensure the American eel's future as a species. Both humans and the American eel evolved to dominate vast swaths of the globe. But this remarkable adaptability does not protect either species from brutal and abrupt anthropomorphic disruption. The sad saga of the passenger pigeon illustrates this seminal principle of conservation biology: that it is not necessary to murder the last individual or mating pair of a species to set that species on an irreversible road to extinction.

THERE ARE MANY LINKS IN the eel's long chain of development, and each of those links is brittle. An American leptocephalus might struggle more than a thousand miles from its birthplace to the coast of Maine, transform from a larva to a glass eel and then to an elver, enter a river and fight its way upstream to a frozen lake, transform once again and hunker down for twenty-five years, turn silver and stock up for the reverse trip home, stop eating and burn its own body for fuel, only to be swallowed by a porbeagle shark before it reaches the breeding grounds. We might agree that this eel is heroic, a wonder of evolutionary grit. But an eel has only one shot at reproduction, and any eel that fails to take that shot is by nature's standards an eel that does not matter.

Canadian environmental physiologist John Casselman has borne witness to this brutal reality. He grew up not far from the St. Lawrence River, for centuries the world's richest habitat for American eel. As a teenager he worked as a fishing guide and, yes, spent moonless nights on the water trapping eels with his father. This practice may or may not have been legal at the time, but what mattered was that it was necessary. Like whales, eels are full of fat, especially silver eels plotting their return to their birthplace. Smoked silver eel has three times the caloric value of smoked salmon, more than any other smoked fish, Casselman told me.

A pantry generously stocked with smoked or salted eel was an insurance policy that ensured his family would eat and eat well through the rough Ontario winters. But his concerns for the creature mounted with industry's growing demand for hydroelectric power: the St. Lawrence was choked with dams and other obstacles that cut off the eel's migration route to the Great Lakes. Eels with the will to fight their way upriver were sucked into the blades of turbines, to which—with their elongated shape—they were even more susceptible than other fish. (If you care to bear witness to this horror, brace yourself and check out the plentiful videos of turbine-shredded eels available on YouTube.) In the United States, nearly a thousand hydroelectric generating plants are within the American eel's range, while Canada, the world's largest producer of hydroelectricity per capita, boasts about 475. Noting this, Casselman determined to find a remedy, but first he needed proof of his own assumptions. Specifically, he needed to know just how many eels had vanished from the river and how many eels remained. That would take time; in fact, half a lifetime. Working with the Ontario Ministry of Resources in 1980, he counted more than twenty-five thousand eels a day on their upriver migration. Three decades later, in 2010, he counted twenty eels daily navigating the same route. A devastating decline, a threat to his heritage and—it seemed to me—his sense of self. "Humans are sadly losing our association with this one-time highly valued and revered species that allowed people to survive when all else failed," he wrote me in an email. "Where does this leave humankind? This should be an ominous warning to us."

Some years ago, a team of scientists analyzed 2,142 American eels sampled from thirty-two distinct locations and were shocked to find absolutely no variation in their genetic makeup. All American eels, the evidence suggested, belong to the same breeding pool, an extraordinary circumstance for a species whose members reside in environments ranging from the tropical Caribbean to arctic Greenland. This breeding strategy offers one distinct evolutionary advantage: free of any genetic or behavioral restrictions on their interbreeding, any American eel is free to breed with any other American eel. But this practice of random mixing, or "panmixia," also comes with risk: when every member of a species has the potential to mate with every other member, the species does not always develop protective traits in response to localized environmental change. For example, it seems only logical that American eels in the northern reaches of their range—say, Casselman's eels in Canada—would evolve into a subpopulation that is better cold adapted than eels in the far southern regions—say, the islands of Trinidad. Likewise, it seems logical that the eels from Trinidad would evolve to be more heat adapted than eels trolling the St. Lawrence River. But while this dimorphism is often true of other widely dispersed species, it is decidedly not true for American eels. Indeed, one American eel is genetically so similar to the next that if it were an agricultural crop, we might call it a monoculture, the cultivation of a single organism across a large area of land. Monocultures present a special challenge, a classic illustration of which reaches back to nineteenth-century Ireland, where most if not all farmers grew but one variety of potato, the Irish "lumper." The absence of genetic diversity left Ireland's entire potato crop vulnerable to attack by *Phytophthora infestans*, the microbe responsible for the Irish Potato Famine and the starvation of a million Irishmen and -women.

It might be argued that unlike American eels, lumpers are clones, meaning that they breed asexually and all share the exact same DNA. So it's a stretch to say that American eels are equally vulnerable. But not a big stretch. For while not all American eels are genetically identical, they all descend from the same breeding pool, which means that a single microbe could wipe out the entire species. Worse yet, unlike the lumpish potato, the eel's far-flung life cycle depends on a variety of habitats in which any perturbation can lead to its demise. A critical implication of this is that preventing further population declines will require international cooperation to protect and revive every environment the American eel inhabits, including freshwater habitats. And that, to put it mildly, is a very heavy lift.

Fresh water makes up just 2 to 3 percent of waters worldwide, and three-quarters of that is tied up in ice. That leaves something like 1 percent of all liquid water, just a drop in the global aquatic bucket, but a critically important drop. Fresh water hosts 40 percent of the world's species, and half of all fish species. Tilapia, carp, trout, and other freshwater fish are a vital protein source for hundreds of millions of people, especially those living in less developed regions of the world. They also account for nearly one-quarter of the value of all commercial fisheries. Scores of millions of people—more than half of them mothers of young children—depend on freshwater fish for their livelihoods. All of which should give us pause when we consider that freshwater habitats are degrading faster than all other ecosystems on the planet.

Over a third of wetlands have vanished since the 1970s, a rate of destruction triple that of the world's forests. As wetlands degrade, freshwater species vanish: in 2021, the World Wildlife Fund and fifteen other conservation groups decried the "catastrophic decline" of freshwater fish brought by pests, pollution, dams, and overfishing. An astonishing eighteen thousand freshwater species are currently under threat, their populations slashed by an average of 94 percent. Perhaps even more concerning is that what doesn't kill individual animals may over time sink the species. That's almost certainly true of the freshwater eel: a recent study linked "non-lethal chemical contamination" to a 50 percent reduction in eel fertility.

Steps have been taken to mitigate these dangers. On one Maine river, I saw ramps installed below dams guiding eels around turbine blades, and racks bolted to the intake of power plants blocking debris and wayward eels. There was talk of power plants powering down when demand declines late at night, especially in the months when eels are at their most active. And as I've mentioned, there is "assisted migration," the trapping of eels in rivers, trucking them around dams, and releasing them upstream. These and other efforts are meant to slow the eel's decline, and in some cases they do. But even taken together, they are not enough to return the American eel to its former abundance.

Still, there is reason for hope. The eel biologist Steven Miller, for one, remains optimistic that in the end, the eel will outsmart even us. "As to the eel being classified as endangered with extinction," he wrote in an email, "to me, that seems like a bit of an insult to the evolutionary adaptability of species that have survived the many changes on earth for many millions of years. Don't you think perhaps it's a bit overconfident to think that we [mere mortals] could put an end to the existence of the mighty anguillid eels on planet earth?" Perhaps. But then again, the eel's soaring popularity—and, more to the point, its soaring price—has made it a target for exploitation at levels difficult for us mere mortals to fathom.

CHAPTER 13

A MOST SLIPPERY BUSINESS

> Who looks upon a river in a meditative hour and is not reminded of the flux of all things?
>
> —Ralph Waldo Emerson, *Nature*

THE NORTH AMERICAN SEAFOOD EXPO, billed as "North America's Largest Seafood Event," takes place every March in the Boston Convention and Exhibition Center. A raucous jumble of fish sellers, fish marketers, fish producers, fish "decision-makers," fish technologists, and their promoters, the gathering claims to offer its nearly twenty thousand attendees a "deep look" into the global seafood trade. I'm not sure about that. But what it does offer is booth after booth of stakeholders hawking oysters from Virginia, salmon from Norway, shrimp from Mexico, catfish from Tennessee, tuna from Spain, salmon from Scotland, grouper from Jamaica, and "veggie seafood" from who knows where. What it doesn't offer is much eel. There is a good reason for this, of course—the EU forbids the exportation of its eel. Still, I wondered, what about Japan or Taiwan or Korea or, for that matter, European eel from Tunisia or American eel from the Dominican Republic or Haiti? Not a chance. Roaming the aisles, I did manage to spot a handful of eel purveyors, all of them from China, and none of them willing to speak with me, let alone allow me to sample their wares.

Andrew Gould, a worldly and debonair investor from New York City I had arranged to meet on the floor, offered some insight. Years earlier, Gould had dabbled briefly in the eel business, which he described as the "worst of all possible worlds: the worst of fish farming combined with the worst of wild harvest."

I knew it was chaotic, I told him, but the *worst*? How so?

"Everything goes through Hong Kong," he said. "You can't have live fish sitting on the docks, so you bribe the custom inspectors to smuggle it over the border into China fast enough to keep the elvers alive. In the eel business, there are crooks everywhere you look."

Gould got too busy shaking hands and scouting deals with fish brokers to expand on this claim, and while his words rang true, they were hearsay. To get the facts, I turned to Florian Stein, head of EU policy and science for Germany's national Angler Association, former director of scientific operations with the Sustainable Eel Group in Belgium, and a world expert on the trafficking of elvers. Stein told me that Gould was correct, and that his own experience of eel crooks hit dangerously close to home. A few years earlier, Stein had received a call from a stranger who claimed to have information linking Jovenel Moïse, then president of Haiti, with a ring of elver thieves with ties to organized crime. (Haiti, then a significant source of eel fry for Asian fish farms, is an even more significant source today.) Stein was home with his wife and young child at the time, so he arranged to meet the caller at a Starbucks in a nearby train station. Before leaving, he strapped on a bulletproof vest and invited two intelligence officers to join him. When the trio arrived at the coffee shop, Stein shook hands with the stranger, ordered a round of cappuccinos, and sat back to listen. In minutes, he'd heard enough.

"It got very hot very quickly," he said. "Too hot for me. I left it for the intelligence officers, and I never followed up. I don't know what happened, or what they learned. I do know that if that man ever found himself in Haiti, he would be murdered."

Stein asked me not to reveal further details of how and where he met the anonymous whistleblower, whose life, even in Europe, remains on the line. I will, of course, honor that request. What I can reveal is that in February 2021, the mayor of Haiti's Port du Paix, a strong ally of Jovenel Moïse, ordered a crackdown on the country's eel trade. According to a *New York Times* investigation, the eel business was used "as a way to launder illicit profits" made by the drug cartels. The *Times* was mostly right. But what the *Times* reporter did not make clear was that Moïse, too, had once been involved in the eel business, which in itself was of enormous value, whether or not the laundering of drug money was involved.

By all evidence, Charles "Kiko" Saint-Remy, brother-in-law of the former president Michel Martelly and allegedly Haiti's most powerful drug trafficker, had gained control over the Haitian eel market. On July 7, 2021, President Moïse was murdered at his residence in Port-au-Prince, allegedly by a gang of foreign mercenaries with rumored links to Kiko. With the government in disarray, Haiti descended into chaos. Since then, the Haitian elver industry has remained firmly under Kiko's ample thumb, as Haiti's export of American elvers to China exploded to what Japanese scientists estimate was an eye-popping one hundred tons in 2022.

Carlos José Then Contín is the director of CODOPESCA, the fisheries authority of the Dominican Republic, Haiti's neighbor on the island of Hispaniola. When I called, he was at home with his young family, and I could hear his daughter pleading for his attention in the background. I suggested we talk another time, but he was eager to speak. He told me that the Dominican elver business was once a small, artisanal industry that—as it did in Maine—exploded in 2012 in response to the moratorium on international trade of the European eel. Elvers are a very important source of income in his country, especially in coastal regions, where dealers stroll beaches handing out as much as $4,400 in cash for every kilogram a fisherman brings them. Dealers deliver the elvers to unmarked warehouses patrolled by armed security guards, to be weighed, dropped gently into plastic bags filled with water and oxygen, and packed on ice to keep them calm. Though some travel through the United States, most are flown to Canada, where the dead are removed, and the rest sorted and consolidated into large shipments to Hong Kong. I asked Then Contín if he was worried that this practice might hasten the decline of the American eel, and if so what that might presage for the local economy. He said that as an environmentalist he was extremely concerned, but that he lacked data to inform his opinion. "All our elvers are for export," he told me, and the only data available is (wholly unreliable) official export numbers. "I wish we could do better."

For years, dealers in the Dominican Republic have smuggled elvers into Haiti, where the eel trade is barely regulated. "They set no quotas for fishermen and require no fishing permits," Then Contin told me. "They allow fishermen to use whatever equipment they want, and any methods they want, such as net systems that entirely block the entrance to rivers" and wreak havoc on the ecosystem. Haitian exporters are granted a quota of 6,400 kilos *each*—substantially more than the total elver quota for the entire state of Maine. But even that wildly inflated "quota" is no impediment to doing even bigger business. Then Contín guessed that Haiti reports only one of every six or seven kilos of elvers it exports. "If you are a businessman, you pay Kiko—which means to export eels, you pay," he said. "Kiko controls the borders, he controls the airports, so we put security on our borders, and at our airports. We try to stop it, but it's very difficult. Trafficking in eels is very, very profitable."

WHEN MOST OF US THINK of wildlife trafficking, we do not think of eels. We think of rare animals and their body parts—tiger paws, rhino horns, leopard skins, tortoise shells, elephant tusks, pangolin scales. We are not wrong; these are all trafficked exotica. But dollar for dollar, illegal dealing in elvers rivals not only that of tiger paws and tortoise shells, but of drugs, guns, and humans. In April 2022, the U.S. Department of Justice denounced eel poaching and smuggling as "one of the world's biggest wildlife trafficking problems, based on both the number of animals and the amount of money that changes hands in the black market."

The Wildlife Conservation Society reports that of the as much as $23 billion in revenue generated annually by wildlife crime, fisheries account for $4.2 billion to $9.5 billion. It's thought that elver smuggling alone accounts for as much as $4 billion.

After habitat loss, the illicit wildlife trade is the world's most powerful driver of species extinctions. And as we've seen, wiping out a single species can lead to a domino effect that devastates entire ecosystems. In the case of the freshwater eel, the repercussions of this are hard to overestimate. As we now know, the American eel must retain very large numbers to survive as a species, and any further decline in this once abundant and ubiquitous animal could trigger a cascade of events that would disrupt life over much of the planet. On a more basic level, elver trafficking threatens not only the livelihood, but the heritage of the world's indigenous people. And nowhere is that truer than in the state of Maine, where the eel traps of Native Americans predate the pyramids of Giza.

CHAPTER 14

TRIBAL MATTERS

Eels do not stutter.
Look, they flow like liquid
They do not take more than they need,
They are the best of us.

—Ben Ray, *The Kindness of the Eel*

I FELT MYSELF LUCKY TO be standing on Pemaquid Falls Landing in the town of Bristol, the first day of elver season. Cloudless and crisp, it was weather of a sort that almost made up for my muddy slog through the path passing as a dirt road. A flock of wild turkeys parted like startled fish to make way, and I could hear birdsong in the distance. Winter was officially over, and a fickle spring was poking through, though this being March in Maine, no one could say for sure where it was headed.

A string of Ford and Chevy pickups lined the rutted strip that sloped down to the Pemaquid River tumbling seventeen miles inland from the sea. A century-old grist mill—then under renovation by the Old Bristol Historical Society—straddled a thundering waterfall. Swarms of fishermen bundled in hooded sweatshirts, puffer vests, and chest-high waders crowded the landing and shoreline, poised to brave the thirty-five-degree water. A trio of marine patrol officers, alert in dark sunglasses and baseball caps, stood by, eyes on their watches.

When noon struck, the eelers pivoted as one, the elders planting their rubber boots almost daintily on the slick rocks, the younger fishers plunging hip—even neck—deep into the churning current, all to claim their carefully chosen spots. For me, the revelations began with the unfurling of the fyke nets, billowing fish traps the size of two-man tents rigged with a series of funnel-shaped openings that make it easy for elvers to enter and nearly impossible for them to escape. In less than an hour, the nets were anchored so densely the riverbank took on the look of a tent city. A few nets nearly touched; a proximity not sought by fishermen jealous of every precious inch of shoreline. (In Maine, elver nets are forbidden in the middle third of any river, stream, or brook to avoid interfering with the water's natural flow.) Across the river, two men faced off in a territorial dispute, neither willing to adjust his fyke net to placate the other. Allies lined up behind each of the angry men, picking sides like seconds in a duel. Voices rose and fists clenched. A fellow bystander in a black sweatshirt embroidered with an eel in Day-Glo pink sidled over to offer this advice: "I wouldn't get too close to those two if I were you." No worries there, I told her. As if on cue, Patrol Officer James Mayotte strode out from a thicket and into plain view. Jacking up his windbreaker to fully expose the Glock 17 holstered on his hip, he placed himself squarely between the feuding pair. I couldn't hear every word of what was said, but whatever it was settled the matter. The men parted ways and returned to fiddling with their nets. The drama was over, at least for now.

"Tempers flare when there's money involved, and eels are all about money," Mayotte told me, stepping back into the chilly shade. The bystander in the eel-embroidered hoodie smirked and rolled her eyes. The dispute was about money, she agreed, but money wasn't the whole story. There was also this: one of the feuding men was Native American, the other was not. That meant trouble. She herself had an elver license, but as a state fisherman—not a tribal fisherman—she had no plans to use it on the opening week of the season. She told me a story I'd heard before, of allegedly unlicensed elver fishermen of the Passamaquoddy Tribe. Apparently, they were confronted by Maine marine patrol officers with a backup of state police on the shores of the Pennamaquan River on an Easter Sunday. This was back in 2013, the year when the river price of Maine elvers stood at $1,850 a pound. With money like that at stake, not every fisherman felt obliged to play by the rules, and many felt obliged to carry a gun. The officers confiscated nets and issued some summonses, she said, but wisely decided to make no arrests that night. "I'm not sure what happened to the Natives, but I do know this," she said. "Whatever they got, they deserved worse for what they did." What she didn't seem to know is that the federally recognized tribe had legal sovereignty and a co-equal government with the feds, and had issued their own permits to fish elvers.

Early the next morning I returned to the fishing grounds to check on the night's catch. On a field of winter-bronzed grass a hundred yards or so above the shoreline, a cluster of Passamaquoddy tribal members gathered in an encampment of campers and pickups. Brothers, cousins, and friends, they'd been hunkered down for the better part of a week, enjoying each other's company and scoping out the best fishing spots. Most were fyke fishermen with long experience of the river and the eel's mysterious ways. But fyke nets are pricey, and not everyone could afford one. The youngest and

Justin Socobasin (center) with cousins and friends drove more than four hours from the Passamaquoddy Reservation at Indian Township to gather at this campsite in Bristol, Maine, on the opening day of elver season. The fishing was so good that the tribal elver quota was met in less than a week. (Ellen Ruppel Shell)

poorest fishermen used handheld dip nets, a far cheaper but more tiresome tactic that required them to remain alert through the night to sweep the nets rhythmically through the moonlit water, a chore they compared to a witch worrying a bubbling cauldron with her broom. I was told you could tell dip net users from fyke net users by their beverage of choice: dip net fishermen drank mostly Arizona iced tea to stay awake; fyke net fishermen drank mostly Mike's Hard Lemonade to stay festive. Either way, it was exhausting work. The fyke fishermen could sleep, but not a lot, as they had to keep watch to prevent a rival from slashing their net to steal the elvers.

Justin Socobasin, a fyke man, stood in the shade of his truck that morning, cleaning sand fleas from the previous night's catch. Tall and square-shouldered, he wore a puffer jacket and high rubber boots tucked into cargo pants. It was broad daylight, but I didn't ask whether he'd forgotten to remove the headlamp still banded tight across his forehead, or if he was just too worn out—or too amped up—to bother. Gesturing me over, he slipped his hand into the seven-gallon plastic bucket of water at his feet and open-palmed a shoal of glass eels, transparent slivers the color of plasma. He urged me to dip a hand in too, and I did, the elvers swarming to the heat. Despite their numbers and frenetic nibbling, they seemed to me barely ripples in the water. Justin smiled. "Don't spread it around," he said, but that bucket—one night's work—held one and a half pounds of elvers. What that meant dollar-wise he wasn't sure;

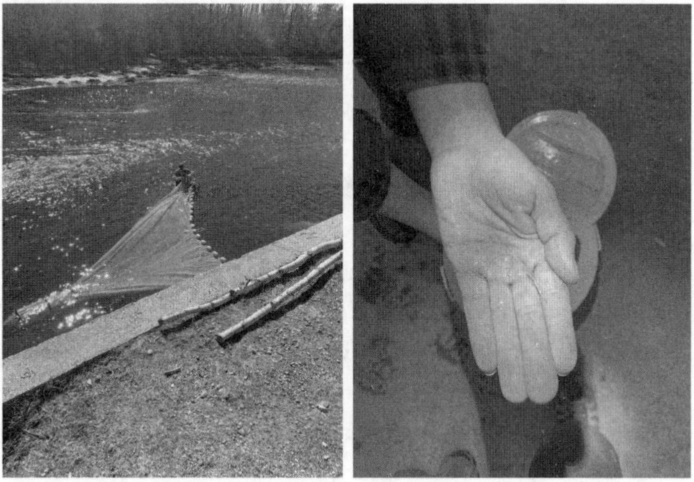

Fyke nets are ungainly, and positioning them along the shore of a rushing river is a challenge typically requiring an hour or more of effort in water so cold that fishermen sometimes don wetsuits. The jackpot—a bucketload of weightless, transparent glass eels—is well worth the effort. (Ellen Ruppel Shell)

he had not yet checked the going rate that morning. But it would certainly add up to at least a full month's pay in his job as a wildlife tech at the tribal warden service.

In Maine, the official elver season runs from noon on March 22 through noon on June 7, with rest periods on Tuesday and Saturday. Some years, the season ends much earlier: once the state quota is met, legal fishing ends regardless of the date. Of the state's 9,688-pound total, 2,070 pounds are reserved for Maine's four federally recognized Native American tribes and allocated according to the number of tribal members—in 2023, the Maliseet were granted 107 pounds, the Micmac 39 pounds, the Penobscot 620 pounds, and Socobasin's tribe, the Passamaquoddy, 1,002.38 pounds (docked 69 pounds for overfishing the previous season). As I mentioned, a number of state fishermen object to this arrangement, especially since—as I will later explain—every tribal member gets a chance at the pot.

Unlike lobster licenses, elver licenses are not transferable. In the rare instance that a state elver fisher gives up his license (or dies), that license is made available through a lottery. The lottery is wildly popular: when thirteen licenses became available in 2022, the Maine Department of Marine Resources was swamped with 8,143 applications. (Application fees—$35 a pop—provide a much-needed source of revenue, most of it slated toward the state's eel and elver management fund.) Native Americans don't use a lottery but rely on a more equitable system that in theory grants all tribal fishermen the same five-pound quota. When the tribe's collective quota is filled, individuals can no longer catch elvers legally, even those who have not yet met their personal five-pound limit. Socobasin and other native fishermen rush to the rivers the first day of elver season to capture as many elvers as they can before their tribal quota runs dry.

The morning before I met Socobasin, Melanie Tibbetts, a

dealer representing Bill Sheldon's Maine Eel Trade and Aquaculture, had set up her station just steps from the river under a sign reading BUYING GLASS EELS HERE. The facility was temporary, carved out of a basement corner of the historic Mill at Pemaquid Falls, a ramshackle nineteenth-century structure purchased in 2020 by the Old Bristol Historical Society. The mill needed a costly overhaul, and I was told that Sheldon, who happens to be Tibbetts's father, chipped in $10,000 toward the renovation in exchange for permission to set up shop on the premises. Dealing eels from a station so close to the river at the kickoff of the season gave the Sheldon clan an edge—the eelers could walk their day's catch just a few hundred feet, get it weighed, and get themselves paid. (Maine Eel Trade and Aquaculture maintains four stations in elver season, the largest one in Ellsworth.)

Tibbetts grew up trapping elvers under the tutelage of her dad and his younger brother, Jonnie, a welder recently retired from Bath Iron Works, where (like so many Mainers) his niece also worked at one time. Tibbetts, who was fifty-two when we met and held a license to fish, said she hadn't missed an elver season in at least forty years, including the previous spring, when she spent two terrifying weeks in intensive care with a raging case of COVID-19. "It felt like my insides were melting," she said. "But I wouldn't miss the season." This year she paid a landowner $500 for permission to walk across his property, to keep her distance from other fishers as she anchored her fyke net. "My dad built my trap for me, it's thirty, thirty-two feet long," she said. (A LinkedIn photo shows her waist-deep in rushing water wrestling the massive contraption to submission.) It's the fishing, not the dealing, that grabs her, and it seemed to me that she was aching to get back to the river, free of the distraction and disappointment humans bring. But today her place was behind a desk, checkbook at the ready.

Elver dealer Melanie Tibbetts and her Goldendoodle, Thor, stay warm in their shop, waiting for the fishermen to arrive. An avid outdoorswoman, Tibbetts has been fishing for elvers for more than three decades. (Ellen Ruppel Shell)

A makeshift wooden stairway led down to Tibbetts's pine-paneled headquarters, a jumble of nets, easy chairs, hip boots and waders, and a trio of blue plastic vats bubbling like outsized hot tubs. (Tibbetts cautioned me not to take photos of the plastic vats, which looked ordinary but apparently were outfitted in some proprietary manner.) A space heater cranked high was not enough to warm the place, and most everyone but me had come prepared with wool hats and thick hooded sweatshirts layered under parkas. Tibbetts's Goldendoodle, Thor (named for the Marvel Comics god of thunder), reclined regally on a cushion at her feet, and a television tuned to Fox spewed objections to the pending appointment of Ketanji Brown Jackson to the Supreme Court. A sign clamped to a clipboard mounted on the wall spelled out the rules:

"Clean Eels. No Fleas. No Dirt. No Junk. Dump Eels in White Bucket. Thank You."

I watched as a fisherman ducked his head low to clear the doorjamb and transferred a fistful of baby eels from his blue bucket into the waiting white bucket. Chris, a tall, athletic-looking man in waist-high waders who introduced himself vaguely as Melanie's assistant ("Nope, no last names"), twisted the waterlogged elvers in what looked like a pastry bag to drain the liquid. ("If I'm not careful, that will be the world's most expensive water," he joked, not for the first time.) When the load was as dry as he could get it, Chris untwisted the bag and poured the mess into a shiny metal bowl to be weighed to a fraction of an ounce on a stainless-steel trade food scale. Tibbetts rose to double-check the scale, entered the amount into her computer, and wrote the fisherman a check. From the look on his face, he got a decent payoff. Later that afternoon, I asked Socobasin whether he, too, would sell to Tibbetts. He shook his head, probably not: her price was too low.

What Socobasin didn't say—and perhaps didn't know—was that Tibbetts's price was not hers to set. That privilege went to the family patron, Mitchell Feigenbaum, principal of Delaware Valley Fish Company of Norristown, Pennsylvania, and president of its Canadian affiliate, South Shore Trading Company. A Philadelphia lawyer by training (and temperament), Feigenbaum is an eclectic entrepreneur: co-owner with his high school buddy Barry Kratchman of the Classic Cake Company, sole owner of an oyster farm, and a dabbler in commercial real estate. His introduction to eels came by way of Kratchman, who happened to be a third-generation fishmonger. A businessman to his core, Feigenbaum sensed the opportunity. He and Kratchman became partners, and in 2000 Feigenbaum moved with his family to New Brunswick, Canada, where today he reigns as the most influential eel mogul in North

Elvers worth nearly $2,000 a pound are cleaned, wrung dry, and weighed to a fraction of an ounce by an assistant while the fisherman (masked to ward off pathogens) stands by anxiously. (Ellen Ruppel Shell)

America. Bill Sheldon—through his wife thought to be the biggest elver dealer in Maine—procures elvers exclusively for Feigenbaum, who told me that his firm handles fully 60 percent of all eels traded in the United States and Canada.

I had caught up with Feigenbaum at Big Sky Resort, in southern Montana, where he spends much of the winter. (The powder was fresh, and I was lucky to catch him between ski runs.) Big Sky is a long way from the South Shore Trading headquarters in New Brunswick, where he also keeps a home. What sort of home? One colleague put it this way: "Eels have been very good to Mitch."

Like Eel Godfather Bill Sheldon, Feigenbaum is an informed and articulate advocate for the elver industry who is most attentive to questions that serve his purpose. When I asked what criteria he used to set the daily price for elvers, he said that it depended entirely on what his customers—most of them Chinese businessmen—were willing to pay. These negotiations are contentious. "They want it as cheap as possible and will engage in predatory practices that would make your head spin," he told me, though he declined to elaborate. At eight P.M. on the night before the start of the 2022 elver season, Feigenbaum had set his price at $1,800 a pound. That was more than triple the going rate of the year previous, when the COVID pandemic had kneecapped the industry. Still, for Maine fishermen aware of a dealer's profit margins, that price wasn't high enough. One of those fishermen was Justin Socobasin. Still, I wondered whether Socobasin had made the right decision: glass eels are fragile and, I thought, not certain to survive the wait. There was truth to that, he agreed, but not enough to change his mind. "Elvers don't live forever in a bucket," he said, not even buckets rigged with battery-powered oxygen pumps. "But I don't mind losing a few. And I don't mind driving a couple of hours to get five hundred to a thousand dollars more [from another elver dealer]." Elvers, he said, were a little like lottery scratch tickets and a lot like life: you take your chances and sometimes you lose.

Socobasin was grateful for his day job as a tech at the Passamaquoddy Wildlife Department, but he spoke with more enthusiasm about his side gig as a hunting guide. He'd hunt most anything, but bear was his forte. To prepare for the season, he lured black bears to a certain clearing in the woods with barrels of stale frosted cookies bought cheap at grocery store bakeries or excavated from dumpsters. ("Donuts work too, but they cost more," he told me.) Bears follow their noses to the bait, eat their fill of sweets, and then amble off in search of more natural fare. Like Pavlov's dogs, they become conditioned to associate the treats with the clearing and return to it regularly. When hunting season opens Socobasin's clients perch camouflaged in elevated tree stands, rifle-ready to pick off the cookie-seeking bears.

Bear baiting is common practice in Maine, though not all agree that it's fair, ethical, or humane. Socobasin called such concerns naive, the worries of vegetarians or other outsiders who don't know what they are talking about. Yes, his family is of the Bear Clan, and his own grandmother disapproved of his vocation. But for him, hunting bear was a public service, and baiting is what made hunting possible. Just over 10 percent of bears in Maine are taken every year by hunters, and baiting is by far the most effective way to harvest them. "Do you know how many bears there would be if we didn't cull them?" he asked. "There'd be no room for us." Also, guiding bear hunts paid well, and Socobasin was a father of five, with a sixth child on the way. When we met on the river in Bristol, that family was a four-hour drive away in Indian Township Reservation, not far from the Canadian border. But Socobasin was pleased to tell me that his wife and children had plans to join him that weekend. That struck me as an iffy proposition: lodged between a busy road and rushing water, the encampment seemed like no place for little kids. Socobasin took a different view. Elvers were for him very much a family affair. His cousins were working the river that week, as were his brothers-in-law. His favorite uncle would have joined them had the cancer not taken him last winter. Actually, his uncle *was* with him; Socobasin had his ashes stashed in his truck. "I'm going to toss them under the falls late tonight, when the elvers are running," he told me. Why would he scatter his uncle's remains so far from home? "For my uncle and for my tribe, this river has a lot of history, and these eels are sacred," he told me.

THE PASSAMAQUODDY AND THEIR ANCESTORS have lived in Maine for at least ten thousand years, most of them in peace. Their custom was this: in winter they went to the woods to hunt large game, and in the spring they returned to the coasts to fish. The tribe's first recorded contact with Europeans came in 1604, when Samuel de Chaplain and his men overwintered on St. Croix Island outside of what is now Calais. In his *Voyages de Champlain*, Champlain declared Indians "sauvages," people of nature who had not been shaped by civilization. Though he pitied them for not yet finding Christ, he also praised them for their expertise and moral character. The Passamaquoddy sided with the French in the French and Indian War and were left to deal with the consequences when that war was lost to the British. Anxious to continue to profit from the fur trade, the British made treaties with the Indians, promising to protect their lands from white encroachment. That promise was promptly and repeatedly broken, but that wasn't the worst of it. In November 1775, Lieutenant Governor Spencer Phips issued to all "his majesties subjects" a thirty-day license to "kill Indians" with a hefty reward for every scalp. Little wonder, then, that the Passamaquoddy united as the main force in securing eastern Maine for the Patriots in the Revolutionary War, a service for which George Washington sent the tribal chiefs a heartfelt letter of thanks.

Over time, whatever gratitude the colonists had for their Native American neighbors curdled into resentment. In 1794, Massachusetts (which governed the district of Maine) signed a treaty with the Passamaquoddy forcing them to cede 12.5 million acres of their holdings—nearly half the district—in exchange for a 23,000-acre plot of protected reservation land and a sum of money. (It's not clear that the state ever ponied up the dough, as there is no record of it.) In 1820, Maine split from Massachusetts and agreed to assume all responsibilities for the Native American population. This did not go well. The Passamaquoddy and its sister nation, the Penobscot, were battered in a siege of cultural genocide: their language banned by the Catholic priests and nuns who oversaw the reservations, their kids lost to a treacherous child welfare system, their land usurped and pillaged.

The Passamaquoddy have a storied reverence for the water world: their name, an anglicization of "Peskotomuhkati," is Algonquian for "pollock plenty place." The tribe constitutes the oldest fishing community in Maine, one of the oldest in the nation, and the American eel has long been a staple of their diet. Every autumn, they speared silver eels on their way to the sea or trapped them in wicker baskets or V-shaped weirs built from stacked river rocks, to be eaten fresh on the spot, or smoked to preserve them for months. Without eel, the Passamaquoddy and other Maine tribes would have likely not survived. Samuel de Champlain, credited with drawing the first map of the Maine coast in 1604, wrote of "a great many . . . fishing for eels, which begin to come about September 15 and go away on October 15. At this time all the savages live on this manna and dry enough of it to last through the winter to the month of February, when the snow is about two and a half feet deep, or three at the most." Thirty years later, Paul Lejeune, a Jesuit missionary who lived among the Innu tribe near Quebec, wrote vividly of the eel smoking process: "This work is done entirely by the women, who empty the fish, and wash them very carefully opening them, not up the belly but up the back; then they hang them in the smoke, first having suspended them upon poles outside their huts to drain. They gash them in a number of places, in order that the smoke may dry them more easily. The quantity of eels which they catch is incredible. I saw nothing else inside and outside of their cabins. They and the French eat them continually during this season and keep a large quantity of them for the time when meat is not eaten; I mean the French, for the Savages usually have no other meat than this until the snow is deep enough for Moose hunting."

Jesuit missionaries made note of the spiritual importance of the eel to the tribes and described rituals in which "sorcerers" threw eels on an open fire to appease the devil. European settlers, by contrast, saw the eel mostly as a commodity. Markets for grain, meat, fish, were tightly regulated and policed. But eels were treated differently, the only fish that could be bought and sold on the shoreline and shipped directly to urban centers abroad. In 1646, the Jesuits reported that "they caught this year, forty thousand eels, most of which sold at half an ecu the hundred." The French Catholic missionary Louis Nicolas encouraged his countrymen to visit the new city of Quebec, "where for three months they [would] be able to feast on eels prepared in a hundred ways." Salted eels were shipped to the Antilles, the Caribbean, and Europe. But soon the eels grew less abundant, and trade in eels slowed. In October 1648, the Jesuits complained, "There were few eels this year, and there was a great tendency to destitution." Apparently, it did not occur to these pious souls that a decline in a once abundant natural resource might be in any way related to the commodification of it by Europeans. It took less than twenty-four months for the Europeans to deplete a fish that had served the region's indigenous people for eons.

Paul Thibeault, an attorney and the managing director of the Maine Indian Tribal-State Commission, has more than thirty years of experience with Federal Indian Law and a deep understanding of its consequences for the state's fisheries. He told me that for the indigenous people of Maine, the eel's significance goes well beyond profits or the vagaries of trade. The elver controversy, he said, "highlights" the difference between Native Americans and other people. In recent decades, elver fishing has taken center stage in the ongoing efforts of Maine tribes to stand as sovereign alongside the state. For tribal members, success of the fishery is measured less by return on investment than on meeting the needs of the present while maintaining a long-cherished resource for future generations.

In June 1924, Congress enacted the Indian Citizenship Act, granting citizenship to all Native Americans born in the United States. The right to vote, however, was governed by state law, and Maine was among the last states in the union to grant Indians the right to vote, in 1954. Thibeault told me that the relationship of Maine with Native Americans "was the worst in the United States," so it was really no surprise when "things really bubbled up when the Passamaquoddy and the state conflicted" in long-held disagreements over who held dominion over the elver harvest. When the elver price spiked in 2012 and the fishery became a chaotic free-for-all, the Maine legislature passed an emergency act to cap licenses issued by the Passamaquoddy Tribe, stipulating 124 licenses allowing one piece of gear (either a fyke net or a dip net), 26 licenses allowing three pieces of gear, and 50 licenses confined to dip-netting a single river, the St. Croix. Tribal leaders quietly overruled that decision to issue 575 elver fishing permits to Passamaquoddy eelers. When 425 of those licenses were pronounced illegal by the state and sixty-eight tribal members arrested, Thibeault gathered a half dozen volunteer lawyers to defend the fishermen in courts from Kittery to Calais. "We resolved every case with no convictions," he told me. Whatever the legal arguments, there was no doubt that the Passamaquoddy were working diligently to protect the eel. And while it was true that far more tribal fishermen than state fishermen were granted licenses, the tribe's catch that season accounted for only 10 percent of the total harvest, with tribal fisherman landing on average less than an eighth of the weight of elvers caught by fishermen licensed by the state. Yet, despite this disparity, more than 25 percent of all criminal and civil charges of elver harvesting violations were levied against the Passamaquoddy. Not even the prosecuting attorneys considered what appeared to be a spasm of racial profiling a good look. "The state and the tribes eventually reached a memorandum of understanding," Thibeault told me. "But fundamental disagreements remain."

Thibeault, who is white and grew up in a working-class neighborhood bordering Boston, attended university in Maine and law school in California. He became familiar with tribal matters in the 1980s, while defending the rights of migrant workers, many of them Native Americans. "Farm labor contractors rounded up people from all over the country, told them lies about the big money they would make raking blueberries in Maine," he told me. "Basically, they ripped them off, but we also had some truly horrendous cases, a lot of injuries, a lot of bad actors. The prevailing attitude toward the tribes was negative, a disproportionate number of the jailed were Indian, and the animosity toward them was high."

In 1980, the federal Maine Indian Claims Settlement Act was signed with a flourish of an eagle-feather quill by President Jimmy Carter. A gesture of appeasement, the settlement was meant as remedy to the long history of exploitation experienced by Maine's four indigenous tribes. It came in response to a suit filed against the U.S. Department of the Interior by the Penobscot and Passamaquoddy, who sought the return of their land, which they argued had been seized without proper constitutional authority, first by the state of Massachusetts and again by the state of Maine.

"When the tribes brought these claims, people in Maine did not expect it," Thibeault said. "Many didn't even know that Natives lived in the state." An even bigger surprise came when the presiding judge agreed with the tribes. The (hotly disputed) outcome was the passage of two laws, one enacted by the state of Maine and the other by Congress, the combined effect of which was to wipe clean the tribal members' claims and redefine the legal relationship between the tribes and the state. The settlement—paid by the feds, not the state—came to $81.5 million, most of it earmarked for the Passamaquoddy and Penobscot to buy back 300,000 acres of tribal lands from large landholders, chiefly paper companies in the state's desolate and thinly inhabited regions.

Having raised—and won—one of the greatest legal challenges ever put before the state of Maine, the Passamaquoddy and the Penobscot were finally granted official federal recognition. But not all was resolved: the state maintained substantial jurisdiction over tribal affairs. Indeed, Maine stands alone among states in the legal sway it holds over Indian tribal lands and members. This has led to escalating clashes over issues of sovereignty, especially in matters of natural resources. Notably, the tribes do not have a clear right to regulate fishing and hunting on their own lands and have no saltwater rights whatsoever. A bill put before the Maine State House would oblige the state to recognize those rights, but while passionately debated, the bill has so far failed to pass.

CONFLICTS OVER RIGHTS TO NATURAL resources—fur, fish, timber, water, land—have for centuries strained relations between Native Americans and non-Natives. In Maine, the American eel is at the center of that conflict, or so it seemed to me when I decided to meet with Justin Socobasin on his home ground at the Indian Township reservation. I made the white-knuckle drive north on what locals call "the Airline" (and the state of Maine calls Route 9), a twisting blur of logging trucks groaning under outsized loads of timber. My ride, a seventeen-year-old Audi with an insatiable appetite for motor oil, lost speed as I approached the top of every hill. There were no gas stations, no convenience stores, not even a shoulder on which to pull over and call for a tow. Approaching what I hoped was the correct exit, I puttered off the highway onto a labyrinth of single-track roads leading to the tribal office, a visually arresting structure that an architect friend later described as "Passamaquoddy Modern."

The August weather was fine, and having no business inside, I warmed in the sun of the parking lot. Socobasin pulled in a quarter hour late, explaining that he'd gone home for an early lunch with the wife and kids. He gestured me into his pickup for a tour of the residential area, a crescent of generously spaced, single-story bungalows, some home to one or more of his relatives. The half circle was flanked by lakes where his kids swam when the weather allowed, and there was an impressive Native American–themed playground. But what struck me was the quiet. It was summer break, and I had anticipated roaming packs of restless teenagers. Socobasin said the teens were probably working, though it wasn't clear what that work might be. There were no coffee shops, fast-food joints, or summer camps in the vicinity, no lawns to mow. The closest grocery store was sixteen miles away. I asked him what it was like for him growing up so far from the hustle. "I always knew I would guide," he said. "Got my license six days after my eighteenth birthday. I also did logging—logging or guiding, depending on the time of year. But I'm thirty years old, and back then we used chain saws. Now there are these giant machines that cut thousands of acres fast—more in two weeks than we could cut in a year. So that job's not available anymore. Potato harvesting is automated, too, so there's no money for us there. Giant corporations pretty much took over everything."

The tour had come full circle. Socobasin parked the truck and ushered me inside to meet his boss, wildlife biologist John

Sewell. A slim, soft-spoken man in early middle age, Sewell had a close-cropped salt-and-pepper beard and a forearm half obscured in a tattoo. “It’s a Newhouse number fifteen,” he volunteered, offering me a chair while Socobasin stood nearby. “Same one my grandfather used.” Oh, right, a bear trap. But Sewell was more of a beaver man. “What beaver meant to tribal members was huge,” he said. “We knew every beaver colony, and we opened them one at a time. Trapping them was very competitive. We managed [the harvest] very well.” That was years ago, when a beaver pelt was worth a dollar an inch, maybe $60 for the whole. But trapping beaver is no longer worth the effort: in Russia or China, where beaver fur is still fashionable, a pelt can sell for as little as $5. “If you are interested in making money these days, elvers are the way to go,” Sewell said.

Sewell recalled a time when he could not give an elver license away. “Only old men wanted them,” he said. “Elvers weren’t worth much, but it gave them something to do before hunting season opened.” Today, everyone wants one, including him. Since he’s not a tribal member, he must procure a license by lottery. He’s tried, but so far, no luck. “I’m mad at myself that I didn’t get one before it got crazy,” he told me. “Elvers free people up, lets them do what they normally can’t do—skip the assistance check, put money back in the community, buy their kid a four-wheeler. It’s a huge boost.”

Socobasin gently interrupted to add that speaking with him and Sewell was fine, but if I wanted the tribe’s perspective, I should also talk to his father, Joseph, who had served in several elected positions, including a four-year term as chief. When I called him, Joseph told me that for most of his lifetime, only a handful of Passamaquoddy elders, maybe twenty, had fished elvers, mainly for the sport of it. But about a dozen years earlier, the number surged to seven hundred, “driven by price.” Soon, more than half of adults on the reservation were dipping and trapping, and it became clear to tribal leadership that regulations to avoid overfishing were necessary. "We believed in conservation, and regulated the fishery well before the state did," he told me. "That made me pretty unpopular with state [non-tribal] fishermen."

As I've mentioned, the Passamaquoddy's standard elver quota averages out to about a pound or two per fisherman, and does not exceed five pounds. Given the far larger quotas allotted to state elver fishers (rumored to be as much as a hundred pounds), this seemed grossly unfair to me. But Joseph explained that what tribal people consider "fair" relates less to the rights of individuals and more to the rights of the tribe as a whole. "Growing up on the reservation, you're taught to look at things in a very different way," he said. "You pay respect to every living thing. You pray to the sun, the moon, the water, the fish. As I've gotten older, I've come to understand why. You see how quickly things can change, and what factors can deplete a resource. The elver does not belong to each of us as individuals. It belongs to us communally, as a tribe. You take only what you need, you don't get greedy." I asked about tribal members who did not honor this no-greed policy. "We elders talk to them," he said. "And we work hard to change their minds."

In 2023, Passamaquoddy elver season in Maine lasted a scant five days, from March 22 to March 27, the day the communal tribal quota was met. The season for state fishermen, by contrast, ran from March 22 through early May. The elvers were still running strong into August that year, and with the price standing at $2,131 a pound, the temptation to poach was powerful. Over the border in Nova Scotia and New Brunswick, poaching was rampant: government authorities made 110 arrests and seized more than half a million dollars' worth of illegally harvested elvers before shuttering the fishery early, citing fears for public safety. Residents complained of mysterious men shrouded in balaclavas driving around in trucks with obscured license plates. Knives and guns were brandished, and at least two people suffered a serious assault, one hit on the head with a pipe, the other shot in the leg. Steele, the budding social scientist who studies eelers and their ways, told me that matters were nearly as dicey in the United States. "Fishermen and dealers have worked out ways to get around using the swipe cards," she told me. The elver wars, thought to be over, seemed to be heating up again.

Joseph Socobasin said that under Passamaquoddy law, this mess would have been avoided. The tribe's idea was to create an "open derby" with unlimited licenses and to close the fishery to all when the agreed-upon weight of elvers had been caught. This way the eel was protected, and everyone who cared to fish got a piece of the action, albeit a smaller piece. But Joseph knew that while this system would likely work well for tribal people, state fishermen would want no part of it: non-Native fishers had made clear they desired more elvers for themselves, not more people fishing elvers. Given this "winner take all" attitude, he said, the best way to protect the eel is to disincentivize illegal fishing, that is, to make elver poaching unprofitable by blowing up the supply chain and ending the sector's reliance on foreign dealers, foreign eel farms, and foreign processors. When I asked for specifics, Joseph went cryptic. "Go talk to Sara," he told me. "Everyone knows that Sara is doing great things for Maine."

CHAPTER 15

CLOSING THE CIRCLE

> To her, they never slithered–
> rather a rustling, the stiff
> texture of their mystery
> still dark and truffled
> on her tongue
>
> —Fiona Wright, "Eel Farm"

AFTER YEARS OF SLOSHING THROUGH the ins and outs of eeldom, I'd heard so much talk of Sara Rademaker that in my mind she had grown into a thing of myth, a towering presence on whom so many had pinned their optimism and hope. Scientists, fishermen, scholars, merchants, and politicians sang her praises, especially in Maine, where like Beyoncé and Madonna she went mostly by her first name. When it came to the American eel, all roads led to Sara, or so it seemed.

Sara's dream was to build and operate America's first-ever full-service eel farm. To those who did not know her, this plan sounded grandiose bordering on delusional, and from all evidence it was. Others with similar ambitions and vast experience had failed and failed miserably. Sara was twenty-seven years old when she proposed the plan and had almost no experience of eels, so what the heck was she thinking? Yeah, well, you know how this fairy tale ends. After eight years of battling crushing odds, Sara's dream came true in the form of American Unagi, the first truly sustainable commercial eel farm in the United States.

Wedged between a maker of doormats and a producer of organic fertilizer in a muddy business park in Waldoboro, Maine, Sara's 27,000-square-foot project bears closer resemblance to a commercial brewery than to the "family farm" she has come to brand it as. Though not, as often claimed, the "first" eel farm in North America, it is by far the largest, and the only one with the slightest chance of toppling the hegemony of China's American eel monopoly.

Sara might be famous, but she is also a hard woman to pin down: she agreed to meet in person only after an exhaustive vetting that included emails, telephone conversations, and my attending a public lecture she delivered at a conference on Maine aquaculture. (For the record, the conference was quite informative.) We finally got together in a café in Rockland, a port city of roughly seven thousand and the self-anointed art capital of Maine. Apparently, Sara considered the café—crowded with patrons—a safe and neutral ground. I arrived early to find her already seated at an outdoor table with her standard poodle, Finn, standing guard nearby. She'd ordered her large coffee to go; not a good omen, I thought.

If one were to score people on how they might best relate to nosy authors, in my view, Sara would not do well. Intensely private about many things (she forbade me to speak with her parents), she seemed determined to maintain control over the narrative that

Sara Rademaker and her standard poodle, Vera, dressed for success in their office at American Unagi. Rademaker, winner of numerous awards and grants, is the first entrepreneur to launch a successful eel farming and processing operation in the United States. (Ellen Ruppel Shell)

had served her so well. According to that narrative, eel aquaculture represents for Sara what interplanetary travel represents to Elon Musk—the future. The main difference, I suppose, is that unlike Musk's, Sara's vision does not trace back to her childhood. "I can't say I started out with eels on my mind," she told me.

Sara was raised in Fort Wayne, Indiana, in a family of doers. Her maternal grandmother, Marian Ward, owned and ran a foundry. Her father, Edward, a veterinarian, specialized in reptiles and taught her how to revive a dehydrated lizard with an eyedropper of electrolytes. Her mother, Beth, a Scoutmaster, specialized in adventure, and taught her to fly-fish and hunt. Sara, a self-described nerd, taught herself to trap mice that she fed live to the family's pet python. "I also bowled," she told me. "In the Midwest, everyone bowls."

The only surprise in all this was the bowling. As a rule, Sara doesn't do what "everyone" else does. When it came time for college, rather than follow her brothers and high school friends to Purdue or Indiana University, she flew the coop to Auburn University in Alabama, a place she'd never visited, let alone knew much about. "The South seemed exotic," she (sort of) explained. Sara has a thing for the exotic: she kept a saltwater aquarium in her childhood bedroom stocked with fish from the Red Sea. "I've always had a soft spot for fish," she told me. Ever practical, she made plans to grow that inclination into a career. "I knew that people would pay a lot of money to treat their pet fish," she said. "I decided to become a fish vet."

At Auburn, Sara took an internship that other students would likely eschew: assessing the impact on fish health of the thermal discharge from a steam-operated power plant on the Mobile River. It was at that power plant that she got her first glimpse of an eel. Three solid days and nights of rain had clotted an intake pipe with leaves, sticks, and other junk, and it was her job to unclog it. She suited up in fluorescent rain gear, safety helmet, and steel-toed boots, but for some reason neglected to don gloves. So it was with a bare hand that she reached up to grab what she thought was a branch, a "branch" that immediately slithered from her grasp. Suddenly, that branch became a water moccasin, or so she thought. "I never scream," she said. "I screamed." With no one there to save her, Sara had no choice but to take a closer look. What she saw, of course, was an eel.

This harrowing experience did not make Sara an eel person, but it did give her second thoughts about attending veterinary school. A course in aquaculture convinced her that it was more fulfilling (and lucrative) to farm fish than to treat them. Graduating with a double degree in aquaculture and fisheries management, she signed on to another internship with Auburn's E. W. Shell Fisheries Center, one of the most prominent aquaculture research institutions in the world. Her adviser and mentor, the renowned marine scientist Karen Veverica, spoke to me from Cambodia, where she kept an apartment in the capital city of Phnom Penh. Veverica said she had first heard of Sara while consulting with fish farmers in Uganda. "I needed help," she recalled. "An Auburn colleague mentioned that he had a student working with him on fish diseases, a young woman who reminded him of me when I was young. I met her, and I had to admit, he was right. In Uganda, there were some very strong local women working in aquaculture. She fit right in."

It was Sara's first experience overseas and a difficult one: she was at once lonely and plagued by the attentions of unwelcome admirers. To compensate, she attacked every task, no matter how menial, as though it were a privilege. One Ugandan fish farmer was so impressed with her persistence and dedication, she described Sara as "a blessing."

When the internship ended, Sara returned to Alabama with plans to enter graduate school and reunite with her boyfriend, a military man just out of special forces training. But Africa had changed her. She felt the need to work on something tangible, something that led to measurable results. She went online and found an opportunity with AmeriCorps teaching marine conservation and aquaculture at Herring Gut Learning Center in Port Clyde, Maine. "My boyfriend told me that I shouldn't move to Maine," she recalled. (One wonders, did he even know her?) Sara ended the relationship, packed her car, and drove north.

Sara knew Port Clyde only as the isolated fishing village where Forrest Gump ended his run across America. Like Alabama and Africa, she found coastal Maine "exotic." And unlike the other places, it was also a perfect fit, a place where whatever judgments and expectations people had of her they kept mostly to themselves. Herring Gut, too, felt right. Founded by the philanthropist Phyllis Wyeth, its mission was to instill a sense of purpose and environmental awareness in kids who were failing in the public schools. Sara had great empathy and respect for those kids, and even more for her patron.

Cherished wife and muse of the realist painter Jamie Wyeth, Phyllis Wyeth worked during her college years for Senator John Kennedy and followed him to the White House, where she served as secretary to his special assistant. Tragically, in 1964 she suffered a head-on collision while driving near her family's farm in Middleburg, Virginia. Paralyzed from the waist down, she walked only with the aid of crutches and was later confined to a wheelchair. Scion to the fabled du Pont family, Wyeth kept a stable of racehorses in Virginia. But she spent her summers on the Maine coast, where later in life she devoted her efforts and considerable resources to reviving coastal communities devastated by the decline of the fisheries. "Phyllis knew that many people in Maine were struggling," Sara said. Sara knew that, too.

AT HERRING GUT, SARA CAME to see aquaculture as her destiny, a way to make her mark. The internship grew into a long-term position, and she spent three mostly happy years there. Then came the call from Tropo Farms in Ghana, another "exotic" locale and one of the largest tilapia farms in the world. The farm was looking for a new assistant hatchery manager, and Sara was looking for an opportunity. She applied, and they invited her to fly to Africa for an interview. "Finn and I got on that plane not knowing what was going to happen," she said. "We stayed a year."

Sara returned to Maine in 2012, when most of the state's commercial fisheries were struggling. The Gulf of Maine, once the richest fishing ground of its size in the world, was by then among the fastest-warming regions of the global ocean. Maine seas were seven inches higher than they were in 1950, and also saltier and more acidic, with sharply reduced concentrations of the phytoplankton on which many fish depend. Overfishing had depleted stocks of cod, northern shrimp, Atlantic salmon, herring, and other fish to levels of scarcity or worse. And Maine's iconic lobster fishery, the backbone of the state's economy, was in the crosshairs.

American lobsters tolerate temperatures of 54 to 64 degrees Fahrenheit, and thrive at the high end of that range, so the warming waters of the Gulf seemed a blessing: from 1994 to 2014, lobster landings grew by 219 percent. But as the landings mounted, the price of lobster declined, meaning lobstermen had to catch more and more lobsters to make their nut, a vicious cycle that did not bode well for sustainability. Another bad sign was that there were fewer juvenile lobsters, suggesting that lobsters were reproducing less. Meanwhile, fishermen had every reason to worry that the water temperature would cross the "stress threshold" of roughly 68 degrees Fahrenheit and send the lobsters north to cooler waters. This left Maine with one question: Could there be economic security after lobster? Sara believed she had at least part of the answer.

"What I saw [in Maine] was people who are constantly changing, people who were thinking ahead," she told me. "More than fifty percent of seafood consumed worldwide comes from farms. When I returned to Maine, I noticed that people were coming to understand and accept that." Well, I thought, maybe some people, but certainly not all. Fishermen realize that the abundance of local species will rise and fall in response to water temperature, weather and an array of other shifting factors to which they are forced to adapt. But that does not mean they are de facto open to novelty. Sara's rose-colored assessment did not account for the great number of Mainers who were—and are—resistant to change, especially change that comes laced with environmental risks. Large commercial fish farms bring pollution, traffic, and other trouble, and are frequently opposed by state residents, advocacy groups and regulatory agencies. Sara needed time and money to build her case. She took a day job at Bioprocess Algae, a startup that converted algae into animal feed, and at night she wrote grant applications and business plans. Her vision was to build a company around a high-value fish with a deep connection to her adopted state. Atlantic salmon, oysters, mussels? Each had its advantages. But in the case of salmon farms the permitting process was fraught, and in the case of oysters and other mollusks the market overcrowded. She sought advice from seafood brokers, fishermen, scientists, and advocates, but in truth she had already made her choice. Before Sara had left to work on the tilapia farm in Ghana, Phyllis Wyeth had gifted her with the book *Eels* by the naturalist and artist James Prosek. Reading that, she said, "planted a seed in my mind."

AS I'VE SAID EARLIER, THE state of Maine is a pleasure dome for visitors, and a challenge for those destined—or determined—to stay. Many are aware of this problem, and some are working hard to address it. But Maine is the most rural state in the nation, and we've all heard the heart-wrenching reports of rural joblessness and deaths of despair. It's become commonplace for thought leaders to advise country dwellers to leave their homes for better opportunities in the city. One Nobel Prize laureate economist went so far as to invoke "powerful forces behind the relative and in some cases absolute decline of rural America" that "nobody knows how to reverse." But while I hesitate to contradict such well-intentioned punditry, personal experience has led me to take a somewhat different view.

I spent my formative years in a farm town in upstate New York, a tight-knit community that opened its arms to my refugee parents. My dad, the only doctor in the area, delivered babies, doled out antibiotics, and patched up the casualties of bucking chain saws. If need be, he took his fee in eggs, apples, or handicrafts, and considered these transactions fair trades. No one mocked his hard-to-place foreign accent or noted my family's absence at church on Sunday mornings. We felt welcome, and I believe we were. But when my younger brothers approached school age, my parents decided to move us closer to what they thought would be better opportunities. My dreams of raising a pony went up in flames. But, more to the point, my dad's patients were abandoned, and he was reduced from a small-town hero to just another doctor in a city full of them.

My parents had every right to do what they thought best for our family. But as a society, we'd be fools to turn our collective backs on "rural America" (whatever that means). I'm not so naive as to advocate that we return to the "good old days" when country docs took their pay in fruit preserves and crocheted oven mitts. But I will argue that we take a step back to reconsider our collective priorities and who—after all—is setting them for us. It's not "rural America" that needs transformation; it's our national dialogue on what constitutes a worthwhile and productive way of life.

In his book *Conserving Communities*, author and humanist Wendell Berry, a fifth-generation Kentucky farmer, mourns the reduction of rural regions to "resource colonies" in service to corporate America's anxious pursuit of profit. The state of Maine has endured a long and tragic history of this problem, with its natural endowments extracted and left as a raw commodity to be sent elsewhere where the real money is made in processing, marketing, and sales of a finished product. This is starkly true in the case of glass eels and elvers, which—as I noted in an earlier chapter—undergo what some have calculated to be a *sixtyfold* increase in value between capture and final sale.

So, you may be thinking, what more might the eel do for the state of Maine? A fair question, and one I put to Dan Perkins, president and CEO of the Gulf of Maine Research Institute, an independent nonprofit created to protect the Gulf and the communities that depend on it. Perkins grew up in Cape Elizabeth, five miles outside Portland, on the coast of Casco Bay. Clearly, he loves his home state, but with an MBA in finance he harbors no illusions about the daunting challenges it faces, especially in the fishing sector. There are many ways to grapple with these challenges, he said, but not many that can leverage the state's special assets and build on its aquatic legacy. In Maine, he said, Sara's eels "could help turn the dial."

A child of the Midwest, Sara did not grow up eating—or even thinking about—eels. But in Maine, her adopted state, eels were part of the landscape, a common if not beloved animal with which locals—especially fishermen—were quite familiar. As Sara tells it, that familiarity is key. "People don't like invasive species," she told me. "And they don't like invasive people. Mainers were much more welcoming when I could connect to their experience." In the course of her research, Sara was shocked to learn that the eel species native to the United States was cultivated and processed in Asia. "Maine eel was making headlines, two thousand dollars and more for a pound for elvers," she told me. "And I thought, *Why the hell are we shipping these adorable creatures to China? Maine is leaving an incredible amount of money on the table.*" She decided she'd be the one to claw it back.

Sara's timing was perfect: in Maine the local food scene had exploded, with Portland boasting more restaurants per capita than any other city in the country. Meanwhile, Maine was riding the "blue wave," with sustainable aquaculture as the next new thing for public and private investors. Oysters, salmon, scallops, clams, and mussels were all part of the mix, but elvers were something closer to the holy grail: a historic fish worth more than its weight in lobster. Tall, rangy, and youthful, Sara was aware that she was not what people expected in a fish farmer. She used that unexpectedness to her advantage, persuading everyone who mattered that she was worthy of their time, attention, and, most of all, their money. "The people of Maine understood the implications of producing local," she told me, in the broad strokes of a politician. "Better for the environment, better for the economy, better for our collective mental health."

Well, yes. But in her pitches to media, investors, and the public Sara failed to mention that the launch of a commercial eel farm had in fact been tried before in the United States, and despite heroic efforts, it had failed. The man behind that unfortunate enterprise, Willy Bokelaar, predicts that Sara's farm will do the same.

WILLY BOKELAAR IS A NATIVE of Zeeland, a province of Holland where eating eel was once as common as eating hot dogs in Ohio. As a schoolboy, Bokelaar worked summers at a seafood market, skinning and cleaning 1,000 pounds of eel a day. "It was a filthy, dirty job," he told me. "No one would do it now." He was only twelve years old when he started, but no one seemed to care—many school chums also spent their weekends ankle-deep in fish guts.

By his mid-teens, Bokelaar had graduated to working nights and weekends, and bit by bit he got pulled deep into the eel world. "It didn't happen right away," he cautioned in measured tones. "But I came to realize that eels are a very intriguing fish."

In the mid-1980s, Bokelaar moved to North Carolina to run Holland Seafood, a company backed by Dutch investors that shipped full-grown American eels to Europe. Back then, North Carolina's Division of Marine Fisheries encouraged eelers, and there were plenty of them. "I had close to one hundred fishermen working for me," Bokelaar said. "The fuel, the bait were really cheap, and everyone made money." He did well enough to buy the US subsidiary of Holland Seafood and shipped eels to Belgium, Italy, Portugal, Germany, and especially Italy, where some epicureans favored American eels over the European species. But as his business grew, the regional American eel population declined, especially eels of the sort for which Europeans would pay good money. "I had an eel business going in three different states in the US, and the eels looked gorgeous," he said. "But a lot of them had an off flavor—to be honest, they tasted like crap because they were living on pollution." In 1998, Bokelaar left Holland Seafood to open his own eel farm in Virginia. "By then, the market in wild eel was pretty much gone," he told me. Like Sara, he saw farming as the future. But to farm eels he needed brood stock, and in Virginia, fishing elvers was illegal. So Bokelaar requested and was issued a special permit to purchase elvers from local fishermen. "It was supposed to be a boon to the Virginia seafood industry," he said.

Bokelaar's eels—he counted 3.5 million elvers—lived in an indoor closed recirculating aquaculture system (RAS), twenty-four fiberglass tanks like so many giant aquariums that featured (among other wonders) a computer-guided contraption by which specialized feed was released in carefully measured sprays as it glided back and forth over each tank. The price of this wizardry was staggering, but he reckoned that his investment of "well over a million dollars" was a good one. "When I planned out my farm, the price of [grown] eels was high, twenty-five dollars a kilogram," he said. Doing the math: 3.5 million elvers grown up to a half a pound—more than 1.7 million pounds of eel at more than eleven dollars a pound—how could he lose? But unfortunately, that math did not account for the competition.

In 1999, the year Bokelaar opened for business, he said there were sixty-seven kabayaki (grilled eel) processing plants in China, each with the capacity to produce 3,000 to 4,000 *tons* of eel product a year. "The Chinese started to overproduce, and the price [of grown eel] dropped to four or five dollars a kilogram," he said. "In Europe, the market slipped away entirely. I fought it, tried to sell eels as bait, but that was too small a market, a joke, really. I just couldn't make it work. I closed my doors almost as soon as I opened them."

Eel farming in Virginia, and certainly in Maine, requires year-round access to warm water, and an expensive setup of the sort that led to Bokelaar's bankruptcy. None of this is needed on the coast of southern China, where summers are hot and winters mild. While China has a handful of indoor eel-growing operations, the vast majority are open ponds, either mud bottomed or lined with cement. To further reduce costs and enhance profits, Chinese farmers use hormones to feminize their eels and hasten their growth, a practice prohibited in Europe and North America. All this, Bokelaar said, makes it nearly impossible to compete with the Chinese for eel market share, especially in Maine, where the spring is colder than are the winters in southern China. "I know Sara, I like her, and I don't want to criticize her," he told me. "She has her dream, her desires, her insights. She has a master plan, and I wish her well. But if I were her, I would not go in that direction."

Sebastian Belle, executive director of the Maine Aquaculture Association, said that he, too, once had his doubts about Sara. "Here this skinny young redhead plunks herself down in my office, and says, Mr. Belle, I'm going to start an eel farm," he recalled. "And I thought, no you're not." Belle was no eel neophyte, his experience of them traced back to the 1970s, when he fished and sold eels to dealers at the Fulton Fish Market in Manhattan. Like Bokelaar and so many others, he told me he became "totally intrigued by the animal." Inspired by the writings of Japanese eel biologist Katsumi Tsukamoto, he headed to college to study fisheries biology and became tutored in the eel's biological peculiarities. "When it comes to farming eels, the biggest challenge is sexual dimorphism," he told me. Eels skew male in captivity and other enclosed spaces, and males are far smaller and grow more slowly than do females. Slow-growing and small are bad for business. "I'm an optimist by nature, but I told Sara you've bitten off the one species that won't work in the US. You are going to fail."

Sara listened respectfully to the advice of her elders, but like the eel, she's a contrarian. She reasoned that Bokelar's farm crashed at a time when the market for American eels was mostly in Europe. But times had changed, and both Americans and Asians had developed a taste for American eel that Sara was determined to satisfy. In 2014, her company American Unagi was born in the dirt-floored cellar of a rental home in Thomaston, Maine. The "company" consisted of two large black Rubbermaid storage containers stocked with a handful of elvers she purchased from a local dealer. Under Sara's administrations, the elvers grew large enough to be cured in a smoker borrowed from a friend. "One taste made me want to build a business around these things," she told me, though my guess was that decision had already been made.

Elvers cost a lot, and Sara was short on cash. She scored a pilot grant to purchase four pounds of elvers from Pat Bryant, the hair stylist–cum–eel wrangler who, like Sebastian Belle, got her start selling eels to vendors at Fulton Fish Market. Boisterous, outspoken, and anything but private, Bryant was the yin to Sara's yang. Sara shrewdly signed her on as a business partner, and with Bryant's help, the elver community rallied behind her. Even Belle was won over. "With eels, she was in with a rough crowd, especially as a woman," he told me. "But she crossed that bridge. She's stubborn, and independent, and in the eel business, those are good things to be." Belle added that Sara, "all piss and vinegar," was a "good example" of the sort of people who succeed in Maine. It seemed to me that Sara would succeed pretty much anywhere. She made a striking presence in the Steve Jobs mold—passionate, erudite, and, when the occasion called for it, no stranger to a black turtleneck. Steadfast and slow to scare, she had an uncanny knack for making the improbable appear inevitable.

Sara rose to celebrity status in aquaculture circles, traveling the northeast to deliver talks, serve on panels, and dish out samples of eel smoked by her boyfriend, Will Rapp, the proprietor of Up in Smoke, then Rockland's premier barbecue joint. The media, too, celebrated Sara, not just local news outlets but YouTube influencers and podcasters, most of them recycling the same rags-to-riches tale of her tenacity, pluck, and knack for "disruptive" innovation. Sara, it seemed, had the magic touch—where others failed, she would triumph.

Frank Simon, a believer, was one of Sara's early investors. We met by chance in Rockland at Suzuki's Sushi Bar, a much-lauded Japanese restaurant where he was sharing a meal with his wife and another couple at a table adjacent to my own. A shameless eavesdropper, I overhead him ask the waiter if the eel on offer that night was local. (To Simon's consternation, it was not, though that has changed.) His inquiry caught my attention, and I leaned toward him to ask whether he knew Sara. Showing not a hint of surprise (or annoyance), Simon told me he not only knew her, he held equity in American Unagi. He returned to his sushi, but the next day I poked around and found that Simon was a veteran fish broker and marketer who owned several successful seafood operations, including a stone crab company he founded in the Bahamas. A few weeks later I called to ask him why he had added eels to his impressive portfolio. "Sara convinced me that the eel has a greater opportunity than salmon and other farmed fish of succeeding in a rural environment," he told me. "And if anyone can make that happen, it's Sara."

In 2015, American Unagi rose from Sara's basement to temporary digs at the Darling Marine Center in the village of Walpole, in South Bristol. While working there one late afternoon, Sara got an unexpected phone call from the sous chef at Eleven Madison Park, a Michelin three-star restaurant later crowned the best in the world. "I had just set up my website, he'd found it, and he asked for my eel," she said. "I shipped it off to him, though I did warn him I couldn't promise him a steady supply." The following year Sara moved her operation once again, this time one hundred miles north to larger quarters at the University of Maine's Center for Cooperative Aquaculture Research, an incubator for commercial marine-related ventures in Franklin, Maine, not far from Acadia National Park. On a gray September morning, I found my way there to have a look. Sara—rocking rubber hip boots and Carhartt bib overalls—greeted me at the door, then race walked us past the dream projects of other aspiring marine entrepreneurs—bubbling tanks of green sea urchins, lumpfish, and ornamental clownfish, all contenders in Maine's high-stakes aquaculture sweepstakes. Her pilot eel farm was housed separately from these, in a series of cavernous spaces carved out of what seemed to be an abandoned greenhouse. The place was wall to wall with two dozen shoulder-high recirculating tanks the diameter of kiddie pools, each roiling with ten thousand eels.

Eels can't be rushed: they grow at their own pace, and it's impossible to know whether an elver will be slow or fast to mature. Some eels reach market size in six months, others in two years or more, and the larger ones have the habit of eating the smaller. To minimize the carnage, elvers are kept separately from adult eels, and eel farmers check their tanks regularly and sort eels as they grow—transferring the larger eels to their own tank to keep the smaller ones out of harm's way. While complicated and confusing, Sara explained that this wide variance in eel size was a blessing: since the eels grow at different rates, they reach market size at different times and are therefore available fresh throughout the year.

Cautioning me to lower my cell phone and to take no photos, Sara explained that her proprietary apparatus provided eels extraordinary support, which was critical given the more than 99 percent fatality rate of elvers in the wild. "I lose very few of these babies," she said, flicking a fingernail of her "secret recipe" feed into a tank. (Hint: it tastes of fish.) "These are very, very happy eels."

With all this coddling, Sara's elvers transform into yellow eels in a month or even less and, she said, continue to grow more than twice as fast as do wild eels. I wondered whether that could be true—eels crowded in small spaces skew almost entirely to slow-growing males, unless, of course, they are dosed with hormones. Sara assured me that she had plenty of fast-growing females and would never consider using hormones, which she said would constitute a "breach of trust with my customers." This puzzled me—and, I'll admit, I later asked around. Not a single scientist I asked thought it possible to grow large numbers of female eels without hormones in a crowded tank; they thought it more likely that Sara's eels are mostly male.

Mitchell Feigenbaum, the businessman who controls most of the North American eel market, has for years planned to open his own eel farm in Canada. "Eel farming is such an incredible economic opportunity," he told me. "I've been to hundreds of eel farms in China, they are covered in black tarps, and eels are in the dark all the time, and because of the density, they are inactive until feeding time. The whole operation is very demanding in terms of water use and effluent. We know that they also use estrogen and growth-enhancing hormones." The problem, he told me, is that it's unrealistic to try to compete with the Chinese without using some sort of "medicated feed." Feigenbaum and other stakeholders in Canada have pooled their resources and formed Nova Eel, a company focused on developing safe alternatives to the banned Chinese hormones. Progress has been made. But after nearly a decade of research and development, no hormones have been approved for use in Canada or the United States.

Under any circumstances, whether to use hormones is a tough choice to make. Eschewing them altogether pretty much ensures that Sara's eels will never be cheap or—for many—even affordable. I asked Sara if that bothers her. "I never said I was going to feed the world," she said. To Sara's way of thinking, it was the quality—not the price—that will bring the American public to American Unagi. And so far, that seems to be right. I had my first taste of her eel at a crowded sushi joint in Cambridge, Massachusetts, in the company of the author Michael Pollan, a colleague with famously wide-ranging tastes in food and other edibles. Michael knew the chef and the menu and ordered several dishes to share, including unagi. What by sheer coincidence turned out to be Sara's eel was unctuous and addictive, something like a cross between bacon and

American Unagi eel smoked over oak and alder wood and tinned in olive oil, served up in an open-faced ELT (eel, lettuce, and tomato) sandwich.

smoked salmon. I could easily imagine that one taste of her eel would change the minds of even the most stubborn eel antagonists.

Maine's support for Sara was personal, but mostly political—she is a poster child in the state's transition to a "blue economy." "Ten years ago, 'aquaculture' was a dirty word, and the granting agencies and research institutes tried to steer clear of it," Belle told me. "Now aquaculture is hot, and Sara is part of that trend."

When I joined Sara once again, in 2021, she had immediate plans to relocate her eels from the incubator in Franklin to the new facility in Waldoboro. But construction projects have a habit of dashing hopes, and this one was no exception. As months and then a year and more passed, Sara stopped responding to my calls and texts. I knew eels were a tight-lipped business, but this was extreme, and I wondered whether her dream had crashed and burned. Since I couldn't reach her directly, I cast around for others who might help, eventually settling on the engineering outfit I guessed Sara had commissioned to design and build her farm. I fired up Google and tracked down the contact information for Rene Remmerswaal, director and owner of Aquaculture Consultancy & Engineering (ACE) in the village of Mill in the Netherlands.

Remmerswaal, driving when I called, was kind enough to pull to the side of the road and fill me in. He told me he had designed and built fish farms in Holland, Lithuania, and Madagascar, among other countries, but that this was his first in the United States. He assured me that Sara's farm was well on its way, though delayed by the pandemic and other factors. He had six people working on the project and had himself just returned from Waldoboro. He and his team loved the town and had rented a house on the Medomak River, where they spoke directly to the elver fishers, who were open and friendly. (Among many other virtues, the town of Waldoboro is reputed to have the nation's highest density of elver fishers, a distinction that springs to life every spring when the river is awash in fyke nets.) One of the challenges of Sara's project, Remmerswaal told me, is that Maine requires that all water discharged from her farm be not only clean but drinkable. "That was quite an expense, and new to us," he said. Remmerswaal has a graduate degree in aquaculture, and I asked him whether he thought Sara knew what she was up against. "It's quite rare for a woman to be in commercial fish farming, certainly rare for one to be an owner/operator," he said. "She's quite special, unique. To be honest, she knows more than I do."

Nearly a year later, in July 2022, I met Sara at the Waldoboro farm, which had finally broken ground that spring. I arrived to find her in deep consultation with a repair guy, who said that some infirmity had slowed the water pump to a crawl, threatening the quality of the water and the eel's oxygen supply. None of this was entirely clear to me, but Sara was in no mood to share the details. As we walked back to the main building, she explained that the youngest eels—the elvers—were still stuck in the Franklin facility, as their tanks here were not yet ready. Still, she forbade me to enter the part of her facility where the elvers would eventually be housed. After further negotiations, I was granted a peek at the tanks of larger eels, slithering in what looked like mad abandon. The tanks were crowded, and reading my mind, she assured me that the eels liked it that way. It's true that many fish are social creatures, but I wasn't convinced that these eels thrived in such close quarters, especially the larger ones. In the wild, eels at the yellow stage are solitary predators, and in overcrowded conditions stoop to eating each other.

As we strolled down the long row of tanks, Sara's expectation, it seemed, was that I portray American Unagi not as what was—a tidy and highly efficient fish factory in a muddy industrial business park—but as something more appealingly Maine, like the scenic photograph featured on the company website. I could understand that impulse, and while I couldn't oblige it, I was impressed by the effort involved in keeping the place afloat. "People don't realize how hard this is," she said, letting down her guard for a moment. "Fish don't take holidays, it's twenty-four seven, and if something breaks in the middle of the night, you have to go out and fix it yourself."

Sara is literally tethered to her workplace, her digital watch linked to sensors that sound an alarm when anything goes awry. And it does: a few months after I first toured the farm, a seal gave way on one of the filtering machines, contaminating the tank. Water is for fish what soil is for grapes, terroir, and with hundreds of thousands of eels crowding her tanks, she knew that a leak boded disaster. Yellow eels are tough, adaptable creatures, but not even an eel will last long swimming in its own waste. While Sara declined to discuss the leak, the investor Frank Simon told me a million dollars in eels was lost that night. "It was a huge deal," he said. "But it could have been worse, much worse. There is no fish farming without challenges." I asked Simon if he saw any serious obstacles going forward, and he drew a breath. "I see two scary risks. One, someone closes the loop, and spawns American eels in captivity, elvers become easily accessible, the competition goes up and the price of eel goes down. That's a long shot." (Yes, we know about that—scientists have tried and failed to efficiently breed the American and European eel in captivity, and while scientists have come closer with the Japanese eel, they have yet to do so in a way that makes economic sense.) "The other risk is that the American eel is put on the endangered species list, and then we're done." To me, that risk sounded even less likely.

Whatever its prospects, no one could deny that American Unagi offered something very special: eel caught and raised in the (idealized) state of Maine. In 2022, the orders were pouring in, as were the accolades, including a "best in show" honor at Maine's prestigious Golden Fork Awards. But the mishap with the water filter had set Sara back, and she needed a financial boost, maybe a partner. Maine was a small state—Sara called it "one big family"—and she had a great reputation. That said, elevating an investor to partner status was risky; she feared losing control of her company, a familiar worry for many entrepreneurs. And then it hit her.

Sara had for five years relied on Native American fishers to provide her with elvers. When I visited Indian Township, several tribal fishers—including Justin and Joseph Socobasin—told me they fished for her, and that she paid them half the going rate. (They of course would have preferred a better deal, but selling to Sara for aquaculture purposes allowed them to exceed the state-mandated quotas by as much as five pounds each.) Over the years, a relationship founded on mutual dependence grew into one approaching mutual trust, a rare thing for Sara, and even rarer for Native Americans in Maine. So when Sara offered the Passamaquoddy Tribe the opportunity to purchase a 12 percent stake in her company, they agreed. In 2023, tribal members were granted a $1.53 million loan to partner with Sara in what became known in Indian Township as the "eel deal."

Stan Meader, director of operations and business development for the Passamaquoddy Tribe in Indian Township, spearheaded the arrangement. He claimed to have met with twenty-five investors, bankers, and venture capitalists across the country to pitch the idea, but not one of them was willing to take the risk. The project finally got backing from the NDN Collective, an organization of indigenous activists and fundraisers with the avowed mission to support and empower Native American communities. (As we know, eel fishing—and eel eating—had been staples of indigenous culture for eons.) Meader convinced the funders that while the elver fishing season lasted no more than ten weeks (and some years just one week for Native Americans), American Unagi held out the potential to employ tribal members year-round in transportation, sales, marketing, and other functions. His winning pitch to NDN was that eels would bring money and stability to the tribe, and, critically, return tribal members to a traditional practice in which generations joined together in common purpose.

"We have a quota of baby eels harvested, but we haven't raised or processed them, we just send them to Asia," Meader said in an NDN Collective–produced video. "So the good jobs are there, in Asia. We thought, why are we allowing China to benefit when our tribe can provide something better here in Maine?"

When I arranged my final visit to American Unagi in September 2023, Sara was, at thirty-eight, an elder stateswoman in Maine's aquaculture world, yet neither her ambition nor her enthusiasm had dimmed. Finn, her standard poodle, was no longer, but Vera, a rambunctious Finn stand-in, bounced between us as we spoke. Sara led me on a quick tour of the tank room, warning me once again not to take photographs. At my request, we stopped briefly to observe a tank of year-old eels clustering at the feeding station. The eels had learned to feed themselves by nosing a trigger on the feeding apparatus, like puppies nuzzling their mother. "They are so cuddly," she said. "And so smart."

Now that American Unagi processed its eel on site, most was sold frozen as butterflied filets, hot smoked, or—to my surprise—shipped to a partner in New Hampshire to be anointed in a shower of virgin olive oil and canned, and sold for more than $100 a pound. That day, Sara had 1.5 million eels in her tank with room for half a million more, enough to satisfy about 6 percent of the US market.

We returned to her office to talk while Sara's newly hired marketing manager, Kelsey Woodworth, sat taking notes of our conversation on her laptop. A graduate of the Culinary Institute of America, Kelsey had worked for nearly a decade as a chef, some of those years in private homes in New York City and Beverly Hills. "Since COVID, private chefs are in huge demand," she said. "It's three hundred sixty-five days a year, twenty-four hours a day taking care of someone else's needs and desires. You can make four thousand to ten thousand dollars a week! But if you take 'fuck you' money, you get a 'fuck you' life. It wasn't for me, and it's not for a lot of young people, who have seen their parents work themselves to death, and then sit out their social security years filled with regret."

Like so many before her, Kelsey came to Maine to find a sort of peace. She described the state with an artist's eye as a "witchy old soul," and she felt embraced by it. Climate change had changed her mind about living in tightly packed, trendy places, and opened her to the delights—and relief—of life in a rural state that was not yet on fire. "I came here knowing no one," she said. "I called Sara and told her I wanted to learn to cut eel, and she took me in."

Sitting between these strong, complicated women, I felt like a page had turned. Yes, the old ways were dying, but something different—something better tailored to withstand the vagaries of the twenty-first century—was trickling into the gap. Sara spoke of old sardine canning factories, once staples of Maine's maritime economy, being repurposed as eel tinning operations manned by employees displaced by the death of the mills. She spoke of eel farms up and down the coast, powered by a young, educated workforce and seeded by the bounty streaming in from the Sargasso Sea to Maine shores every spring. She spoke of rural regions escaping their past as "resource colonies" and bringing the value of what nature had granted back home. She spoke of rekindling the traditions of tribal peoples, and the rejuvenation of tribal economies. And she spoke of all this with the hard-won hope and determination of someone who had made her own way in a blisteringly competitive, even treacherous business, blasting through the doubts and judgments of everyone who tried to dissuade her. So, you may ask, will she ultimately succeed? With no crystal ball to guide me, I can offer only another question: Has she not already done so?

EPILOGUE

THIS INCOMPREHENSIBLE WORLD

When we try to pick out anything by itself, we
find it hitched to everything else in the Universe.
—John Muir

RACHEL CARSON COMPOSED ESSAYS WITH the heart of a scientist and the soul of a poet. Though she never learned to swim, she felt at home in the water, and forged a visceral connection to it. Carson studied biology at Johns Hopkins University and graduated with her master's degree in 1933, a year or two behind schedule. Her 108-page thesis, "The Development of the Pronephros during the Embryonic and Early Larval Life of the Catfish (Ictalurus punctatus)," revealed a remarkable understanding of her subject and its ways. But it was while spending a postgraduate summer at Woods Hole Oceanographic Institution on Cape Cod that Carson stumbled upon the species that would truly animate her. In an unpublished letter, her friend Dorothy Thompson Seif recalled Carson's words: "'Eels are fascinating creatures. How they can adapt as larvae to living in fresh water and then to sea water is not well-known. Did you know that as almost elvers they migrate hundreds of miles from the seas, where they are born, into the freshwater streams and ponds of our forests?'" Carson went on like this for far longer than she normally would, then caught herself: "'That was quite a spiel. I do get carried away.'"

In Carson's first major work of nonfiction, *Under the Sea Wind*, the spiel continues through the eyes of Anguilla, a female eel readying for her final migration. We meet Anguilla growing restless in the early days of autumn, when "the cold rains shed off the hard backbones of the hills." Carefully and with purpose, Anguilla makes her way downstream, ducking into the dark recesses of a waterfall to hide from a strange eel she senses intends harm, then exiting the pool to proceed downstream. She is one of "thousands [that] passed the lighthouse that night, on the first lap of a far sea journey . . . And as they passed through the surf and out to sea, so also they passed from human sight and almost from human knowledge." The critical word in this passage is "almost." Carson first published these thoughts in 1941. Since then, more has been learned about the eel than was known in the many eons that proceeded her fine book's publication.

For Carson, the eel was both protagonist and passion, as it was for many before her and for many who have followed and will follow. For me, then, the "eel question" is not how and where it propagates, navigates, or congregates. Nor is it why the eel bothers to fight its way up freshwater rivers rather than bed down in brackish estuaries, or even whether European and American eels actually breed in the Sargasso Sea. To me, the deepest mystery is why and how the eel has over so many centuries entangled so many human hearts and minds.

Unlike the brainy octopus, the playful dolphin, or the majestic salmon, the eel is uncharismatic and—though Carson came close—nearly impossible to anthropomorphize. Slimy, scaly, and utterly carnivorous, it offers humans few if any lessons. The centuries-long quest to unlock its secrets, then, does little to indulge the human innate tilt toward narcissism. On the contrary, the pursuit of its secrets reflects an ineffable curiosity about the world and its ways. We are fascinated by the eel for the very reason we are fascinated by nature itself: it is within our reach, yet never fails to surprise us.

More than two decades ago, the British historian, travel writer, and angler Tom Fort published *The Book of Eels*, a poignant, insightful, and—as critics noted—peculiar volume. A resident of South Oxfordshire on the River Thames, Fort wrote mainly on the European eel and the fishermen who sought it. In his book, first published in 2002, he observes that "eel fishing is slowly dying," including on Lough Neagh in Northern Ireland, the largest eel fishery in the European Union. In his view, "the survival of the two species of Atlantic eel is not at stake. They are too widespread, too adaptable, too resilient to be at that kind of risk. But what is under threat—doomed, more likely—is something precious and irreplaceable: the interaction between the eel and humankind."

With the wisdom of 20/20 hindsight, I can say with some certainty that Fort was wrong on both counts.

First, the eel is very much at risk. Globalization has made the exotic far less so for many of us, especially in matters of food. My grandchildren—ages four and six—eat sushi with abandon, a delicacy that their doting grandparents had heard of but never seen as children, and to which their parents had at best rare access. The global explosion in sushi's popularity contributed to a demand for eel that in recent decades has sent its price soaring. Were scientists able to breed Atlantic eels in captivity, this problem might be mitigated, but for now this holy grail remains far out of reach, while overfishing looms as a gnawing temptation.

A fish capable of thriving for thousands of years in everything from arctic to tropical conditions would seem not to suffer the impact of global warming. But that theory fails to account for several variables, prime among them the eel's migration path. The Atlantic eel's epic twice-taken odyssey—both from and to its presumed spawning grounds in the Sargasso Sea—is so meandering and mysterious that it's not known just how or to what degree that path is disrupted by climate change. Nonetheless, scientists have shown that the warming of the seas has altered the ocean currents in a way that is misdirecting eels on their journey, and almost certainly contributing to their decline. As well, rising levels of carbon dioxide in the atmosphere brought by the burning of fossil fuels underlies ocean acidification that inflicts a sensory loss in infant eels, making it more difficult for them to find their way out of the ocean and into freshwater rivers, lakes, and streams. Most eels that fail to enter fresh water become male, thereby tipping the gender scale and reducing reproductive capacity.

Eels that do make it to fresh water and become female are still very much at risk from inland dams, pumping stations, and other obstacles that block their way and impede their migration. This problem is being actively addressed in the EU, and actively discussed in the United States. On my travels, I met with many advocates of "eel ladders," man-made ramps that allow eels safe passage around hydroelectric dams and generating stations. And I saw them working. Though not yet common, implementation of these and similar protective measures is on the rise in both Canada and the United States. These measures seem to have brought a resurgence of eels in some regions. Unfortunately, these victories are conditional; though helpful in enabling the eels' return to some locations, these efforts have not much slowed the American eel's decline overall.

On a happier note, Fort's second prophesy—a loss of "the interaction between the eel and humankind"—has not stood the test of time. On the contrary, in the United States and Europe, those interactions have multiplied. True, we may see fewer two- and three-foot-long monsters being wrestled out of lakes and streams by crusty fishermen. The reason, of course, is money: what was for the previous generation a "trash fish" for the poor is today a delicacy for those who can afford it, and those who can afford it vastly prefer the more refined (and often safer) cultivated eel. Elver fishing may lack the machismo of *Deadliest Catch*—it requires little gear and more cunning than brute strength—but it is fishing nonetheless.

In Maine, any sea creature—be it lobster, cod, or eel—is said to have no better steward than an honest fisherman. Whether or not you agree, the reasoning behind this platitude stands: without fish, the fisherman is out of business. In the case of eels, this brings both bad news and good. The bad news is that people who once had absolutely no interest in eels are now among their most ruthless predators, some even demanding the lifting of quotas and the relaxation of other regulations. The good news is that people who once had absolutely no interest in eels are now among their most ardent advocates, some demanding crackdowns on poachers and the enforcement of preservation measures. As the eel scientist Reinhold Hanel told me, when eels were plentiful and cheap, few people noticed them or worried about their survival. Now that baby eels are less plentiful and worth their weight in caviar, their future is of much greater concern, not only to fishermen, but to stakeholders around the globe. The paradox is this: eels are under threat because they are desirable, but their very desirability also curbs their risk of extinction.

I began this book by admitting that I came to this project with almost no experience of eels. Since that time, I have watched them, played with them, eaten them, and spoken to scores of people who can't get enough of them. Yet by most measures I am not an "eel person." I cannot write of eels in the way of Rachel Carson, which is to say, with empathy and love. And unlike the scientist Caroline Durif, I will never snorkel with eels. But what has changed is my regard for the courageous souls who've devoted such large parts of their lives to decoding the wily ways of the slippery beast. For centuries, people of every rank strove to peel back the layers of the eel's strangeness. Their revelations were and are relative; we do not know everything about the eel. But thanks to these indomitable seekers, we understand so much more than we otherwise would, and not only about the eel. I believe it is not the eel's riddles that truly matter, but the unstoppable human drive to interrogate our world. Even if we learn nothing more of these boggling and beguiling creatures, is the very fact of this uniquely human quest not miracle enough?

ACKNOWLEDGMENTS

MY THANKS TO THE SCORES of "eel people" who contributed so much to this book—Passamaquoddy Tribal members, zoologists, naturalists, social scientists, attorneys, visionaries, dreamers, rascals, economists, fishermen, elver dealers, advocates, environmentalists, historians of eels and of Maine—not all of whom appear by name in the text. Your generosity and openness made tackling this challenging project something close to a joy.

Special thanks to Caroline Durif, who not only reviewed the section on eel navigation for accuracy but also hosted me in her lovely home on the Norwegian coast. Thanks also to Reinhold Hanel and Marko Freese in Germany, Alexandro Cresci in Norway, Sylvie Dufour in Paris, Eric Feunteun in Dinard, Steven Miller in Toyoko, Florian Stein in Belgium, Mitchell Feigenbaum in New Brunswick, William Casselman in Ontario, Julian Dodson in Quebec, Chris Flook and Fae Sapsford in Bermuda, Carlos Then Contin in the Dominican Republic, and Karen Pinchin in Halifax. In the United States, I am especially grateful to David Sykes, Pat Bryant, William Sheldon, John Sanders, Esq, Steven Rappaport, Paul Thibeault, Esq., Eric Holmes, Catherine Morse, Darrell Young, Sheila Eyler, Justin Socobasin and his dad, Joe Socobasin, Joel Llopiz, Kenneth Oliveria, Don Perkins, Desmond Kahn, Frank Simon, Shane Waller, Sebastian Belle, and John Wyatt (Taylor Swift) Greenlee.

Special thanks to Sara Rademaker, whose hard-earned privacy I so frequently invaded. Also to Catherine Morse, who kindly shared her unpublished undergraduate thesis on the eel culture of Japan, and to Kristen Steele, who knows more about the eel hunters of Maine than perhaps she should.

For Michael Carlisle, an agent of such wit, grace, loyalty, and integrity one wonders how he survives—let alone thrives—in this unforgiving business, I owe you far more than I can ever begin to repay. Thank you. And to Michael Mungiello, the man from New Jersey, thanks for the bracing "tough love" that helped me see the forest through the trees.

For Jamison Stoltz, editor and one-man support team, thanks so much for your wise counsel, patience, and encouragement.

As always, I owe my friends for their thoughtful suggestions, their enthusiasm, their good humor and unwavering (if perhaps deluded) faith in me, and most of all, their tolerance—there's nothing more aggravating than a writer in the thick of it.

As is customary, my little family suffered the most, but from long experience I trust they will over time forgive the mood swings, obsessions, and late-night rants. Thank you, Alison, Joanna, Jake, and Luke; you are the critics who truly matter.

For Marty—my support in tech and everything else—I can't imagine this book, let alone this world, without you.

NOTES

vi **"I discovered in nature":** Vladimir Nabokov, "Butterflies," *New Yorker*, June 12, 1948.

Prologue

1 **"Alone / In her millions":** Ted Hughes, *A Ted Hughes Bestiary* (New York: Farrar, Straus and Giroux, 2016), 143–44.

5 **South Carolina's was too small:** In South Carolina, the elver fishery is confined to a small section of the Cooper River, and only ten fishermen are issued a license.

Introduction: Love's Arrow

7 **"the selfsame eel":** Eugenio Montale, "The Eel," in *The FSG Poetry Anthology*, eds. Jonathan Galassi and Robyn Creswell (New York: Farrar, Straus and Giroux, 2021).

8 **three out of every four:** Accounts vary from as little as 60 percent to as much as 80 percent of all species going extinct in this event. See, for example, J. David Archibald and David E. Fastovsky, "Dinosaur Extinction," *The Dinosauria*, ed. David Weishampel (Berkeley: University of California Press, 2004), 672–84.

Half of the total freshwater fish biomass: The freshwater eel once constituted a very large percentage of the biomass in some lakes and rivers in Europe and the Americas. See, for example, R. MacGregor et al., "Recovery Strategy for the American Eel (Anguilla rostrata) in Ontario," Ontario Recovery Strategy Series, prepared for the Ontario Ministry of Natural Resources, Peterborough, Ontario.

See also Daniele Bevacqua et al., "A Demographic Model for the Conservation and Management of the European Eel: An Application to a Mediterranean Coastal Lagoon," *ICES Journal of Marine Science* 76, no. 7 (December 2019): 2164–78, https://doi.org/10.1093/icesjms/fsz118.

8 **Counts of the European eel:** Estimates of the freshwater eel's decline vary tremendously, which is quite understandable given the elusiveness of the genus. The 90 percent estimate lies at the low end of these but is often cited by scientific publications. See, for example, Juan German Herranz-Jusdado et al., "Eel Sperm Cryopreservation: An Overview," *Theriogenology* 133 (2019): 210–15, https://doi.org/10.1016/j.theriogenology.2019.03.033.

9 **strict regulations:** The EU measures for eel recovery were adopted in 2007 and are implemented by all member states assessed to be within the current geographical range of eel, excluding the Black Sea states and some inland countries. Member states must establish eel management plans for river basins identified as natural habitats for European eels, or may designate all of their national territory as one "eel river basin," resulting in a very variable approach across the EU. The recovery measures are accompanied by an EU trade ban put in place in 2010, halting all trade in eel with countries outside the EU, in addition to the more recent temporary eel fishing closures intended to protect eel migrations. In 2017, the European Commission, under the advice of scientists, proposed the closing of all fishing for eel larger than twelve centimeters in length in EU waters. However, the EU member states rejected this proposal. Instead, the first of a series of three-month eel fishing closures was part of a political compromise agreement to further strengthen measures for eel recovery.

"You Americans don't give a damn": Conversation with Dr. Reinhold Hanel, Institute of Fisheries Ecology, Thunen Institute.

11 **"In the United States":** Gertrude Stein, *The Geographical History of America* (New York: Random House, 1934; Vintage reprint, 1973).

12 **top states for business:** CNBC, "Top States for Business: 39. Maine," July 11, 2023, https://www.cnbc.com/2023/07/11/top-states-for-business-maine.html.

"most valuable export": Joseph W. McDonnell, "The Political Geography of Maine's Economic Future: Cities and Their Metro

Regions," *Maine Policy Review* 29, no. 2 (2020): 102–10, https://digitalcommons.library.umaine.edu/mpr/vol29/iss2/14.

12 **11 million pounds:** Nicole Ogrysko, "A New Waldoboro Eel Farm Appears to Be First Facility of Its Kind in US," Maine Public Radio, April 18, 2023, https://www.mainepublic.org/business-and-economy/2023-04-18/a-new-waldoboro-eel-farm-appears-to-be-first-facility-of-its-kind-in-us#.

most lucrative fishery: "2022 Commercial Fisheries Value Returns to Levels More in Line with Recent Years," Maine Department of Marine Resources, March 3, 2023, https://www.maine.gov/dmr/news/fri-03032023-1200-2022-commercial-fisheries-value-returns-levels-more-line-recent-years

13 **all but worthless:** Jessica Hall, "Maine's Most Lucrative Fishery Closes the Season at an Eye-Popping $2,100 a Pound," Mainebiz, April 25, 2022, https://www.mainebiz.biz/article/maines-most-lucrative-fishery-closes-the-season-at-an-eye-popping-2100-a-pound; and J. A. Gephart, H. E. Froehlich, T. A. Branch, "To Create Sustainable Seafood Industries, the United States Needs a Better Accounting of Imports and Exports," *Proceedings of the National Academy of Sciences* 116, no. 19 (2019): 9142–46.

other drugs: Mitchell Feigenbaum, whose company is the largest exporter of infant eels in North America, told me that hormones are widely used in China to enhance growth. Several scientists mentioned that eel was a bioaccumulator of toxins, both from natural sources and from additives. For example, in May 2023, the businessman Kevin Sheng Hsiang Fang, a high-volume importer of frozen eel from China, and Fang's City of Industry–based food wholesale business, Yong Chang Trading Co., Ltd. (dba Heng Xing Foods, Inc.), each pleaded guilty to one count of smuggling and one count of introducing adulterated food into interstate commerce. Fang admitted that the frozen roasted eel he tried to import and distribute in the United States was adulterated with gentian violet, leucogentian violet, and malachite green, substances shown to be carcinogenic in humans and thought to increase antimicrobial resistance in human pathogens.

15 **Many eels spend their formative years**: In one study of wild eels, the concentration of mercury was just over a gram per kilogram in one specimen of the 120 samples examined, and in 16 specimens

it exceeded half a gram per kilogram. Lucyna Polak-Juszczak and Stanisław Robak, "Mercury Toxicity and the Protective Role of Selenium in Eel, Anguilla anguilla," *Environmental Science and Pollution Research* 22, no. 1 (2015): 679–88, https://doi.org/10.1007/s11356-014-3382-x.

16 **against eating it:** Kenneth Oliveira, an ecologist at the University of Massachusetts, Dartmouth, was one of several scientists to warn me of the dangers of consuming wild eel meat.

98 percent: Yuan Yuan et al., "Development Status and Trends in the Eel Farming Industry in Asia," *North American Journal of Aquaculture* 84, no. 1 (2022): 3–17, https://doi.org/10.1002/naaq.10187.

"The majority subsist": Kostas Ganias, Charikleia Mezarli, and Eleni Voultsiadou, "Aristotle as an Ichthyologist: Exploring Aegean Fish Diversity 2,400 Years Ago," *Fish and Fisheries* 18, no. 6 (November 2017): 1038–55, https://doi.org/10.1111/faf.12223.

the practice spread: Mari Kuroki and Katsumi Tsukamoto, *Eels on the Move: Mysterious Creatures over Millions of Years* (Hadano-shi, Japan: Tokai University Press, 2012), 168.

90 percent: Yuan et al., "Development Status and Trends."

Guangdong Province: For a campaign to promote local seafood in April 2020, Guo Ningning, then vice governor of the Fujian Province and described by *Time* magazine as "a rising star in the Chinese Communist Party," stood before a camera to feast on eel on a livestreamed show. The broadcast attracted more than a million viewers, and the government claimed it prompted a 628 percent spike in eel sales that year.

Customs data indicate: Hiromi Shiraishi and Kenzo Kaifu, "Early Warning of an Upsurge in International Trade in the American Eel," *Marine Policy* 159 (November 2023).

17 **two-thirds of eel eaten:** The British biologist Andrew Griffiths, lead author of a study of eel products in both the United States and Europe, told me that two-thirds of the samples his team analyzed turned out to be American eels, which he said might actually be an underestimate. Interestingly, one-third of the eel analyzed in the United States was European eel, which is not legal for export outside the EU. See: Amy Goymer, Kristen Steele, Freddie Jenkins, et al., "For R-eel?! Investigating International Sales of Critically

Endangered Species in Freshwater Eel Products with DNA Barcoding," Food Control 150 (August 2023).

17 **export-focused eel supply chain:** China is the world's largest importer of seafood, but nearly 75 percent of these imports are processed and reexported to other countries. This makes it extremely difficult to track the origins of individual catches. See, for example, Frank Asche et al., "China's Seafood Imports—Not for Domestic Consumption?," *Science* 375, no. 6579 (January 7, 2022): 386–88, https://doi.org/10.1126/science.abl4756.

Ease the pressure: See, for example, Zhixin Zhang, "Rural Revitalization and China's Eel Industry," *Global Citizen*, November 23, 2022.

18 ***sixtyfold increase*:** Interview with Florian Stein.

traveled to Guangdong: I heard of these travels through conversations with Sebastian Belle, executive director of Maine's Aquaculture Association.

Chapter 1: The Eels of Maine

21 **"Fricasseed frogs":** C. S. Lewis, *The Silver Chair* (Chronicles of Narnia #4; New York: Macmillan, 1954).

22 **"tens of millions":** Charles J. Cornish, *The Naturalist on the Thames* (London: Seely and Company, 1902), 104.

"a cold backward summer": Humphrey Davy, *Salmonia or Days of Fly Fishing* (London: John Murray, 1869), 195.

24 **preferred eel to lobster:** Libby O'Connell, *The American Plate: History in 100 Bites* (Naperville, IL: Sourcebooks, 2015), 47.

cockroach of the sea: D. Koczanowicz, "Taste and Its Value: Cultural Hierarchies," in *The Aesthetics of Taste: Eating within the Realm of Art* (Leiden, The Netherlands: Brill, 2023), 52.

"a gourmet's dream": O'Connell, *The American Plate*, 47.

400,000 pounds: The earliest detailed account of US eel fisheries was provided by George Brown Goode (1884) for the period of 1877 to 1880. Historical commercial landings data from 1888 to 1940 were transcribed from online US Fish and Fisheries Commission annual reports. See for example: George Brown Goode, *The Fisheries and Fishery Industries of the United States* (1884–87, Washington, Government Printing Office).

24 **"I don't mind eels":** Ogden Nash, "The Eel Poem," *A Critical Handbook of Children's Literature*, ed. Rebecca J. Lukens (Oxford, OH: Miami University Press, 1976), 198.

industrial-age contaminants: By the 1930s, a variety of agro-chemicals were commonly used, and food additives were becoming common in processed foods.

25 **"taste like chicken":** Helene York, "How to Get Americans to Eat Fish," *The Atlantic*, November 13, 2012.

26 **closer to 1900:** The culinary historian H. D. Miller is a man I'd love to meet, but alas, I have not. So I follow his marvelous blog—*An Eccentric Culinary History*—on Substack, where I found his take on the history of sushi under the title "The Great Sushi Craze of 1905," in parts 1 and 2.

"the principal feature": *Los Angeles Herald* society pages, August 18, 1904.

first modern sushi bar: Daniel Miller, "This Little Tokyo Restaurant Is Long Gone. But It Changed L.A.'s Food Scene Forever," *Los Angeles Times*, May 3, 2023.

27 **Vintage Kawafuku menus:** Miller, "This Little Tokyo Restaurant Is Long Gone."

a "trend": Craig Claiborne, "Restaurants on Review; Variety of Japanese Dishes Offered, but Raw Fish Is Specialty on Menu," *New York Times*, November 11, 1963.

four-star review: Mimi Sheraton, "Sushi and Sashimi, the Best in the City," *New York Times*, April 15, 1983, C22.

28 **catches plummeted:** The Japanese Ministry of Agriculture, Forestry, and Fisheries reported that the global catch of Japanese elvers plummeted from an average of more than two hundred tons in the mid-1960s to twenty tons in the 1980s.

organized crime: Kaori Shoji, "Expensive and Unsustainable, 'Unagi' Remains as Popular as Ever," *Japan Times*, October 6, 2018, https://www.japantimes.co.jp/life/2018/10/06/food/expensive-unsustainable-unagi-remains-popular-ever/.

today Japan imports: I got this data point online at the data portal Trendeconomy.com, a subscription service that offers trade statistics by nation.

29 **"unknown" sources:** Ryo Imaizumi and Yomiuri Shimbun,

"Catch Certificates Eyed to Stamp Out Eel Poaching," *Japan News*, November 27, 2021.

29 **"unofficial channels":** Imaizumi and Shimbun, "Catch Certificates Eyed to Stamp Out Eel Poaching."

three years in prison: See, for example, "Poaching Shall Never Be Forgiven: Anti-Coastal Poaching Measures," a publication of Japan's Rec. Fishing and Coastal Fisheries Office, Fisheries and Resources Management Division Resources Management Department of Fisheries Agency, available here: https://www.maff.go.jp/e/policies/fishery/attach/pdf/nopoaching-6.pdf.

it remains to be seen: Imaizumi and Shimbun, "Catch Certificates Eyed to Stamp Out Eel Poaching."

"critically endangered": Check out the IUCN website, or see the European Commission on Food Farming and Fisheries available here: https://oceans-and-fisheries.ec.europa.eu/ocean/marine-biodiversity/eel_en.

30 **the greater the incentive:** Aitor Ibáñez Alonso and Daan P. van Uhm, "The Illegal Trade in European Eels: Outsourcing, Funding and Complex Symbiotic-Antithetical Relationships, *Trends in Organized Crime* 26 (2023): 293–307, https://link.springer.com/article/10.1007/s12117-023-09490-5.

Gilbert Khoo: Cahal Milmo, "Surrey Fish Broker Becomes First in UK Convicted of Involvement in £2.5bn Endangered Eel Smuggling Racket," *the i*, February 7, 2020, https://inews.co.uk/news/long-reads/surrey-fish-broker-old-bailey-convicted-endangered-eel-smuggling-racket-395109.

31 **300,000 live elvers:** U.N. Office on Drugs and Crime, World Wildlife Crime Report, "Trafficking in Protected Species" (Florian Stein contributed the chapter on freshwater eels), 2020.

100 tons: Europol does a reasonable job of tracking eel poachers, though critics worry that their estimates are low. See, for example, "49 Individuals Arrested in Major Blow to Eels Trafficking," published on the agency's website: https://www.europol.europa.eu/media-press/newsroom/news/49-individuals-across-europe-arrested-in-major-blow-to-eels-trafficking.

Spain's Civil Guard: Sam Jones, "Police in Spain and France Break Up International Eel Smuggling Gang," *Guardian*, May 12, 2023.

31 **nineteenfold:** The state of Maine's Department of Marine Resources keeps a running tally of annual elver catch and prices under the heading "Historical Maine Fisheries Landing Data," available online: https://www.maine.gov/dmr/fisheries/commercial/landings-program/historical-data.

32 **China's extraordinary eel production:** See: United Nations Office on Drugs and Crime, *World Wildlife Foundation Crime Report, Trafficking in Protected Species* (Vienna: United Nations, 2020), chapter 7.

33 **"species in the world"**: Hiromi Shiraishi and Kenzo Kaifu, "Early Warning of an Upsurge in International Trade in the American Eel," *Marine Policy* 159 (January 2024):

Chapter 2: The Kingpin

35 **"preliminary, pre-world creatures":** Alice Oswald, "Eel Tail," *Granta*, January 7, 2008.

37 **first glimpse of Sheldon:** Peter Smith, "The Eel World: Inside Maine's Wild Elver Turf War," BuzzFeed, August 29, 2013.

41 **twenty-five-page manifesto:** William Sheldon, "Elvers in Maine: Techniques of Locating, Catching and Holding," a Sea Grant publication, State of Maine Marine Resources, April 1974.

42 **casting a wider net**: For background on W. R. Livingston, I relied on Pat Bryant's memories and also on Tom Hamrick, "Sante Eels Tittillate Zuider Zee Gourmands," *Sandlapper: The Magazine of North Carolina*, February 1973, 21–25.

51 **Tommy Water Zhou:** I interviewed several Fish and Wildlife agents about Mr. Zhou. For general information on the Zhou case, see "Maine Fisherman Sentenced for Illegally Trafficking American Eels," U.S. Department of Justice Office of Public Affairs, November 3, 2017, https://www.justice.gov/opa/pr/maine-fisherman-sentenced-illegally-trafficking-american-eels-0.

53 **"only a small portion":** Transcript of Proceedings, United States District Court District of Maine, United States v. William Sheldon, May 3, 2018.

"unique among the defendants": United States v. William Sheldon.

53 **"Sheldon knew eels":** It is something of an irony that wildlife traffickers who deal in live animals are often near experts on the care and feeding of the species they steal. In some sense, they feel entitled to take the animal, as they believe they understand its needs far better than do most "ordinary" people.

54 **"I will forever feel":** United States v. William Sheldon.

maintained executive status: In a filing with the U.S. Securities and Exchange Commission, both Cindy Sheldon and Mitchell Feigenbaum are listed as executive officers and directors of Maine Eel and Trade Aquaculture; see "Maine Eel Trade & Aquaculture," CapEdge by Finsight, accessed December 19, 2023, https://capedge.com/filing/1651161/0001651161-15-000001/D.

Chapter 3: Nuns of the Water

57 **"It is very strange":** As quoted from Voltaire's *Questions sur l'Encyclopédie,* "The Story of Eels," in J. E. Greaves, "Some Interpretations of Life Phenomena and their Practical Significance," *Monist* 33, no. 1 (January 1923): 4.

"To a person not acquainted": Leopold Jacoby, "Der fischfang in der Lagune von Comacchio nebst einer darstellung der aalfrage," translated in Spencer F. Baird, "Part I: Report on the Condition of the Sea Fisheries on the South Coast of New England in 1871 and 1872," United States Commission of Fish and Fisheries, https://oceanconservancy.org/wp-content/uploads/2015/10/COF_1871-1872-1.pdf.

58 **Genomic analysis:** The debate over the ancestorial line of the eel and other ray-finned fishes has raged for fifty years, but newly available genomic techniques have allowed scientists to trace eels back to the oldest known group. See, for example, Elise Parey et al., "Genome structures resolve the early diversification of teleost fishes," *Science* 379(2023): 572–75.

59 **Even then, the eel was caught between worlds:** World Ocean Review (Maribus, Hamburg, 2021), available at: https://worldoceanreview.com/en/wor-5/coastal-dynamics/on-the-origin-and-demise-of-coasts/evolution-of-the-eel-a-matter-of-continental-drift/.

eel population was parted: World Ocean Review.

59 **The Atlantic widened:** World Ocean Review.

60 **Aristotle offers:** Aristotle, *The History of Animals*, trans. Richard Cresswell (London: George Bell and Sons, 1887).

61 **Aristotle's contributions:** Aristotle, *The History of Animals*.

62 **Pliny the Elder theorized:** Pliny the Elder's position on eels is common knowledge among scientists and historians of science—see, for example, A. Vasemägi, "Eel Mystery: Time Makes a Difference," *Heredity* 103 (2009): 3–4, https://doi.org/10.1038/hdy.2009.38.

Oppian built on this theory: J. Perry Land, "Eels and Their Utilization," *Marine Fisheries Review* 40, no. 4 (April 1978): 1–20.

Each winter: This insight comes thanks to the delightful and ever-generous John Wyatt Greenlee, PhD, independent medievalist and self-proclaimed Surprised Eel Historian.

63 **"a grand scale":** M. C. Marsh, "Eels and the Eel Question," *Popular Science Monthly*, vol. 61, September 1902.

from rotten material: "Hair Eels," *Scientific American* 39, no. 14 (October 5, 1878): 217–18.

"bred of a particular dew": Izaak Walton, *The Compleat Angler* (New York: E. P. Dutton & Co., 1906), 157.

the valorization of certainty: Joshua Landy and Michael Saler, eds., *The Re-Enchantment of the World: Secular Magic in a Rational Age* (Redwood City, CA: Stanford University Press, 2009).

64 **"guardian angel":** Sir Gavin de Beer D.Sc. Hon. D.-ès-L. F.R.S. (1954) "Jean-Jacques Rousseau: Botanist," *Annals of Science* 10, no. 3 (1954): 189–223, DOI: 10.1080/00033795400200214.

absorbed the personalities: Linnaeus actively campaigned to end the popular practice of middle- and upper-class women employing wet nurses to feed their infants, and it is thought that this concern played a role in his choice of the term *Mammalia* for the class of organisms that raise their young on mothers' milk.

"viviparous": G. Brown Goode, "The Eel Question," *Transactions of the American Fisheries Society* 10, no. 1 (1881): 81–124.

mistaken an eel's bladder: Antony van Leeuwenhoek, "Part of a Letter from Mr Antony van Leeuwenhoek, Concerning the Worms in Sheeps Livers, Gnats, and Animalcula in the Excrements of Frogs," *Philosophical Transactions* 22 (1700): 509–18, http://www.jstor.org/stable/102744.

65 **dutiful observations:** Paul E. Hatcher and Nick Battey, *Biological Diversity: Exploiters and Exploited* (Hoboken, NJ: Wiley-Blackwell, 2011).

"a fiend armed with a sharp hatchet": Tom Fort, *The Book of Eels* (London: William Collins, 2002), 230–31, quoting Leopold Jacoby.

a thousand tons: Vassilis George Aschonitis et al., "Long-Term Records (1781–2013) of European Eel (*Anguilla anguilla* L.) Production in the Comacchio Lagoon (Italy): Evaluation of Local and Global Factors as Causes of the Population Collapse," *Aquatic Conservation: Marine and Freshwater Ecosystems* 27, no. 2 (November 2016): 502–20.

66 **Valisneri prepared:** Leopold Jacoby, "The Eel Question," trans. Herman Jacobson, *Report from the Commissioner of Fish and Fisheries* (Berlin, 1880).

Renowned for many things: As were so many "natural scientists" of his day, Valsalva was a remarkable polymath—see, for example, Nathan Jacobs, Michele Bossy, and Amish Patel, "The Life and Work of Antonio Maria Valsalva (1666–1723)—Popping ears and tingling tongues," *Journal of the Intensive Care Society* 19, no.2 (May 2018): 161–63.

67 **remedy for deafness:** Jane Francesca Agnes, mother of Oscar Wilde, recorded this ancient Irish recipe for deafness: "Nothing is esteemed better than the constant anointing with the oils of eels, used perfectly fresh." See Jaipreet Vivdi, *Hearing Happiness: Deafness Cures in History* (Chicago: University of Chicago Press, 2020), 39.

68 **determined to settle:** Anonymous, "The Life History of the Eel," *Nature Journal*, April 27, 1882, 610–11.

as discovered by Mondini: Carl H. Eigenmann, "The Annual Address of the President: The Solution of the Eel Question," *Transactions of the American Microscopical Society* 23 (1902), 5–18.

a skeptic raised concerns: Eigenmann, "The Annual Address of the President."

69 **"The constant efforts":** *The Letters of Sigmund Freud to Eduard Silberstein, 187–1881*, ed. Walter Boehlich, trans. Arnold J. Pomerans (Cambridge, MA: Harvard University Press, 1990), 149.

one of several scientists to disprove it: Annalisa Ariatti and

Paolo Mandrioli, "Lazzaro spallanzani: A Blow Against Spontaneous Generation," *Aerobiologia* 9 (December 1993): 101–107.

70 **"a mystery of nature":** United States, Report of the Commissioner, U.S. Commission of Fish and Fisheries (U.S. Government Printing Office, 1872), 483.

description of a pregnant eel: J. J., "The Life History of the Eel," *Nature* 110, no. 716 (1922). https://doi.org/10.1038/110716a0.

Chapter 4: Freud's Eel Encouter

73 **"It is surely possible":** Sigmund Freud, *Beyond the Pleasure Principle,* trans. James Strachey (New York: W. W. Norton, 1961), 53.

In a Noah's Ark conception of life: I shamelessly borrowed that lovely phrase from Eliot Schrefer, "Queen Animals Are Everywhere," *Washington Post*, June 30, 2022.

"parthenogenesis": Alpheus Spring Packard Jr., "The Breeding Habits of the Eel," *The American Naturalist* 13, no. 1 (1897): 25–30.

74 **three noted Italian scientists:** M. Perkins-McVey, "A Portrait of the Neurophysiologist as a Young Man: Claus, Darwin, and Sigmund Freud's Search for the Testes of the Eel (1875–1877)," *History of Psychology*, 25, no. 4 (2022): 367–84.

"not the slightest trace": Leopold Jacoby, "The Eel Question," trans. Herman Jacobson, *Report from the Commissioner of Fish and Fisheries* (Berlin, 1880), 471.

"increased size": As quoted in Kevin Padian and John R. Horner, "Darwin's Sexual Selection: Understanding His Ideas in Context," *Comptes Rendus Palevol* 13, no. 8 (November–December 2014): 709–15. Also see Charles Darwin, *The Descent of Man, and Selection in Relation to Sex*, 2nd ed. (London: John Murray, 1874).

75 **"some remote progenitor":** Charles Darwin, *The Descent of Man, and Selection in Relation to Sex* (London: John Murray, 1901), 249.

"too many good observers": Charles Darwin, *The Descent of Man*, vol. 1 (American Home Library, 1902), 216.

76 **Syrski's finding:** The saga of how the male and female organs of eels were discovered and first described comes in many versions, of which I found that of eminent fish scientist Dr. George Brown Goode the most convincing. Goode (1851–1896) filled many roles, including assistant secretary of the Smithsonian Institution

and—for a brief time—U.S. fish commissioner. See in particular: G. Brown Goode (1882), "Notes on the Life-History of the Eel, Chiefly Derived from a study of Recent European Authorities," *Bulletin of the United States Fish Commission*, 71–124.

76 **physical proof:** Rodrigo Cornejo, "Origins of a Theory of Psychic Temporality in Freud: The Study of Eels and the Darwinist Influence of Carl Claus," *The International Journal of Psycho-Analysis* 99, no. 2 (2018): 450–67.

"eels keep no diaries": Sigmund Freud to Eduard Silberstein, April 5, 1876, *The Letters of Sigmund Freud to Eduard Silberstein, 1871–1881*, ed. Walter Boehlich, trans. Arnold J. Pomerans (Cambridge, MA: Harvard University Press, 1990), 149.

77 **a cartoon sketch of an eel:** Freud to Silberstein, April 5, 1876, *Letters of Sigmund Freud to Eduard Silberstein.*

He disemboweled four hundred eels: Rodrigo Cornejo, "Origins of a Theory of Psychic Temporality in Freud," 377.

a mixed blessing: For a fascinating account of young Freud's adventures in Trieste see: Laurence Simmons, *Freud's Italian Journey* (Amsterdam and New York: Edition Rodopi BV, 2006), 51–79.

78 **one scholar mused:** Siegfried Bernfeld, "Freud's Scientific Beginnings," *American Imago* 6, no. 3 (September 1949): 163–96.

every German-language journal: Jacoby, "The Eel Question," 474–75.

79 **"Most of the senders":** Jacoby, "The Eel Question," 475.

"extraordinary means": Jacoby, "The Eel Question."

80 **"To catch a river eel":** Jacoby, "The Eel Question."

Chapter 5: Oh, What a Lucky Man

83 **marine life was his passion:** As a junior scientist, from 1900 to 1909, Schmidt was part of the Scandinavian research team behind the International Council on the Exploration of the Sea in 1902. See, for example, this excellent historical account: Bo Poulsen, *Global Marine Science and Carlsberg: The Golden Connections of Johannes Schmidt* (Boston: Brill, 2016).

Strait of Messina: In 1896, the Italian scientists Giovanni Grassi and Salvatore Calandruccio captured a few eel larvae and studied their metamorphosis. The specimens had been caught in the Strait of Messina, and it was assumed that the spawning ground was somewhere off the coast of Italy. Schmidt's catch of a freely flowing larva in the Northern Atlantic all but mooted that theory.

83 **"I had little idea":** Johannes Schmidt, "The Breeding Places of the Eel," *Philosophical Transactions of the Royal Society of London, Series B, Containing Papers of a Biological Character* 211 (1923): 181.

keep a lookout for eel larvae: While Schmidt credits Petersen in an early report of the larvae finding, by 1912 in accounts of the discovery Petersen's role was sharply diminished, hence Schmidt's claim that he found the larvae by "sheer luck." See, for example, Paulsen, *Global Marine Science and Carlsberg*.

84 **"it fell to my lot to take charge of the work":** Schmidt, "The Breeding Places of the Eel," 181.

"enamors Professor Schmidt": Casper Bruun Jensen, "The Anthropocene Eel: Emergent Knowledge, Ontological Politics and New Propositions for an Age of Extinctions," *Anthropocenes* 1, no. 1 (2020): https://doi.org/10.16997/ahip.11.

86 **"more intricate than ever":** Schmidt, "The Breeding Places of the Eel," 200.

"True, the technical difficulties": Schmidt, "The Breeding Places of the Eel," 200.

87 **"Given the many difficulties":** Bruun Jensen, "The Anthropocene Eel," 1.

He knew the risks: For an eye-opening—if rather technical—critique of Schmidt's claims, see Jans Boetius and E. F. Harding, "A Reexamination of Johannes Schmidt's Atlantic Eel investigations," *Dana* 4 (1985): 129–62. Also, for general background on Schmidt's voyages, see Helen M. Rozwadowski, *The Sea Knows No Boundaries: A Century of Marine Science under ICES* (Seattle: University of Washington Press, 2002), 70–71.

"it most often will not come back": Poulsen, *Global Marine Science and Carlsberg*, 425.

tectonic plates: Alfred Wegener, the father of continental drift theory, noted the relevance to his theory of eel behavior—writing that "the gradual drift of this ocean basin, plus America away from Europe" explained the fact that the larval stage of European eels lasted as long as three years, while the American eel larval stage was closer to one year. See B. F. Skinner, "The Shaping of Phylogenic

Behavior," *Journal of the Experimental Analysis of Behavior* 24 (1975): 117–20.

88 **"an uncontrollable force":** Poulsen, *Global Marine Science and Carlsberg.*

the notable exception: Carl Eigenmann, "Annual Address of the President," *Transactions of the American Microscopical Society* 23 (August 1901): 7.

Chapter 6: Tales from the Uncanny

89 **"hypothesis and dream":** Louise Glück, "Theory of Memory," Faithful and Virtuous Night (New York: Farrar, Straus and Giroux, 2014).

92 **"start with the eels":** Alex Thompson, "The Eels: Best Thing about a Cure for Wellness," *Horror Homeroom*, February 23, 2017, http://www.horrorhomeroom.com/eels-best-thing-cure-wellness/.

93 **essay on animal metaphors:** Ryan J. Stark, "Cuttlefish Rhetoric," *Rhetorica: A Journal of the History of Rhetoric* 35, no. 1 (Winter 2017): 52–74.

a superstitious man: Graham Swift, *Waterland* (New York: Vintage, 1992), 2.

Swedish journalist: Patrik Svensson, *The Book of Eels: Our Enduring Fascination with the Most Mysterious Creature in the Natural World*, trans. Agnes Broome (New York: Ecco, 2020), 50.

94 **"curious enticement":** Aurel Kolnai, Carolyn Korsmeyer, and Barry Smith, *On Disgust* (Chicago: Open Court, 2003).

Chapter 7: Don't Call Him Ahab

95 **"true places never are"**: Herman Melville, *Moby-Dick* (Boston: St. Botolph Society, 1892), 57.

98 **"melody of nightingales"**: See, for example, Myron Gordon, "Sargasso Sea Merry-Go-Round," *Scientific Monthly* 53, no. 6 (December 1941): 542–49.

"a perfect meadow": Jules Verne, *20,000 Leagues Under the Sea* (Summit, NJ: Start Publishing, 2013), 301.

"render it useless": John H. Ryther, "The Sargasso Sea," *Scien-*

tific American 194, no. 1 (January 1956): 98, https://doi.org/10.1038/scientificamerican0156-98.

98 **"Who could know"**: C. C. Dixon, "The Sargasso Sea." *Geographical Journal* 66, no. 5 (1925): 434–42, https://doi.org/10.2307/1782665.

99 **"I do not like the nothing":** Klein's blue, a reflection of his boundless vision of the world, pretty much captures the (literally) boundless Sargasso Sea.

103 **the seamounts of the Mid-Atlantic Ridge**: Yu-Lin K. Chang et al., "New Clues on the Atlantic Eels Spawning Behavior and Area: The Mid-Atlantic Ridge Hypothesis," *Scientific Reports* 10 (2020): https://doi.org/10.1038/s41598-020-72916-5.

outside the Sargasso: Chang et al., "New Clues on the Atlantic Eels."

105 **"they tried to calm us down"**: Reinhold Hanel, Lasse Marohn and Håkan Westerberg, "No New Evidence for an Atlantic Eels Spawning Area Outside the Sargasso Sea," *Scientific Reports* 12 (2022): https://doi.org/10.1038/s41598-022-14882-8.

106 **data modelers had overestimated**: Leander Hohne et al., "Overestimating Management Progress Modelled vs. Monitored Silver Eel Escapement in a North Sea Draining River," *ICES Journal of Marine Science* 80, no. 7 (September 2023): 1936–48, https://academic.oup.com/icesjms.

an international consortium: European Inland Fisheries and Aquaculture Advisory Committee, Rome, March 28–29, 2023.

Chapter 8: Shapeshifters

109 **"You're all a bunch of Melun eels":** François Rabelais, *Gargantua and Pantagruel* (New York: W. W. Norton, 1990), 108.

"hybrid" eels: In the late 1980s, a team of scientists documented the existence of hybrid eels in Iceland, which, as one author of the paper put it, "came as a real shock." See J. C. Avise, W. S. Nelson, J. Arnold, et al., "The Evolutionary Genetic Status of Icelandic Eels," *Evolution* 44 (1990): 1254–62.

110 **until the late nineteenth:** In 1886, French zoologist Yves Delage kept leptocephali alive in a laboratory tank until they matured into eels, and in 1896, Italian zoologist Giovanni Battista Grassi observed the transformation of a leptocephalus into a glass eel

in the Mediterranean Sea and recognized the importance of salt water to the process.

110 **"marine snow":** Michael J. Miller et al., "Morphology and Gut Contents of Anguillid and Marine Eel Larvae in the Sargasso Sea," *Zoologischer Anzeiger* 219 (March 2019): 138–51, https://doi.org/10.1016/j.jcz.2019.01.008. Some scientists have raised the possibility that, like most fish larvae, eel larvae feed on zooplankton. Sree Lakshmi, a master's degree candidate in marine biology at the University of Bremen in Germany, told me that in captivity, eel larvae appear unable to survive on a diet of marine snow, and she and other scientists are currently investigating the question by looking at the gut contents of wild captured larvae. However, most other experts I spoke with agreed that all evidence points to marine snow as the primary diet of Anguilla larvae.

calcium reservoir: Conversation with Katherine Dale, postdoctoral fellow in marine ecology at East Carolina University.

111 **computer simulations published:** Irina I. Rypina et al., "Dispersal Pathways of American Eel Larvae from the Sargasso Sea," *Limnology and Oceanography* 59, no. 5 (September 2014): 1704–14, https://doi.org/10.4319/lo.2014.59.5.1704.

112 **0.3 percent:** Håkan Westerberg et al., "Modeling the Drift of European (*Anguilla anguilla*) and American (*Anguilla rostrata*) Eel Larvae During the Year of Spawning," *Canadian Journal of Fisheries and Aquatic Sciences* 75 (2018): 224–34, https://doi.org/10.1139/cjfas-2016-0256.

114 **while there is some early evidence**: Scott A. Pavey et al., "RAD Sequencing Highlights Polygenic Discrimination of Habitat Ecotypes in the Panmictic American Eel," *Current Biology* 25, no. 12 (June 15, 2015): 1666–71, https://doi.org/10.1016/j.cub.2015.04.062.

116 **Less by genes:** Andrew J. H. Davey and Donald J. Jellyman, "Sex Determination in Freshwater Eels and Management Options for Manipulation of Sex," *Reviews in Fish Biology and Fisheries* 15 (2005): 37–52.

117 **"Now it was autumn again":** Rachel Carson, *Under the Sea Wind*, 50th anniversary ed. (New York: Truman Talley Books/Dutton, 1991), 213.

118 **alimentary tracts:** Caroline Durif, Aymeric Guibert, and Pierre Elie, "Morphological Discrimination of the Silvering Stages of

the European Eel," *American Fisheries Society Symposium* 58 (2009): 103–11, https://fisheries.org/docs/books/54058C/7.pdf.

120 **satellite tags slowed them down:** Eric Burgerhout and Sebastian Brittijn et al., "Dramatic effect of pop-up satellite tags on eel swimming," *The Science of Nature* 98, no. 7: 631–34.

"first direct evidence": Rosalind M. Wright, et al., "First Direct Evidence of Adult European Eels Migrating to Their Breeding Place in the Sargasso Sea," *Scientific Reports* 12 (2022): https://doi.org/10.1038/s41598-022-19248-8.

121 **"mystery unraveled":** Helen Briggs, "Ancient Eel Migration Mystery Unraveled," BBC, October 14, 2022, https://www.bbc.com/news/science-environment-63259738.

122 **"deeper darkness than ever":** J. Schmidt, "Breeding Places and Migrations of the Eel," *Nature* 111, no. 2776 (January 13, 1923): 52.

Chapter 9: Animal Magnetism, or Snorkeling with Eels

123 **"her sweat":** I borrowed this snippet from an online poetry site, Hello Poetry (HePro for short). I believe "Irate Watcher" is a pseudonym, but I was unable to find the author's actual name. See: https://hellopoetry.com/words/eel/.

124 **switched direction:** Caroline Durif et al., "Behavioural Study of Downstream Migrating Eels by Radiotelemetry at a Small Hydroelectric Power Plant," *Biology, Management, and Protection of Catadromous Eels*, American Fisheries Society Symposium 33 (2003): 343–56, https://scholarworks.umass.edu/fishpassage_conference_proceedings/170/.

128 **Consider the flounder:** Thanks for the flounder example go to ethnologist Jonathan Balcombe, author of *What a Fish Knows: The Inner Lives of Our Underwater Cousins* (New York: Farrar, Straus and Giroux, 2017).

a few drops of rose water: See Frederick W. Tesch, *The Eel*, trans. R. J. White (Oxford, UK: Blackwell, 2003), 67.

129 **invented by the Chinese:** Li-Jun Ji, Albert Lee, and Tieyuan Guo, "The Four Great Inventions of China," *Oxford Handbook of Chinese Psychology* (2010): 155.

von Middendorff theorized: Gregory C. Nordmann, Tobias Hochstoeger, David A. Keays, "Magnetoreception—A Sense

Without a Receptor," *PLoS Biology* 15, no. 10 (October 23, 2017): https://doi.org/10.1371/journal.pbio.2003234.

130 **"biophysically impossible":** Donald R. Griffin, "The Sensory Basis of Bird Navigation," *Quarterly Review of Biology* 19, no. 1 (March 1944): 15–31, https://doi.org/10.1086/394685.

Merkel and his student: Ed Yong, *An Immense World: How Animal Senses Reveal The Hidden Realms Around Us* (New York: Random House, 2022), 303.

Other scientists have since found: Yong, *An Immense World*, 309.

131 **"living compass needles":** See, for example, Sönke Johnsen, "Open Questions: We Don't Really Know Anything, Do We? Open Questions in Sensory Biology," *BMC Biol* 15, 43 (2017): https://doi.org/10.1186/s12915-017-0385-3.

132 **magnetite found in salmon noses:** M Renee Bellinger et al., "Conservation of Magnetite Biomineralization Genes in All Domains of Life and Implications for Magnetic Sensing," *PNAS* 119, no. 3 (January 18, 2022): https://doi.org/10.1073/pnas.2108655119.

the new moon: Alessandro Cresci et al., "The Relationship Between the Moon Cycle and the Orientation of Glass Eels (*Anguilla anguilla*) at Sea," *Royal Society Open Science* 6, no. 10 (October 2019): https://doi.org/10.1098/rsos.190812.

133 **"isoline":** As Caroline Durif kindly explained to me, an isoline is an imaginary line that provides a visual representation of various features of a terrain—in the case of aquatic environments this might mean temperature, salinity, or—for our purposes—magnetic field strength. The hypothesis for eels and other migrating fish is that they imprint on the magnetic field of their home areas when young and then use this information to return as adults. During the past decade, strong evidence has accumulated to support this idea.

134 **impact of light:** John B. Phillips and S. Chris Borland, "Behavioural Evidence for Use of a Light-Dependent Magnetoreception Mechanism by a Vertebrate," *Nature* 359 (1992): 142–44, https://doi.org/10.1038/359142a0.

137 **"We thought it incredible":** Alessandro Cresci et al., "Glass Eels (*Anguilla anguilla*) Imprint the Magnetic Direction of Tidal Currents from Their Juvenile Estuaries," *Communications Biology* 2, no. 366 (2019): https://doi.org/10.1038/s42003-019-0619-8.

138 **"has been plagued":** Yong, *An Immense World*, 316.

138 **light-dependent magnetic compass:** Patrick A Guerra, Robert J Gegear, and Steven M Reppert, "A Magnetic Compass Aids Monarch Butterfly Migration," *Nature Communications* 5, 4164 (2014): https://doi.org/10.1038/ncomms5164.
Studies in humans: Connie X. Wang et al., "Transduction of the Geomagnetic Field as Evidenced from Alpha-Band Activity in the Human Brain," *eNeuro* 6, no. 2 (March 18, 2019): https://doi.org/10.1523/ENEURO.0483-18.2019.

Chapter 10: Dr. Eel and the Lovely Maidens

141 **"We are two eels":** Mary Rokonadravu's gorgeous and courageous short story "Famished Eels," first published in *Granta* in 2015, took first prize for the Commonwealth Award that year. My favorite line in that story seems somehow apt to quote here: "*As long as someone remembers, we live.*"
"Fact and truth": While often attributed to William Faulkner, this exact quote doesn't appear in any of his known works or writings. There's a possibility that it might have been misattributed to him, but it's more likely to be a paraphrase or interpretation of some ideas expressed in his works—in particular his belief that fiction expresses truth more powerfully (and in some sense more accurately) than fact.

142 **Unagi Sensei:** Dr. Tsukamoto is a beloved figure in Japan, where he is often referred to as Dr. Eel. See, for example, Christina Couch, "The Utterly Engrossing Search for the Origin of Eels," *Haiku,* September 26, 2022.
mark its breeding ground: Katsumi Tsukamoto, "Discovery of the Spawning Area for Japanese Eel," *Nature* 356 (1992), 789–91, https://www.nature.com/articles/356789a0.

143 **always during the nights of the new moon:** Katsumi Tsukamoto et al., "Oceanic spawning ecology of freshwater eels in the western North Pacific," *Nature Communications* 2, no. 179 (2011): https://www.nature.com/articles/ncomms1174.
The selection committee wrote: "The 38th (2022) International Prize for Biology is awarded to Dr. Tsukamoto Katsumi," The Japan Society for the Promotion of Science, accessed December 19, 2023, https://www.jsps.go.jp/english/e-biol/38_awardee.html.

144 **Perusing his text:** Mari Kuroki and Katsumi Tsukamoto, *Eels on the Move: Mysterious Creatures Over a Million Years* (Tokyo: Tokai University Press, 2012).

"bordering on the totemic": Thanks to environmental scientist and scholar Catherine Morse, whose magnificent honors thesis, "Elvers to Kabayaki," is a testament to the eel in itself.

145 **national holiday:** Doyo-no Ushi-no Hi is one of the traditional dates on the lunar calendar that varies from year to year but generally takes place in July. Eel is eaten as a cure for "summer weariness." Legend has it that in the mid-1700s, a freshwater eel restaurant advertisement for the Day of the Ox transmogrified the word "ox" into "eel." Another theory is that Day of the Ox was simply a marketing ploy to encourage people to eat eel.

"placed eels on a par": Alexandre Dumas, *Le Grand Dictionnaire de Cuisine*, ed. Alphonce Mederre (1873), 168. Thanks to Google Translate.

progenitor of all eels: Leopold Jacoby, "The Eel Question," trans. Herman Jacobson, *Report from the Commissioner of Fish and Fisheries* (Berlin, 1880), 463.

"O my sweetest": Georges Cuvier, *History of the Natural Sciences: Twenty-Four Lessons from Antiquity to the Renaissance*, ed. Theodore Wells Pietsch (Paris: Publications Scientifiques du Muséum, 2019).

"lovely maidens": Pliny the Elder mentioned Crassus's fondness for eels in his work "Natural History," and it is said that Crassus kept a pond of eels as pets and took great pleasure in feeding and caring for them. The quote "so many lovely maidens" is from Marcus Tullius Cicero's famous oration "Pro Caelio," which he delivered in defense of Marcus Caelius Rufus, a Roman politician who was accused of various crimes. The specific line refers to the allure of the city of Rome and the distractions it presents, including the presence of many attractive women.

wept bitterly: Pliny the Elder, in his work *Natural History*, mentions Quintus Hortensius and his affection for an eel. Here's the passage from book 9, chapter 9 of *Natural History*, translated into English: "Quintus Hortensius, the orator, who was consul with the younger Marius, had so strong a passion for keeping these animals, that when one of them died he actually had it carried forth on a litter, and was greatly affected by its death, exhibiting all the tokens of deep and unfeigned sorrow."

146 **"field of pleasure":** John Wilkins and Shaun Hill, *Archestratus: Fragments from the Life of Luxury* (London: Prospect Books, 2011).

Eel Historian: The Surprised Eel Historian, John Wyatt Greenlee, holder of a PhD in medieval studies from Cornell University and professional cartographer, taught me the historical significance of the eel across European cultures. A generous and courageous sage of cultural history, he is a treasure trove of information and insight.

149 **family crests:** According to John Wyatt Greenlee, there are fewer instances of eels on family coats of arms on the European continent, though the arms of the Spanish Guzman family does include a basket of eels.

"surfeit of eels": The story of King Henry I of England's death due to consuming a surfeit of the eel-like fish—the lamprey, appears in various historical accounts. The following reference comes from historian William of Malmesbury in his work "Gesta Regum Anglorum" (The Deeds of the Kings of England): "At a subsequent period, in the sixty-seventh year of his age, and the thirty-fifth of his reign, partaking too freely of lampreys, against which he had been cautioned, he was seized with sudden illness; and when he perceived his end to be near, he summoned to his presence the person who he imagined would aspire to the throne after his decease, and made him take a solemn oath, that in the event of his dying without issue, he would not withhold the crown from his daughter Matilda."

from merchants "over seas": Thanks once again to Dr. John Greely, who quotes King Richard III thus in one of his online missives.

Shakespeare: In *King Lear*, Shakespeare famously juxtaposes the King's towering rage with the Fool's account of a ludicrous kitchen scene in which a silly woman struggles to beat down with a stick the live eels she's neglected to kill before covering them in pastry. See for example this alarming excerpt from *King Lear*, act 2, scene 4: "Cry to it, Nuncle, as the cockney did to the eels when she put 'em i' th' paste alive." Eels also make cameo appearances in *Henry IV*, *King John*, *The Taming of the Shrew*, *Love's Labor's Lost*, and *Pericles, Prince of Tyre*, where in act 2, scene 1, the character Thaisa, who is pregnant, expresses a craving for eels, much as does the character Agnes Matzerath in *The Tin Drum.*

150 **Leonardo da Vinci:** John Varriano, "At Supper with Leonardo," *Gastronomica* 8, no. 1 (2008): 75–79, https://doi.org/10.1525/gfc.2008.8.1.75. It's written that Da Vinci believed that eating eel frequently "can cause madness."

"a delicacy": W. Doose, "Eine wenig bekannte Aalfangmethode" [A less well-known technique for catching eel], *Allgemeine Fischerei-Zeitung* 33, no. 18 (1908): 393–94.

Basque Country: Reinhold Hanel et al., Research for PECH Committee Environmental, Social and Economic Sustainability of European Eel Management, European Parliament, 2019.

with torches: Harriet V. Kuhnlein and Murray Humphries, "American Eel," Traditional Foods of Indigenous Peoples of North America, accessed December 21, 2023, at http://traditionalanimalfoods.org/fish/searun-fish/page.aspx?id=6450.

Eel skin: William A. Allen, *The American Eel: Driving a Shift in Power*, presentation at Barrier Management Session, A.D. Latornell Conservation Symposium Nottawasaga Inn, Alliston, Ontario, November 20, 2008, http://www.latornell.ca/wp-content/uploads/files/presentations/2008/2008_T2F_William_A_Allen_delivery.pdf.

151 ***Mayflower* colonists:** Thanks to Charles Mann, author of the magisterial *1491: New Revelations of the Americas Before Columbus* (New York: Vintage, 2006), for sharing this background on the Pilgrims in a personal conversation. Also, see Mark Kurlansky, *Cod: A Biography of the Fish That Changed the World* (New York: Penguin Books, 1997), 68–70, in which the author says of the Pilgrims: "Not only couldn't they fish, they didn't know how to hunt. They were also bad at farming."

"went at noon": As written in *Mourt's Relation: A Journal of the Pilgrims at Plymouth*, authored primarily by Edward Winslow, although William Bradford appears to have written most of the first section. Written between November 1620 and November 1621 and published a year later, the booklet describes in detail what happened from the landing of the Pilgrims at Cape Cod, through their exploring and eventual settling at Plymouth, to their relations with the surrounding Indians, up to the First Thanksgiving and the arrival of the ship *Fortune*. *Mourt's Relation* was first published in London in 1622, presumably by George Morton (hence the title).

151 **New England winters:** While it's often claimed that the Native Americans taught the Pilgrims how to fish for eels, it's far more likely that the Pilgrims learned the practice in their home country—where eels were both popular and plentiful. Still, the "treading up of eels" from river bottoms with one's feet may indeed have been new to the Pilgrims.

152 **"I never eat better":** John Josselyn, *An Account of Two Voyages to New England, Made During the Years 1638, 1663* (Boston: William Veazie, 1865), 87.

"form and colouring": W. F. Nelson, "Eels," *Time* (London) 16 (March 1887): 347–53.

Chapter 11: The Night Mind of Water

153 **"Like a sprat":** This line is from Sylvia Plath's "You're," first published in 1961 and collected in *Ariel* in 1965. It was reprinted in Sylvia Plath, *The Collected Poems* (New York: HarperCollins, 2008).

"an extreme position": M. C. Marsh, "Eels and the Eel Question," *Popular Science Monthly* 61 (September 1902).

"unclean": Eels are not kosher, it is written, because their scales are embedded in their skin. I'm not convinced by this explanation. Jewish law dictates that a fish possessing even a single scale is kosher, and does not make reference to the location of those scales or how said scales are attached to the fish. My guess is that the decision was made when it was not yet known that eels do have scales, as religious rulings of this sort tend to stick regardless of the facts.

154 **harbingers of famine:** This historical tidbit comes thanks to Dr. Neil Buttery, British food historian, author, and chef, and his blog: https://britishfoodhistory.com/.

"would sooner eat": P. Anderson Graham, "Pallinsburn Gull Pond," *Longman's Magazine* 27, no. 167 (November 1895), 75–81.

155 **"The investigation of poisons":** G. C. Frankland, "The Toxicity of Eel-Serum, and Further Studies on Immunity," *Nature* 58 (1898): 369–71, https://doi.org/10.1038/058369a0.

155 **criminal poisonings:** Joan Acocella, "Murder by Poison," *New Yorker*, October 14, 2013, a review of Sandra Hempel, *The Inheritor's Powder: A Tale of Arsenic, Murder and the New Forensic Science* (New York: W. W. Norton, 2013).

forerunner to the fMRI: Stefano Sandrone et al., "Weighing Brain Activity with the Balance: Angelo Mosso's Original Manuscripts Come to Light," *Brain* 137, no. 2 (February 2014): 621–33, https://doi.org/10.1093/brain/awt091.

156 **no demonstrated ill effect:** Cooking and smoking neutralizes the poison, and humans are generally cautioned never to eat eel raw. I was unable to find hard evidence that eating raw eel is dangerous to humans with a healthy digestive system but also unwilling to put this to the test—and suggest you don't either.

160 **do not fare all that well:** H. Froehlicher et al., "Eel Translocation from a Conservation Perspective: A Coupled Systematic and Narrative Review," *Global Ecology and Conservation* 46 (October 2023): https://doi.org/10.1016/j.gecco.2023.e02635.

That said, it was Dufour's own mentor: M. Fontaine, "Sur la maturation complete des organes genitaux de l'anguille male et l'emission spontanee de ses produits sexuels," *Comptes Rendus de l'Académie des Sciences* 202 (1936): 1312–15.

162 **"We got lucky":** K. Oliveira and W. E. Hable, "Artificial Maturation, Fertilization, and Early Development of the American Eel (*Anguilla rostrata*)," *Canadian Journal of Zoology* 88 (2010): 1121–28, https://doi.org/10.1139/Z10-081.

163 **on a commercial scale**: Scientists have been able to reproduce the Japanese eel in the laboratory for more than two decades. See, for example: Hideki Tanaka et al., "The First Production of Glass Eel in Captivity: Fish Reproductive Physiology Facilitates Great Progress in Aquaculture," *Fish Physiology and Biochemistry* 28, no. 1 (2003): 493–97, https://doi.org/10.1023/B:FISH.0000030638.56031.ed. More recently, scientists have even managed to induce eels grown in the laboratory to produce a second generation of eels. See, for example: Hideki Tanaka, "Progression in Artificial Seedling Production of Japanese Eel *Anguilla japonica*," *Fisheries* Science 81 (2015): 11–19, https://doi.org/10.1007/s12562-014-0821-z. But despite the success at "full-life-cycle eel culture," so far technical

difficulties have foreclosed all attempts to produce Japanese eels on a commercial scale.

Chapter 12: This River Is Full of Money

165 **"Oh beloved eel, you!":** Aristophanes, "Aristophanes" (425 BCE), Poetry in Translation, accessed December 28, 2023, https://www.poetryintranslation.com/PITBR/Greek/Acharnians.php.

166 **the price of Maine-caught elvers:** The price of elvers is a matter of enormous interest in Maine, and the Maine Department of Marine Resources keeps a tally—"Historical Maine Fisheries Landings"—on its website: https://www.maine.gov/dmr/fisheries/commercial/landings-program/historical-data.

172 **"a phenomenal amount of glass eels":** Nora Flaherty, "Why Maine is the Only State in the U.S. with a Significant Elver Fishery," Maine Public Radio, May 1, 2018, https://www.mainepublic.org/business-and-economy/2018-05-01/why-maine-is-the-only-state-in-the-us-with-a-significant-elver-fishery.

9,688 pounds: James McCleave told me that this quota was essentially arbitrary, saying that there was "no data to back it up," but nor is the data strong in support of raising it.

fourteen lucky veterans: Interview with Darrell Young.

174 **"In my opinion, that makes them worse":** When we last spoke, Waller had left his job in the Department of Justice to found Star in the Valley, an estate vineyard he runs with his wife, Cara Mroczek, who is also an attorney, and a fourth-generation grape farmer.

175 **reinforced that ruling:** "2023 Winter Meeting," Atlantic States Maine Fisheries Commission, American Eel Management Board, February 1, 2023, http://www.asmfc.org/files/Meetings/2023WinterMeeting/AmericanEelBoard_Feb2023.pdf.

176 **2.2 billion:** Wilson estimated the pigeon parade to be at minimum a mile wide and 240 miles long with three birds per square yard of space throughout. From this, he calculated the flock to consist of more than 2.2 billion birds, a number he believed to be far lower than its actual size.

"the light of noonday": Audubon's essay, "Watching the Devastation," written in 1813, can be found reprinted here: https://www.laphamsquarterly.org/animals/watching-devastation.

176 **"I have satisfied myself":** This is from another of Audubon's essays on the passenger pigeon: John J. Audubon, "Passenger Pigeon," John J. Audubon's Birds of America, accessed December 19, 2023, https://www.audubon.org/birds-of-america/passenger-pigeon.

select committee: See, for example, "Passenger Pigeon: Species Profile," Pennsylvania Game Commission, accessed December 19, 2023, https://www.pgc.pa.gov/Wildlife/EndangeredandThreatened/Pages/PassengerPigeon.aspx.

177 **toppled dead:** Dolly Jogensen and Isla Gladstone, "The Passenger Pigeon's Past on Display for the Future," *Environmental History* 27, no. 2 (2022): 347–53.

"The complete extinction of the species": Charles Darwin, *Origin of Species: A Facsimile of the First Edition*, (Cambridge, MA: Harvard University Press, 1964), 318.

178 **"Are fisheries exhaustible?":** Thomas Huxley, Inaugural Address, Fisheries Exhibition, London, 1883, http://alepho.clarku.edu/huxley/SM5/fish.html.

"the death-rate": Huxley, Inaugural Address.

will remain plentiful: Thanks for this insight go to David Secor, fisheries ecologist at the Institute of Marine and Environmental Technology at the University of Maryland, who studies factors that boost resilience in exploited species.

179 **irreversible road:** Interestingly, the monarch butterfly presents a parallel case. Since the 1980s, the monarch has declined by 90 percent, and in 2022, the IUNC listed it as endangered. But the species is not listed as endangered in the United States, and is therefore not protected under the federal Endangered Species Act.

180 **blades of turbines:** In 2022, one industry-sponsored study reported "stressors that fish may face in passage through turbines include blade strike, entrapment between rotating and stationary components of the turbine, rapid pressure changes, and shear forces." See Sterling Watson et al., "Safe passage of American Eels through a novel hydropower turbine," *Transactions of the American Fisheries Society* 151, no. 6 (November 2022): https://afspubs.onlinelibrary.wiley.com/doi/epdf/10.1002/tafs.10385.

182 **Tilapia, carp, trout:** Chrissy Sexton, "The Nutritional and Economic Value of Freshwater Fish Have Been Underestimated,"

Earth.com, September 2019, https://www.earth.com/news/value-freshwater-fish/.

182 **"catastrophic decline":** See *The World's Forgotten Fishes*, World Wildlife Foundation, March 2021, https://europe.nxtbook.com/nxteu/wwfintl/freshwater_fishes_report/index.php#/p/2.

eighteen thousand freshwater species: Interview with Florian Stein, currently in a new position as the director of policy and science, German Angler Association.

183 **"chemical contamination":** Bastien Bourillon et al., "Anthropogenic Contaminants Shape the Fitness of the Endangered European Eel: A Machine Learning Approach," *Fishes* 7, no. 5 (2022): 274, https://doi.org/10.3390/fishes7050274.

"assisted migration": For example, since 2008 scientists have trapped elvers in the Susquehanna River and trucked them past hydroelectric dams for release in freshwater creeks upstream. This has led to a resurgence of both juvenile eels and freshwater mussels. But trucking the large mature eels on their return trip is considered logistically impractical, so it is unlikely that many mature eels make it home to spawn.

Chapter 13: A Most Slippery Business

185 **"Who looks":** Ralph Waldo Emerson, *Nature* (Boston: James Munroe & Company, 1849), 24.

187 **ordered a crackdown:** Maria Abi-Habib, "Haiti's Leader Kept a List of Drug Traffickers. His Assassins Came for It," *New York Times*, December 12, 2021, https://www.nytimes.com/2021/12/12/world/americas/jovenel-moise-haiti-president-drug-traffickers.html.

rumored links to Kiko: Abi-Habib, "Haiti's Leader Kept a List of Drug Traffickers."

Haiti's export of American elvers: Hiromi Shiraishi and Kenzo Kaifu, "Early Warning of an Upsurge in International Trade in the American Eel," *Marine Policy* 159 (January 2024): https://doi.org/10.1016/j.marpol.2023.105938.

188 **6,400 kilos:** Jean Anderson, "National Report – Haiti: Fishing for American Eel, Anguilla rostrata," International Oceanographic

Commission, United Nations Educational and Scientific and Cultural Organization, 2021.

189 **"the black market":** "Major Seafood Dealer and Eight Individuals Indicted for International Wildlife Trafficking," U.S. Department of Justice, Office of Public Affairs, https://www.justice.gov/opa/pr/major-seafood-dealer-and-eight-individuals-indicted-international-wildlife-trafficking.

Wildlife Conservation Society: See: "Why We Should Care about Wildlife Trafficking," Wildlife Conservation Society, https://wildlifetrade.wcs.org/Wildlife-Trade/Why-should-we-care.aspx.

the pyramids of Giza: The oldest known eel weir in the U.S. is in Maine at the Sebasticook Lake Fishweir Complex, where wood recovered from a capture basket has been radiocarbon dated to 3000 BC. The Pyramids of Giza were built around 2500 BC.

Chapter 14: Tribal Matters

191 **"Eels do not stutter":** Ben Ray, *The Kindness of the Eel* (Smith Doorstop Books, 2020).

193 **issued their own permits:** The Passamaquoddy Tribe, prior to the opening of the 2013 elver fishing season, issued around 575 elver-fishing licenses to its members, a number that far exceeded the licenses prescribed by State. The DMR determined that in order to comply with the law, the first 150 licenses would be considered valid, with all licenses numbered above 151 considered invalid. See: Joseph O. Gribbin, "The Glass Eeling: Maine's Glass Eel and Elver Regulations and Their Effects on Maine's Native American Tribes," *Ocean and Coastal Law Journal* 20, no. 1 (2015).

196 **official elver season:** "The Maine Eel and Elver Fishery," Maine Department of Marine Resources, accessed December 19, 2023, https://www.maine.gov/dmr/fisheries/commercial/fisheries-by-species/eels-and-elvers/the-maine-eel-and-elver-fisheries.

federally recognized: https://legislature.maine.gov/statutes/12/title12sec6302-B.html

8,143 applications: The 8,143 number is for total number of applications—some applicants made multiple applications. See

Laurie Schreiber, "Out of 2,600 applicants, 13 Mainers get Licenses for Elver Harvesting This Season," Mainebiz, March 7, 2022.

200 **"Eels have been very good to Mitch"**: Conversation with Neil Ross, PhD, research head of Nova Eel.

203 **first recorded contact:** I write "extensive" because it is possible that the Passamaquoddy had at least a brief encounter with Europeans prior to their first encounter with Champlain in 1604.

reward for every scalp: The notorious "Phips Bounty Proclamation" is available online: Upstander Project, accessed December 19, 2023,https://upstanderproject.org/learn/guides-and-resources/first-light/phips-bounty-proclamation.

heartfelt letter of thanks: "From George Washington to the Chiefs of the Passamaquoddy Indians, 24 December 1776," Founders Online, National Archives, accessed December 19, 2023, https://founders.archives.gov/documents/Washington/03-07-02-0340.

204 **"a great many":** Samuel de Champlain, *Voyages of Samuel de Champlain, Vol 2*, translated from the French (Forgotten Books, 2018).

"This work is done": Reuben Gold Thwaites, *The Jesuit Relations and Allied Documents: Travels and Explorations of the Jesuit Missionaries in New France, 1610–1791,* vol. 5, 1897, https://rla.unc.edu/Louisiane/jesuit.html.

205 **"they caught this year":** Reuben Gold Thwaites, *The Jesuit Relations and Allied Documents*.

"a hundred ways": François-Marc Gagnon, ed., *The Codex Canadensis and the Writings of Louis Nicholas* (Montreal: McGill-Queens University Press, 2011), 375.

207 **"fundamental disagreements remain":** For in-depth legal analysis see: Joseph O. Gribbin, "The Glass Eeling: Maine's Glass Eel and Elver Regulations and Their Effects on Maine's Native American Tribes," *Ocean and Coastal Law Journal* 83 (2015) and John Sanders, "A Tiny Fish and a Big Problem: Natives, Elvers, and The Maine Indian Claims Settlement Act of 1980," *William & Mary Law Review* 57 (2016): 2287. Also, thanks to John Sanders for speaking with me to clarify his cogent review.

208 **right to regulate:** See, for example, Maine Indian Tribal State Commission Special Project, June 17, 2014: "Assessment of the Intergovernmental Saltwater Fisheries Conflict Between Passamaquoddy and the State of Maine." Also, John M. R. Paterson, "The

Maine Indian Land Claim Settlement: A Personal Recollection," *Maine History* 46, no. 2 (June 2012).

Chapter 15: Closing the Circle

213 **"To her, they never":** Fiona Wright, "Eel Farm."

225 **processing plants in China:** Interview with Willy Bokelaar, a seasoned consultant to Asian eel farms.

To further reduce costs: Bokelaar said it is "a fact" that the Chinese use hormones and antibiotics, and that seems to be the case. Some eels reimported to the United States contain residues of the antimicrobial substance malachite green and the banned antibiotic chloramphenicol. In April, 2018, the U.S. Food and Drug Administration warned of contaminants in eels, and other seafood products exported from China. At one point, as much as 25 percent of sampled eel and other fish from China tested positive for drug residues.

235 **the "eel deal":** NDN Fund put together this mini documentary on what it calls the "eel deal," which it says follows the "revitalization of the Passamaquoddy Tribe and the Indian Township traditional eel harvesting." See Angelica (Angie) Solloa, "What's the Big Eel?," NDN Collective, https://ndncollective.org/whats-the-big-eel/.

Epilogue: This Incomprehensible World

239 **"When we try":** John Muir, *My First Summer in the Sierra* (1911; New York: Dover Publications, 2004).

240 **"'I do get carried away'":** Gabriel Popkin, "Right Fish, Wrong Pond," *Johns Hopkins Magazine* 65, no. 2 (Summer 2013).

"the cold rains shed": Rachel Carson, *Under the Sea Wind*, 50th anniversary ed. (New York: Truman Talley Books/Dutton, 1991)

241 **"the survival of the two":** Tom Fort, *The Book of Eels: Their Lives, Secrets and* Myths (London: William Collins, 2020), 329.

242 **sensory loss in infant eels:** Francisco O. Borges et al., "Ocean Warming and Acidification May Challenge the Riverward Migration of Glass Eels," *Biology Letters* 15, no. 1 (January 2019): https://doi.org/10.1098/rsbl.2018.0627.

INDEX